D0782408

The Definition of a Profession

✤

The Definition of a Profession

THE AUTHORITY OF METAPHOR

IN THE HISTORY OF

INTELLIGENCE TESTING, 1890–1930

✤

JoAnne Brown

153.93
B878

REMOVED FROM THE
ALVERNO COLLEGE LIBRARY

PRINCETON UNIVERSITY PRESS

PRINCETON, NEW JERSEY

ALVERNO COLLEGE LIBRARY
MILWAUKEE, WI

Copyright © 1992 by Princeton University Press
Published by Princeton University Press, 41 William Street,
Princeton, New Jersey 08540
In the United Kingdom: Princeton University Press, Oxford
All Rights Reserved

Library of Congress Cataloging-in-Publication Data
Brown, JoAnne, 1954–
The definition of a profession : the authority of metaphor in the
history of intelligence testing, 1890–1930 / JoAnne Brown.
p.   cm.
Includes bibliographical references and index.
ISBN 0-691-08632-X
1. Intelligence tests—United States—History. 2. Psychology—United
States—Language—History. 3. English language—Social aspects—
United States—History. 4. Professions—United States—Psychological
aspects—History. 5. Medicine and psychology—United States—
History. 6. Engineering—United States—Language—History.
7. Progressivism (United States politics)   I. Title.
BF431.5.U6B76   1992   92-1147
153.9′3′0973—dc20

This book has been composed in Linotron Baskerville

Princeton University Press books are
printed on acid-free paper, and meet the guidelines
for permanence and durability of the Committee
on Production Guidelines for Book Longevity
of the Council on Library Resources

Printed in the United States of America

1   3   5   7   9   10   8   6   4   2

Who saw what ferns and palms were pressed
Under the tumbling mountain's breast
In the safe herbal of the coal?
But when the quarried means were piled,
All is waste and worthless, till
Arrives the wise selecting Will,
And, out of slime and chaos, Wit
Draws the threads of fair and fit.
Then temples rose, and towns, and marts,
The shop of toil, the halls of arts;
Then flew the sail across the seas
To feed the North from tropic trees;
The storm-wind wove, the torrent span,
Where they were bid the rivers ran;
New slaves fulfilled the poet's dream,
Galvanic wire, strong-shouldered steam.

    (Ralph Waldo Emerson, "Wealth")

❖ *Contents* ❖

❖ *Acknowledgments* ❖

LIKE EVERY WRITER, I have many people to thank. I hope that this formal gesture of acknowledgment is the smallest of the many expressions of appreciation that I have made to each of you.

My family made sure that while I have rarely doubted the importance of intellectual work, I know that it is but one of many conversations. They have taught me that beauty and justice, rigor and humor, politics and faith, work and pleasure, are inseparable.

Faculty, staff, and friends at the University of Wisconsin made my five years in Madison happy and productive. Murray Edelman has changed the way I see the world, by introducing me to the ideas that motivate my work. Paul Boyer's critical encouragement and moral commitments have enriched my understanding of historical practice. Allan G. Bogue has given me a sense of place in the profession. Carl F. Kaestle offered steady guidance and friendship. Michael Apple first made me question the uses of expertise, and the members of the Department of Educational Policy Studies supported me in material and intangible ways. In the Department of History, Thomas Archdeacon, John Cooper, Stanley Kutler, and John Dower all provided timely criticism and encouragement. I wish especially to thank Judy Cochran, Jean Kennedy, and John Palmer. Steve Kretzmann, Liz Keeney, Edward Gale Agran, Charlotte Fairlie, Mo Strype, Sam Crane, David Rich Lewis, Earl Mulderink, and Nancy Isenberg made Madison difficult to leave.

The generous support of the University of Wisconsin, the American Association of University Women, the Lilly Endowment, and the Smithsonian Institution gave me the means to complete this work. I am indebted to the curators and scholars of the National Museum of American History, especially Barbara Melosh and Raymond Kondratas, for easing transitions both personal and intellectual. Charlie McGovern, I can't begin to thank.

The directors of and participants in the 1986 Summer Institute at the Center for Advanced Study in the Behavioral

Sciences, especially George S. Stocking, Jr., David Leary, James Farr, Andrew Kirby, Shank Gilkeson, Walter Jackson, David van Keuren, Ray Seidleman, Leigh Star, Antoine Joseph, Robert Proctor, Gail Hornstein, Robert Richards, Jeff Biddle, and Jill Morawski, all forced me to defend my ideas about language against excellent criticism. Director of the Center Robert Scott gave us the opportunity to engage one another. I also wish to thank David Hollinger for our conversations.

I am indebted to the expertise and generosity of the librarians and archivists of the University of Wisconsin, the Wisconsin State Historical Society, the Archives of the History of Psychology at the University of Akron, Yale University's Sterling Memorial Library, Harvard University's Widener Library, the Boston Public Library, the Stanford University Archives, the University of London, the Library of Congress, the National Archives, and the National Museum of American History.

Gail Ullman of Princeton University Press has guided this project with insight and sensitivity; my debt to her is enormous. The readers of the manuscript provided challenging criticism, for which I thank them. Annette Theuring edited the manuscript with great skill, intelligence, and sensitivity.

Michael Sokal, Leila Zenderland, Robert Wozniak, Henry L. Minton, Ray Fancher, and other members of Cheiron provided critical support at the beginning of this project.

My colleagues at Johns Hopkins have been generous with their time and energies. I especially appreciate the expert support of Betty Whildin, Sharon Widomski, Shirley Hipley, and Sharon McKenney. Louis Galambos, Bill Leslie, and John Russell-Wood have offered terrific intellectual example, company, and counsel. Vernon Litdke, Jeffrey Brooks, David Campbell, and Harry Marks all provided timely critical readings of the manuscript. Ron Walters' unfailing collegiality, shrewd criticism, and wit have made all the difference. Judy Walkowitz has appreciated my intellectual intentions, her critical comments made the more powerful by her sisterly support. J.G.A. Pocock profoundly influenced my work before we met; my appreciation is multiplied by affection. Toby Ditz and Dorothy Ross have given me their friendship as well as their insight, without which both the book and I would be much the poorer.

The Definition of a Profession

✥

❖ *Introduction* ❖

In the inevitable specialization of modern society, there
will become increasing need of those who can be paid
for expert psychological advice. We may have experts
who will be trained in schools as large as our present
schools of medicine, and their profession may
become as useful and as honorable.
(James McKeen Cattell, "The Conceptions and
Methods of Psychology" [1904])

AT THE INTERNATIONAL CONGRESS of Arts and Sciences,
held in conjunction with the Louisiana Purchase Exposition of
1904, Americans lined up to have their mental and physical capacities measured by the latest scientific techniques. In celebra-
tion of the occasion, psychology's entrepreneur James McKeen
Cattell set forth his vision of the fledgling profession in an
address on "The Conceptions and Methods of Psychology."
"Control of the physical world is secondary to the control of
ourselves and our fellow man," he proclaimed, at length con-
cluding, "If I did not believe that psychology affected conduct
and could be applied in useful ways, I should regard my occupation as nearer to that of the professional sword-swallower
than to that of the engineer or scientific physician."[1] In this address, Cattell set forth the dual model of engineering and medicine that would define, defend, and advertise the enterprise of
psychological measurement in the new century, and establish
the profession he imagined.[2]

This is a book about the ways professionals use language to
gain authority. Under study are the psychologists who formed
the core of the early movement toward intelligence testing in
the United States. These mostly academic psychologists envisaged mental testing as the basis for social progress and social
order in the Progressive Era: Robert Mearns Yerkes (1876–
1956), Lewis Madison Terman (1877–1956), Henry Herbert
Goddard (1866–1957), and Edward Lee Thorndike (1874–
1949) among the younger generation, variously inspired by

3

James McKeen Cattell (1860–1944), Wilhelm Wundt (1832–1920), William James (1842–1910), G. Stanley Hall (1844–1924), Alfred Binet (1857–1911), Francis Galton (1822–1911), and Hugo Münsterberg (1863–1916) among an older generation.[3] The language at issue is a vocabulary borrowed from medicine and engineering. These psychologists used this authoritative language to assert professional control over the logic of public education and, by extension, over the very logic of democratic rule, through the definition of popular conceptions of intelligence.[4]

This study spans the period from the closing of the American western frontier in 1890, when James McKeen Cattell first defined mental tests in a scholarly article, through the Great War, when 1.7 million U.S. Army recruits underwent tests of mental ability and achievement, to the early years of the Great Depression, when commercial publishers sold an estimated four million intelligence tests annually. Yet it was not until 1908 that Henry Herbert Goddard translated and revised the Binet scale of intelligence, upon which most intelligence testing depends, and it was in 1917–1919 that psychologists used intelligence tests on a sufficiently large population to validate the results. By 1925 the entire public educational system of the United States had been reorganized around the principles of mental measurement, and the psychological profession had produced more than seventy-five tests of general mental ability.[5] Although it has antecedents in nineteenth-century medicine, anthropometry, and phrenology, the testing enterprise developed in practical form within about a decade (1908–1918) and was fully implemented in public schools within another decade.[6] This rapid transformation needs to be explained, given the intransigence of the educational and social problems that testing was intended to address, given the currency of many component ideas throughout the nineteenth century, and particularly given the institutional inertia of the public educational system at the turn of the century.[7] The development and commercialized implementation of psychological testing was given momentum, I argue, by the cultural authority of medicine and engineering, which the psychologists invoked to advertise their own enterprise. Authoritative medical and engineering vocabularies tended to legitimate psychologists' elitist, hereditarian, and racialist assumptions by glossing the political contradictions between democratic ideals and the logic of social efficiency.[8]

This is a theoretically focused study of the semantic construction of the intelligence testing enterprise within the "new psychology." It is not intended to be a comprehensive history of mental testing.[9] I am interested in the historical, semantic processes by which a social group within the larger profession of psychology coalesced around a new technology, and by which the technology was itself socially, semantically, and historically constructed. I begin with the assumption that despite the self-imposed autonomy of professions, professionals act in other social worlds as well, and while total, long-term identification with the group is a marker of professionalism, multiple social roles impinge on this autonomous ideal. This may be especially true in the formative years of a new profession or discipline; I therefore focus on the extraprofessional and interprofessional aspects of psychologists' professionalization. Their successful self-advertisement as competent authorities over the measurement of intelligence allowed them to institutionalize a social technology with far-reaching and long-lasting implications. However, insofar as this investigation describes a complex historical interplay among private experience, metaphorical language, and the production of public knowledge, the principles at work here may pertain to all of us.[10] In a broad sense, this book is about the political uses of tradition, as implemented through metaphorical language.[11]

Between 1890 and 1930, as psychology became a profession, standardized mental tests constituted its practitioners' primary claim to a scientific and utilitarian knowledge base.[12] The general mental test became "the most important single contribution of psychology to the practical guidance of human affairs."[13] As such it was the technical foundation for psychologists' claim to professional status. Although early efforts in mental testing were greeted with skepticism by many older psychologists, by the early 1920s most such criticism emanated from outside the psychological profession, with psychologists reserving their skepticism for private correspondence.[14] Mental testing became the technology in which many American psychologists vested their aspirations for a profession as useful as engineering and as honorable as medicine. On this profession, they argued, rested most, if not all, solutions to social problems.[15]

Professionalism did not follow directly or inevitably from the development of expert psychological knowledge, as James McKeen Cattell assumed it would.[16] Professionalization depends on the creation and maintenance of at least three things: knowledge, practitioners, and clientele.[17] Psychologists in the testing movement developed a discrete body of technical expertise, based on self-consciously "scientific" knowledge, but this alone did not constitute profession. Only insofar as psychologists were able to advertise the new tests to a potential clientele, without thereby relinquishing their monopolistic ownership of the knowledge represented by the new tests, did this scientific knowledge contribute to professionalization in psychology.[18] The test psychologists' expert knowledge about human intellect, encoded in mental tests, did not itself generate practitioners and clientele; rather, I am arguing, psychologists defined the social value of their expert knowledge, created a virtual monopoly over it, and identified a school-based clientele, largely through the figurative, historically referenced language in which they modeled their inchoate profession. Much of this they accomplished in advance of the means to practice testing, even in advance of scientific data.[19] Metaphor and analogy—semantic models predicated on historical example, on other professional traditions—created for the psychologists, in forms much of the public was primed by the culture of progressivism to accept, the three requisites of profession: practitioner, knowledge, and clientele.[20] The psychologists modeled themselves, through their public discourse, upon the historical examples of the two established professions of medicine and engineering.[21]

The particular social problems that these academic psychologists identified as dangerous in their time were crime, disease, racial degeneracy, cultural diversity, and labor unrest. They understood both the prevalence of "feeblemindedness" and the waste of unrecognized talent as fundamental causes of all of these social problems.[22] They saw mental testing as a clear parallel to the larger social science of eugenics; both were typically progressive social technologies that emphasized prevention over cure, conservation over production, and efficiency over economic redistribution.[23] In these emphases the psychologists shared a larger vision of technological progressivism with an entire generation of business leaders, politicians, educators, engineers, physicians, and intellectuals.[24] This progressive vision entailed a belief that American ingenuity (generalized as human intelligence) was a great untapped natural resource, provided by God to replace the exhausted or endangered resources of cheap, tractable labor and cheap, fertile land.[25] The mobilization of this intelligence was the essence of Progressives' emphasis on improving the articulation between capitalist business enterprise and educational institutions, at both the grade-school and the university levels; of their efforts to bring university research into the service of the state; of their efforts to reform municipal government; and of their attempts to apply social-scientific research to "human engineering" in labor practices.[26] The psychologists of the testing movement, through their participation in educational reform and in business management, recycled these principles for their own professional uses, and in doing so participated in shaping progressive ideology.[27]

The political ideals subsumed under the banner of progressivism were not monolithic, nor even always compatible; neither were the political motivations, such as they can now be discerned, of the psychologists involved in the testing movement. The technological language with which the psychologists framed their professional agenda served, in fact, largely to remove their enterprise from the domain of politics and thus from the reach of its strongest critics.[28] The bracketing of divisive political issues also strengthened the apparent (and therefore effective) consensus within the discipline. This removal from the larger political domain of questions of intelligence and social worth, of personal labeling and social assignment, was the most powerful effect of the professionalization process that psychologists furthered by comparing their work to medicine and engineering. It was not until the early 1920s, several years after intelligence tests were mass-marketed, that a chorus of political dissent arose around the issues of democracy, mental testing, and "educational determinism."[29] The semantic banishment of these social questions, questions that many critics of mental tests later saw as pertaining directly and essentially to democracy itself, bought psychologists and their school clientele time to institutionalize and commercialize their techniques for mental measurement, by which time in the early 1920s critics were hard-pressed to mobilize sufficient counterevidence to remove the tests from the schools.[30] By making the measurement of intelligence a technical matter akin to gauging temperature, tensile strength, or volume, thereby fostering their own opportunities as politically "neutral" scientists to test the tests on a large number of subjects during World War I, these professionals established a data base that was, by virtue of its sheer size, nearly impossible to challenge.[31]

The psychologists' ability to assume this kind of persuasive cultural authority, to use it to get the resources they needed from the state and from private enterprise, and to meet professional challenges to their technological monopoly on "intelligence" was thoroughly dependent upon economic and social structures of power, but it was through the psychologists' semantic appeals to these structures of corporate capitalism and constitutional democracy that those structures became thoroughly implicated in the intelligence testing project. "The impact of factual reality," Hannah Arendt observes, "like all other human experiences, needs speech if it is to survive the moment of experience, needs talk and communication if it is to remain sure of itself."[32] To Marx and Engels, "language is practical consciousness."[33] Semantics defined who would partake of the new testing enterprise, and in what capacity: the dual metaphorical script projected a future psychological profession, and defined social roles for the actors therein.

The psychologists used analogy to link their inchoate enterprise to extant, allegedly politically neutral, professions, capitalizing on the order of things both to alter and to reinforce that order.[34] The metaphors drawn from engineering and medicine fortified the value of the new psychologists' numerical language into which the tests themselves translated mental

8

characteristics newly quantifiable as "intelligence," at the same time minimizing the value of teachers' traditional, qualitative, descriptive language pertaining to children's directly observed abilities.[35] The metaphors of medicine and engineering both established the cultural authority of quantitative methods and universal norms over qualitative methods and firsthand, local knowledge.[36]

Increasingly, historical scholarship on the professions has had to contend with the immaterial aspects of cultural authority, with the vague yet undeniably powerful realm of ideology, legitimation, and persuasion. In this context, nearly every recent writer on the history of the professions has had something to say about professional language, but very few have featured language in their analysis of professional authority.[37] This study, of a small but successful professionalizing effort on the part of American psychologists, is an attempt to bring the language of profession into a central position in a theory of professionalization, admittedly at the temporary and provisional expense of other analytical categories that have been the conventional foci of historical and sociological scholarship on the professions.[38] The socialized and historicized concept of language used in this analysis, which rejects language as epiphenomenal to social action, inherently allows material conditions, personal experience, historical circumstance into the picture; language, I believe, is practically inseparable from experience. Under this definition, there is no question of attributing "too much" to "mere language." Such a critique is founded on a much narrower definition of language than I, and most scholars of the linguistic turn, find plausible: language as fundamentally distinct from both private thought and social action. My understanding of language is that it is founded on metaphor, which makes it the primary means by which we make public—and therefore historical and social— our private experiences. We can only rarely make sense of even these innermost experiences without resort to a socially learned language of some kind. We are only able to think new thoughts in terms of the finite (but extraordinarily numerous) possible juxtapositions of our own historical experiences and those conveyed to us by other people, usually through language.[39] The language itself is a storehouse of collected experience.[40]

In the United States, few practicing historians until recently have considered language as the sociolinguists and philosophers tend to do, as action in itself and not merely a record of "real" action. Traditionally, historians have treated most language either as rhetoric—by which they mean a special, tricky form of speech, an anomaly confined to the public discourse of politicians and other deceivers—or simply as synonymous with thought.[41] More recently, the linguistic turn in philosophy, current in the 1950s, has at last reached history departments, via departments of English, sociology, anthropology, and political science, with confusing results.[42]

Language, it might be argued, has become the prevailing analogy governing avant-garde research in the humanities and several social sciences in the last twenty years.[43] From the vantage point of many traditional practitioners of history, the metaphors "history is literature," "history is fiction," and "the world is text" seem to dominate the new scholarship, to the apparent exclusion of other analytical possibilities. If historians work under the assumption that "reality" and "fiction" are mutually exclusive categories, then clearly this sort of analogical claim is a threat to the historian's ideal of objectivity, if not a cheap insult. If, however, historians view fiction, rhetoric, legal discourse, scientific texts, newspapers, advertisements, and gossip as different sorts of human social activity, speech-acts within specific historical, cultural, political, and economic contexts, then the equation of history and fiction is neither insulting nor threatening, but a shorthand reminder of the degree to which these human activities involve imagination, invention, interpretation, and persuasion along with observation, documentation, and proof. The philosophical burden (at the moment) is both upon the narrow positivist who would deny that creativity enters into the writing of history and upon those literary theorists who fail to recognize that "the world is text" is a rich, historically specific analogy, with epistemological, political, and professional implications.

This study began as a much more conventional investigation of the mental testing movement, seeking to explain how this particular solution to educational problems succeeded so quickly where others had faltered.[44] I read a great deal of what the mental test psychologists had written, from textbooks and dissertations to private diaries and letters, and noticed something that had not been mentioned in the secondary literature: a pervasive appeal in the published material to two particular analogies, in which psychologists compared themselves to physicians and to engineers. These analogies appeared time and time again in published sources, particularly in those addressed to nonpsychologists, almost never in private intraprofessional correspondence, and fairly regularly in diaries. What significance might this language have? Historians of psychology were silent on the subject. The literature on professions held almost no clues, with the exception of passing notations in Wilensky's famous article "The Professionalization of Everyone?" and a book by British sociologist Kenneth Hudson, *The Jargon of the Professions*.[45] I set the metaphor issue aside and continued to study the other activities of these psychologists. When the secondary and primary sources had given me a chronology that linked mental testing both to the earlier school hygiene movement and to the human engineering projects of both World Wars, I saw new social and historical significance in the metaphorical systems the psychologists shared. The metaphors had made the social linkages more salient to my historian's eye; I wondered whether the language had served the psychologists in similar ways. What were they *doing* when they employed these medical and engineering models? Medical and engineering models cropped up in psychological treatises whenever psychologists were called upon to explain their own professional identity against challenges to it; to defend or explain the validity of their knowledge base; or to claim authority over a particular clientele. This explained some of the rhetoric, but why a heavily metaphorical style, and why these particular metaphors, rather than other available models? Literary criticism, the obvious place to seek answers to these questions, seemed oblivious to the historical, referential side of the metaphorical equation.

I needed to read about the social and political uses of language, and through my teacher Murray Edelman I was introduced first to the Anglo-American, German, and Italian and

11

Soviet political-philosophical traditions rather than to Franco-American literary poststructuralism. The result is a theoretical perspective owing much more to George Herbert Mead, Edward Sapir, J. L. Austin, Ludwig Wittgenstein, and Antonio Gramsci than to Michel Foucault, Jacques Derrida, Hayden White, or Dominique LaCapra, although the shared insight among these thinkers has been obscured by the tensions among their followers. All are challenging positivist conventions that hold language apart from reality.[46] The advantages of this political-theory approach over a more literary approach have been to make it somewhat easier to keep social relations in focus while discussing the meanings of metaphor. This historical-semantic method that I develop in this book specifically historicizes linguistic evidence, rather than abstracting and generalizing it. Thus medical and engineering terms are not seen merely as symptoms of a more general scientism (though, as many have noted, they are also that) but as tracers of specific social relationships and personal experience. The method also has a striking potential to surprise the investigator, to make salient historical relationships that conventional methods have not disclosed, and that one may not expect. It supports and enriches, rather than subverts, other kinds of historical investigation and interpretation. More difficult to admit is that the political theorists who inform this study, as opposed to some of the literary critics, have not openly and aggressively challenged the very fundamental assumptions of the historical discipline, and that has been useful to someone writing for other historians.[47]

From excursions into political-semantic theory, I returned to the sociological literature on professions for a second look, having judged the "classic" work of Talcott Parsons unlovely and arrogant, enmeshed as it is in modernization theory.[48] The linguistic ride had taken me from my historical home, and I wished to root the semantic analysis of mental testing in a theoretical context indigenous to historical scholarship. It has seemed to me essential that this historical-semantic study be permeated by the study of private and social experience, not only to give the story verisimilitude, but to avoid the twin hazards of positivism and nihilism that threaten the entire philosophical enterprise.[49] On second examination, a different literature on professionalization appeared, which did not seem to preclude a historical-semantic revision.[50] The three accomplishments that sociologists had deemed requisite to professionalization were the establishment of the practitioner community; of expertise; and of a clientele.[51] These categories corresponded to the apparent functions of metaphor I had noticed in the published work of the testing psychologists. The question remained, however, why a more "scientific," expository vocabulary was not used in place of these medical and engineering analogies.

The literature on professions fell into two general types according to the priority given by its authors to the question of professional self-definition and monopolistic control over expert knowledge, versus the question of popularization and advertisement of that expertise to an actual or potential clientele: in short, the problem of monopoly versus popularity.[52] Very few scholars of the professions have dwelt on the contradiction inherent in the professionalization project as defined by the bifurcated sociological literature: the contradiction between popularization and monopoly of professional knowledge. The contradiction becomes salient only when the two kinds of studies are forced to address one another. Approaching the culture of professional psychology through its language, I viewed these two professional activities as contradictory but inseparable. The social, epistemological, and economic contests that make up the histories of professions seemed to me to stem from the professional imperative to continually maintain monopolistic control over expert knowledge while continually expanding a market for it. The prevalence of metaphors that explained the social usefulness, the moral goodness of intelligence testing while giving away nothing of its technical secrets, seemed consistent with this view, and this tension between monopoly and popularity, so well met by metaphorical discourse, is the centerpiece of my argument.

The very vagueness and multiplicity of metaphorical meaning is what makes it so powerful a social adhesive. Metaphor, through its familiar literal referent, appears to offer self-evident, socially shared meaning to the unfamiliar. Yet it invites each listener to interpret its meaning personally, even pri-

13

vately.[53] Metaphor thus softens contradictions and differences because it encapsulates a whole social system of meanings in one term, while the comprehension of specific aspects of the metaphor nevertheless may remain a very private mental act. Thus each listener is likely to interpret a given metaphor differently, yet also perceive that interpretation to be widely shared, without ever realizing that the consensus is created by the vagueness of the metaphor itself. In this way, metaphor creates a powerful illusion of consensus, but it is a fragile consensus, a "conversation of gestures" that may easily break down under scrutiny, which a socially powerful metaphor tends to obviate. Conversely, political controversies usually involve the discovery and explication of such differences in interpretation of a previously unquestioned symbol. That is, a metaphor that calls upon widely shared social experience makes other metaphors difficult to imagine.[54]

By identifying and tracing to experiential referents the generative metaphors that gave psychologists their professional logic, I do not imply that there was anything nasty, dishonest, foolish, or even unique about this usage of metaphorical language or about these people. On the contrary; I have chosen to avoid the terms *rhetoric* and *ideology* precisely because they have accumulated inescapable negative connotations, and imply that somehow we may dispense with both language and political commitments, in favor of Truth.[55] Nonetheless, I do argue that *particular* metaphors have particular sociopolitical implications and consequences that are dictated by their literal referents, and that it is appropriate to evaluate these specific consequences in ethical terms. Everyone uses language, all of which is fundamentally metaphorical, and its effects as political action are potentially both creative and stultifying, depending on *a priori* political and moral questions of value, and on which metaphors—storehouses of collective historical knowledge—are brought to bear on a given political situation.[56]

If all language is at base metaphorical, then what is distinctive about the language herein identified as medical and engineering "metaphor"? Clearly, the category is a moving target for the historian no less than for the linguist. What distinguishes the apparently metaphorical systems of reference to medicine and engineering, used by early psychologists, from the subtler analogies embedded in now-conventional professional discourse on intelligence is that the early psychologists were at great pains to elaborate their new ideas by specific and protracted references to the contemporaneous social worlds of medicine and engineering.[57] Half a century or more later, the same usage is accomplished without explication, on the tacit assumption that the professional psychologist fully shares the analogical assumptions on which the original metaphors were constructed. The distinction is as much historical and social as semantic or linguistic.[58]

The prevailing metaphors of medicine and engineering transformed mental testing from a disorganized philosophical and scientific tradition into a professional enterprise, from private vision to social system. This language advertised to all prospective consumers and sponsors of the psychological technology what was good and true and practical about it, in terms of what psychologists presumed was good and true and practical about contemporary engineering and medicine.[59] Such explication, such professional advertisement, became essential as the system of education and employment in an industrial America became more and more attenuated, less and less reliant on intimate, personal, local, firsthand knowledge transmitted between teacher and student, graduate and employer, officer and soldier, physician and patient, psychologist and client.[60]

Moreover, the intelligence quotient per se can be understood as an advertisement of the self that in a more local economy of human talent would be redundant. Although, as I point out, all measurements of intelligence were standardized against received subjective wisdom about group or individual capacities, psychologists insisted tautologically on the independence of their mass data from the errors of subjective judgment, the so-called personal equation. The "IQ" became for the individual entering a rationalized educational and employment system a sort of normative certification, analogous to professional certification, or to a brand name.[61] The quotient came to represent the entire logical system by which intellectual power would be described not as a personal attribute but ultimately with reference to a universal standard. The quotient comparing

15

chronological age to mental age ultimately advertised psychology as succinctly as it advertised the mental capability of the individual.

This book has two beginnings, and different readers may choose different chapters with which to begin. Chapter 1, which was written last, sets forth the semantic theory of professions that I derived from this study of mental testing. It can profitably be read first, with the caveat that it did not determine my historical research strategy in advance, but rather comprises the general conclusions of that research; it can also be read as a summary methodological chapter. The chapter was originally published as "Professional Language: Words That Succeed," in a special issue on language and work of *The Radical History Review* in January 1986.

Chapter 2, the chronological beginning of the book, briefly describes the larger discipline of psychology as it emerged in the nineteenth century from allied pursuits. The chapter also addresses the centrality of psychological technologies to the ideology of progressivism, with its emphasis on mental resources.

Chapter 3 portrays the schools into which standardized mental tests were introduced, explaining how the social realities of education at the turn of the century were viewed by teachers, school administrators, educational reformers, social critics, and even the occasional parent or child in such a way that standardized tests were more welcomed than feared. This chapter also addresses the importance of the school hygiene and medical inspection movements in clearing the way for medical-like interventions by psychologists.

Chapter 4 explains the personal sources and resonances of the medical and engineering analogies that bound the psychologists into a community of discourse. The emphasis is not on conventional biography but on (public and private) experiential commonalities captured by the shared vocabularies.

Chapter 5 contains closer analyses of the medical language used by psychologists, and of the historical references inspiring this language. Metaphors are not self-explanatory; for historical purposes, it is necessary to ask what possible references to shared experience the psychologists could have been claiming by evoking these, and not other, metaphors.

Chapter 6 parallels Chapter 5 in exploring the psychologists' professional use of engineering language. This chapter also examines similar use of an efficiency model among teachers, school administrators, and educational reformers.

Chapter 7 loosely parallels Chapter 4 in examining the social-historical components of the engineering metaphor as it developed in the context of World War I, and the significance of the war in creating a mass data base and patriotic propaganda for universal testing.

Chapter 8 examines the significance of numbers as a special kind of language whose importance was reinforced and elaborated by the logic of medical and engineering analogies. This chapter was originally published as "Mental Measurements and the Rhetorical Force of Numbers," in *The Estate of Social Knowledge*, ed. JoAnne Brown and David van Keuren (Baltimore: Johns Hopkins University Press, 1991).

The Bibliographic Essay is offered as a brief guide to the several theoretical literatures on which this study draws, and to the archival and secondary sources on the history of psychology and mental testing. A comprehensive bibliography of primary sources appears in JoAnne Brown, *The Semantics of Profession* (Ann Arbor, Mich.: University Microfilms, 1986).

17

The Semantics of Profession

A THEORY

> There was a painter became a physician, whereupon a
> citizen said to him: "You have done well; for before
> the faults of your work were seen but
> now they are unseen."
> (Attributed to Francis Bacon)

THE EARLIEST MEANING of the term *profession* was religious, and referred to a proclamation of faith. A great "professor" was one whose religious devotion was unimpeachable: during the Salem witchcraft trials, Goody Nurse was termed an "old professor" in her defense, for she had long professed her devotion to God.[1] By 1675, the term had acquired secular significance, meaning "having claim to due qualifications." The newer professions drew sustenance from the old: medics and lawyers drew authority from the clergy, and both medical and legal practices were, until fairly recently, the province of clerics.[2]

The shift in the connotations of the word *profession* from religious to secular—such that the term came to include first medicine and law, then nearly everyone—is a fair recapitulation of the history of work in Western countries.[3] The word *profession* is not a mere reflection of this history, but an integral and active part of it. The term is a reminder of the way in which each succeeding generation, and each new group of would-be professionals, used the examples of history in order to define, organize, and publicize their own particular expertise and cultural authority. In successive generations of would-be professionals, the language of predecessors became, through the ingenious use of metaphor, ready-made and usable tradition. Moreover, as the words *profession* and *professional* (and *laity* and *lay*, and all of the more particular emulative terms employed) were used by new secular groups to draw upon established authority for

18

their own purposes, the meanings of the words changed and expanded.

Professionals are now defined as workers whose qualities of detachment, autonomy, and group allegiance are more extensive than those found among other workers. The difference is one of degree; professions differ from other occupations in attributes that are common to all work. Among professionals, these attributes include a high degree of systematic knowledge; strong community orientation and loyalty; self-regulation; and a system of rewards defined and administered by the community of workers.[4]

One flaw in this definition is that it does not distinguish professional work from skilled craft-work. Sociologist Eliot Freidson argues that a discrimination can be made on the basis of the more extensive higher learning required for the professions, but this distinction seems weak.[5] A more telling difference between craft-work and professional work lies in the relations among work, practitioner, and client. Craft-work, unlike professional work, is inherently and historically its own publicist. The standards of a craft-worker's skill are defined by the clientele, and the quality of a given piece of work is judged by the client directly. A cabinetmaker is judged by how well the cabinets look and function; a plumber's skills, a roofer's skills, are known directly by the householder who can see that the pipes are fixed and the roof no longer leaks. Craft-work is work that needs little or no further interpretation in order to be judged good or bad. In other words, craft-work entails no argument, no interpretation on the part of the worker, in order that the client may know, without resorting to specialized knowledge, that the work in question has been completed to a given standard.[6] The work-product speaks for itself. These distinctions are clearly not hard and fast, and under some modern conditions of work, many crafts have acquired some of the attributes of professions, largely owing to the atrophy of manual skills and craft-knowledge among the general population.

Professional work is work that, for complex reasons related to the changing technological and social situations in which it is performed and evaluated, needs some interpretation in order to be appreciated by a clientele. Medicine is a prime example.

Because disease can kill or maim people in spite of the best medicine, results are not adequate definition of medical competence. Both doctors and patients need protection from this uncertainty—good doctors need to survive (professionally) the deaths or chronic illnesses of their patients; patients need to discriminate between good and bad doctors without recourse to crude mortality and morbidity statistics. In short, professionals must somehow interpret, translate, or mediate the results of their work in order that the public, their clients, may appreciate its value. Mechanisms for mediating among work, practitioner, and client have developed with doctors' and patients' changing expectations of therapeutic efficiency. These expectations, in turn, depend both on advances in therapeutic efficacy (e.g., theoretical and technological advances such as asepsis and vaccination) and on the meanings of illness, death, cure, and expertise that are culturally defined and historically specific. As Paul Starr has documented, therapeutic efficacy does not translate automatically into cultural authority.[7] Conversely, as Charles Rosenberg has shown, ineffective—even dangerous—therapies may inspire patients with great respect for the physician.[8] "People are obliged," writes sociologist Erving Goffman, "not only to carry out their tasks and routines, but also to *express* their competence in doing so."[9] Often, particularly under highly bureaucratic conditions, the expression of competence is all that matters.[10]

The changing character of work in twentieth-century America has led sociologist Harold Wilensky to speculate about "the professionalization of everyone."[11] Clients cannot make effective judgments as to the quality of professional work when they are utterly removed from the institutional context in which that work is performed, and when the professional work-product is vague and diffuse. Accepting for the moment that professional work is work that requires mediation between practitioner and clientele, it is easy to see that the increased technical specialization, bureaucracy, geographic mobility, attenuation of community, and division of labor that characterize modern work also create conditions in which interpretation is necessary. Under these conditions, many kinds of practitioners (Wilensky's "everyone") seek the protection of professionalization, and many clients acquiesce.[12] An occupation will have difficulty claiming the monopoly of skill essential to professionalism if its technical base "consists of a vocabulary that sounds familiar to everyone."[13] There is thus a social pressure on would-be professionals to create a closed and esoteric vocabulary. The more historical circumstances and the intrinsic logistics of a given kind of work conspire to make difficult the client's assessment of the worker's competence, the more workers will devote time and effort to expressing (as opposed to merely demonstrating) their own competence. The complex institutional results of this expression are what we call professionalism.[14]

Professional associations, educational systems, restrictive licensing, and legal sanctions against unlicensed practice can all be seen as efforts to express competence indirectly, by creating a community of authority among practitioners that will supplant the client's personal judgment. These institutions develop out of the accumulated arguments that workers offer clients to convince clients of their legitimacy in the absence of work-products that "speak for themselves."[15] That is, the social institutions that characterize full-blown professions are the formal products of practitioners' efforts to express their competence. There is nothing inherently illegitimate about these efforts. These institutions become self-perpetuating as they continue to generate arguments on behalf of their members. Individual practitioners then offer advice, as Paul Starr explains, "not as a personal act based on privately revealed or idiosyncratic criteria, but as [representatives] of a community of shared standards."[16]

Groups of practitioners trying to establish new professional institutions have first to establish the value of their work in the eyes of a clientele. At the same time, however, these would-be professionals have to keep their specialized knowledge from becoming common knowledge. Within societies that idealize both capitalism and democracy, an inherent tension arises between the twin tasks of *popularizing* one's contribution to society, so that it is comprehensible enough to be appreciated, and *monopolizing* one's knowledge, so that it is incomprehensible enough to be marketable. In highly developed, well-established professions, monopoly is the main concern, while in new pro-

21

fessions, popularity is more important. The two pose continual problems for professionals, who must publicize their work without "giving away" their expertise. In the course of solving this dilemma, professionals create special forms of argument that explain the profession to its clientele without revealing its secrets. The most common and effective way professionals do this, I am convinced, is through the use of metaphor.[17] Professional language, therefore, holds a position of supreme importance in the resolution of this chronic difficulty.

This linguistic or semantic approach to the historical processes of professionalization fits the social-historical formulation developed by historians of medicine in recent years. The formation of a new profession involves both the creation of a body of knowledge and the maintenance of professional controls over that knowledge. As Starr and others have explained, professionalism rests on the "twin supports" of dependency and legitimacy. Dependency is a function of professionals' ability to monopolize their knowledge; legitimacy is a function of their ability to popularize it. The "project" of professionalization involves balancing these two functions such that professional knowledge is appreciable by a clientele, yet not entirely demystified. Professionalization, I argue, is thus a fundamentally contradictory undertaking. Metaphor, as a rhetorical form of political action, is uniquely suited to resolving the contradictions inherent in the project of professionalization. Bridging the functions of "dependency" and "legitimacy," metaphor enables professionals to explain themselves and their work to a clientele, without relinquishing to that clientele the esoteric knowledge in which they trade.

LANGUAGE AND PROFESSION

According to Kenneth Hudson, "If one wished to kill a profession, to remove its cohesion and its strength, the most effective way would be to forbid the use of its characteristic language."[18] Because professional work is not its own publicist, but must be interpreted by its practitioners to their clientele, an elaborate semantic system evolves around any profession. So much in a profession depends on language that, as Hudson argues, the professions could not exist otherwise.[19] Moreover, the maintenance of a balance between professional monopoly on expert knowledge and a sufficient popularity stimulates would-be professionals to borrow authority and image from other, precedent professions. If professionals did not do this borrowing, their authority would necessarily rest wholly on an exegesis of their own expertise, and they would risk losing their monopoly over their specialized knowledge, and hence the market for their expertise. This borrowing takes the form of linguistic mimicry and modeling, evident in professionals' prolific use of metaphor. It is a creative process.

Physicians thus draw upon clerical authority in distinguishing themselves from "laymen," in making a convention of confidentiality, and, especially in earlier centuries, in adopting moral theology as the basis of disease etiology.[20] More recently, psychologists of the early twentieth century drew linguistically upon the cultural authority of medicine in order to advance their claims to a new profession. Psychologists compared themselves to medical doctors, mental and social problems to bodily disease, and their methods, such as the "IQ" test, to diagnostic instruments like the thermometer, the x-ray, and the blood count. In using the social and epistemological powers of language, psychologists were not alone among middle-class American professionals. Other professions have taken other metaphors as their primary legitimation: nurses have used the ministry; social workers, both the ministry and medicine; teachers, agriculture, industry, and engineering; engineers, law and medicine; psychoanalysts, surgery; lawyers, the ministry; medical scientists, the military. Professionals may use different metaphors as their intellectual and political status changes, but most favor some reference to the archetypal professions, using medical, military, or theological metaphors and returning to these models in times of professional crisis. Professionalizing engineers, for example, at the turn of the century frequently likened their profession to a priesthood: "We are the priests of material development," proclaimed the leader of the American Society of Civil Engineers in 1895.[21] Physicians and other health professionals have long favored both theological and

23

military metaphors; Cotton Mather spoke of ministers' practice of medicine as "an angelic conjunction."[22] Early-nineteenth-century health reformers continued to cast their ideas in religious terms: *The Catechism of Health*, published in 1819, was a family medical guide.[23] Military language overtook, but did not supplant, religious language in medicine sometime in the mid–nineteenth century.[24] Officials of the U.S. Public Health Service called the early-twentieth-century medical inspection of immigrants "the first line of defense" against disease and eugenical "taint."[25] Following earlier public health discourse on tuberculosis, medical journalists still write of the "crusade" against cancer, a term at once religious and military.[26]

The phenomenon of linguistic modeling—the use of metaphor to found a new enterprise upon the cultural authority of an old one—is in fact so common as to seem to require no comment. But the phenomenon is no mere curiosity; it becomes important historically (and politically) when a group of professionals begins to use a single metaphor systematically and repeatedly in accomplishing the demanding tasks of creating its knowledge base, defending its practice against encroachment and charlatanism, and popularizing its social role among a clientele. When this happens, the vision of the profession narrows and coalesces around the logic of the chosen metaphor, and its daily operations, its group decision-making, and individual members' practices become routinized, and their responses to change and to challenge become stultified. When a single metaphor becomes dominant, it tends to lose its metaphorical qualities and, in becoming part of a literal vocabulary, loses its creative potential. To remain "alive," a metaphor must retain, in use, its *dis*similarities to the thing signified, as well as its similarities.[27]

The widespread, uncritical acceptance of a professional, metaphorical vocabulary—such as "the war on cancer"—has social consequences, human consequences.[28] Alternative constructions of the problem become difficult to entertain; certain questions are made irrelevant, certain evidence disallowed, certain witnesses disqualified. A profession may also quickly gain inordinate power over its clientele and over competing practitioners on the basis of its borrowed authority. Its driving metaphors may become so persuasive that neither internal nor external criticism is possible; such dissent is, in a powerful sense, heretical.

It would be patently absurd to insist that anyone—even professionals—abandon metaphor and other characteristic language; there *is* no language that is not fundamentally metaphorical.[29] Nonetheless, inquiries into the metaphorical bases of professions' cultural authority are to be welcomed for introducing alternative models, with alternative sociopolitical implications. Such alternatives can moderate the power of professions and loosen obsolescent habits of practice.

LANGUAGE, POWER, COMMUNITY, AND MIND

Historians, anthropologists, political scientists, social psychologists, and sociologists seem to agree that language is somehow intertwined with the creation of power. But because the historiographic, anthropological, political, psychological, and sociological vocabularies with which scholars discuss language are not unified, this cross-disciplinary consensus is easily missed. One scholar may write of "communities of discourse," another of "jargon," another of "symbol," another of "rhetoric," another of "persuasion" and "argument," another of "hegemony," another of "ideology." All are describing their observations that language seems to have something to do with power relations within and among communities.[30]

That language should have something to do with profession is therefore hardly surprising, insofar as professions have been termed "communities within communities" whose social power is the gist of their fascination to scholars. Sociolinguists, particularly anthropological scholars, have long accepted that language is one of the bases of community and individual identity, perhaps *the* basis. As anthropologist Edward Spicer writes, "the specialized vocabulary is a vital part of the mechanism of social separation." This specialized vocabulary defines who belongs to the community and who does not: "It includes words for self-identification and reference, and for defining the opposition." Spicer is drawing on a long tradition of research on language and community that informed the work of George Herbert Mead and Leonard Bloomfield and has continued with that of Charles Hockett and Dell Hymes.[31]

In addition to its well-documented social functions in defining community, language obviously is a preeminent feature of mind. George Herbert Mead writes, "Language, as made up of significant symbols, is what we mean by mind."[32] In particular, metaphor and other forms of analogy have been understood as the basis of creative intelligence; some have argued that this is because of the metaphorical basis of all language.[33] If the historians and philosophers of science are correct in taking models, analogies, and metaphors to be *the* bases of scientific knowledge, then again it should not surprise us to find that metaphorical language is a fundamental aspect of professionalization, since the development of specialized knowledge is central to the professional project.[34] Language, then, is a vital principle of both the social (political) and the epistemological (scientific) aspects of profession, defining both professional community and professional knowledge.

WORDS ABOUT LANGUAGE: A HISTORIOGRAPHIC PROBLEM

If language is salient in both important aspects of profession, why have historians of the professions paid so little systematic attention to professional language?[35] Few scholars have recognized the centrality of language to profession, largely because scholarly language itself contains so many verbs that denote linguistic acts without emphasizing their linguistic character. That is, many verbs that seem to describe nonverbal physical "action" in fact denote acts that are essentially linguistic. The dichotomy between words and deeds is profoundly embedded in Western cultural tradition, and in English scholarly discourse. It is therefore easy for historians to write about the past conduct of professionals without emphasizing, or even recognizing, that most of what they report is what professionals in the past *said*.

One finds in scholarly work a subtle obfuscation of the linguistic aspects of any political action, including the political action that occupies professionals. This unconscious and innocent concealment derives from the vocabulary in which history is conventionally written. The historian's vocabulary overflows with words that denote linguistic actions and transactions, but that seem instead to describe some other, possibly more "real," activity. A close reading of any history of the professions yields countless such terms, used by the historian to enliven his or her prose. Professionals, when they are expressing (as opposed to demonstrating) their competence, are mostly just saying things, but the historian is doomed stylistically who recounts the proceedings of a professional congress with only a "he said" and a "she said." In a concerted effort to make history come alive, historians who study the professions mask the essentially linguistic aspect of the past professional activities that are their historical subject. When, for example, historian Barbara Melosh writes, "Established professionals must polish up their image periodically," she evokes a kind of busyness that is more palpable than the activities she is describing. Professionals don't actually *polish* their *images*; they make various kinds of persuasive statements in trying to convince their public of their continued competence and unique importance.[36] The "polishing up" is, first and last, linguistic, but Melosh, working under the stylistic constraints of *her* profession, and of English-language scholarship in general, uses other verbs to describe these acts. There is nothing foolish or nasty (or even unique) in the way that historians use figurative language to describe the linguistic actions of professionals; as emphasized earlier, it would be silly to insist that historians limit themselves to a literal vocabulary. But the way that historians write about language has made it difficult for us to recognize its importance to the social and intellectual processes of professionalization.

The same conventions hold true for sociologists, with similar consequences. Thus sociologist Magali Sarfatti Larson uses the term *translate* apparently without attending to its literal, linguistic sense, as a kind of dead metaphor, a mere synonym for *transform*. "Professionalism," Larson writes, "is thus an attempt to *translate* one order of scarce resources—special knowledge and skills—into another—social and economic rewards."[37] *Translate* is the key word here; it describes the kind of transformation, a fundamentally linguistic one, that takes place when special knowledge and skills are presented to a public. Because the word *translate* is such a common metaphor in scholarly discourse, Larson uses it without necessarily intending it to mean "a linguistic transformation." In a somewhat similar manner, Paul Starr discusses the bases of professional authority, stressing "argument" as one of the "twin supports" for medicine's cultural authority (the other being force). Very quickly, however, he turns from "argument" to "persuasion," then to "legitimacy," and the linguistic aspect of these nouns fades from the reader's consciousness.[38] Larson and Starr are exceptions among scholars of professionalism in that they acknowledge the role of language, though they do not feature it as language per se in their analyses.[39]

In a series of lectures delivered in 1955, philosopher J. L. Austin investigated this phenomenon (which I see as a special historiographic problem), whereby verbs hide the linguistic nature of many human actions. Austin listed these verbs, and differentiated among several kinds of action that words could accomplish.[40] Some of his words appear below (I have added others).

accept	bet	finagle	join	quash
accuse	bless	fine	judge	rank
adopt	certify	grade	license	report
advertise	charge	grant	locate	revise
affirm	choose	greet	marry	rule
agree	christen	guarantee	mention	solicit
annul	convince	hedge	name	swear
apologize	deny	impeach	object	testify
appoint	disavow	impute	pardon	thank
ask	dismiss	indict	pray	urge
ban	draft	interpret	promise	vote
bequeath	explain	introduce	protest	welcome

Austin points out that uttering the phrase "I promise" or "I christen thee" or "I give and bequeath" is an act, and not a description or report of an act. He notes that U.S. law recognizes a secondhand report of such language as an eyewitness report of an act, and not as hearsay.[41] Each of these verbs denotes a complex act involving speaking, writing, or signaling: an act of communication. Such verbs are common in the English language, and appear particularly often in historical discourse. These "linguistic" verbs are even more prevalent in histories of the professions, since most of past professional actions that historians describe are linguistic actions. As noted earlier, these words lend a sense of physical action to otherwise dry historical descriptions of past professional proceedings.

Because professional work demands interpretation, professionals talk a lot. Professional meetings are devoted not only to the exhibition of research, but to the passing of resolutions, the naming of committees, the election of officers, the ousting of charlatans, the congratulation of peers, the declaration of principles, and the definition of professional prerogatives.[42] All of these activities are designed to maintain the cultural authority of the profession, and are part of the vast interpretive task necessitated by the nature of professional work. Professionals may form associations, and may join such organizations. They may appoint or elect officers, after certifying their credentials. They may congratulate, even toast, the new officers, who in turn swear to uphold the association's constitution and bylaws. On occasion they may draft new rules, and void old ones, after due debate; they may disagree. They may excommunicate heretical members, and ban others altogether. The officers may themselves be impeached, and their policies disavowed. The professional association may publish a journal, in which their proceedings are printed, appointments announced, and jobs posted. All of these acts are primarily linguistic, though they do not immediately or commonsensically appear so.[43] The variety of verbs used to describe linguistic acts tends to create the illusion of another, vague kind of busyness. Nonetheless, the professional community and the ideas it stands for are created and maintained through these linguistic acts. When uttered (or published) in the appropriate social contexts, certain words are, in and of themselves, deeds. Though they are fundamentally linguistic acts, "electing" and "annulling" are just as much definite actions as "punching" or "embracing." Like punching and kissing, these linguistic acts are heavily dependent on context for their meaning—*but not more so*. In arguing that their linguistic character has often been ignored, I do not imply that these linguistic acts are less real, less powerful, or less definite than punching or embracing.[44] Nor are they more so. On the contrary, the point is that there is not as much difference between talk and action as we have enshrined in our homilies; therefore, historians should desist from treating language as if it were usually merely a record of nonlinguistic action. This applies particularly to historians of the professions, because most of the action carried out by the professionals they study is linguistic.

The sense of busyness created by verbs that denote linguistic acts is largely a product of the way language itself is conceived. George Lakoff and Mark Johnson have shown that in the English language, argument is conceived of as war. The war metaphor offers a discrete lexicon by which to discuss and describe argument, including the arguments that occupy professionals: "Your claims are indefensible," "Her criticisms are right on target," "They shot down my arguments," "You disagree? Okay, shoot!"[45] In the busyness of professional activities, much of the movement comes from this and other active metaphors through which argument and other language is described. In the editorial column of a professional journal, or in a convention address, one professional "attacks" another, "buttressing" his or her argument with weighty facts. Others may "rally to the defense" of the victim; some may "stay out of the fray." The entire "battle" may take place without the combatants' ever meeting one another, further demonstrating that it is this shared conversation, rather than actual physical contact, that creates the community of professionals.[46]

HEGEMONY AND LEGITIMATION

Linguistic communities can and usually do transcend temporal as well as geographic constraints. Like the spatial dimension of these problems, the historical dimension has been somewhat neglected by observers concerned with professional language, or with the more general problems of hegemony and legitimation. Some historians and sociologists who concern themselves with the professions focus on professional hegemony and the processes of legitimation. Like the words in Austin's list, these two terms obfuscate the linguistic nature of the phenomena they describe.[47] Both denote the complex operations by which economic power is "translated" into cultural authority, and vice versa. In *The Social Construction of Reality*, Peter Berger and Thomas Luckman discuss the historical and linguistic aspects of legitimation, but they unfortunately illustrate most of their discussion with ahistorical hypothetical examples that are insensitive to the historical, "time-binding" functions of language.[48] Berger and Luckman point out that "language bridges different zones within the reality of everyday life and integrates them into a meaningful whole. The transcendences have spatial, temporal and social dimensions."[49] Berger and Luckman's prose is overburdened with abstract nouns and verbs that leave the reader whirling in a discourse of symbols, signs, and "objectified and objectivated sedimentations," all of which conspire to obliterate the reader's understanding that the "social construction of reality" is fundamentally linguistic.[50]

Antonio Gramsci developed his concept of cultural hegemony, as exercised by professionals and others, in an effort to explain how power is exerted in the absence of coercion. Gramsci recognizes both the historical dimension of hegemony and the role of language in transmitting historical meaning from one generation to the next.[51] Unfortunately, his readers have adopted as Gramsci's fundamental theoretical contribution the more diffuse notion of hegemony, and have set aside his insights on language. Gramsci explains how hegemony is partially maintained through the uncritical acceptance of an inherited, "verbal" conception of the world: "But this 'verbal' conception is not without consequences. It binds together a specific social group, it influences moral conduct and the direction of will, in a manner more or less powerful, but often powerful enough to produce a situation in which the contradictory character of consciousness does not permit any action, any decision or any choice, and produces a condition of moral and political passivity."[52] Thus the ability of language to transmit ideas from one generation to the next is, in Gramsci's thinking, the essence of what subsequent scholars have called "hegemony." For Gramsci, the effects of language are to undermine private or class conviction in the lived experience, to negate personal experience. Language can have a massive stultifying effect on other political actions. But language also has tremendous liberating potential. To confound analysis even further, what is liberation to one group or person is oppression to another. It becomes important to study these phenomena historically, to judge under what circumstances language is empowering, and to whom and for what ends, and under what circumstances it is disempowering, and to whom and for what ends. Since social-historical context ultimately determines the function of language, while language is a major part of any social context, there seems as little point to arguing for one over the other as to arguing in favor of studying eggs over chickens. In the case of professional psychology detailed in the following chapters, language and social context are seen as inextricably linked, mutually determinative. One learns more about each by studying both, and, as in studying chickens and eggs, there are moments when the two are indistinguishable.

Two scholars in particular, J.G.A. Pocock and Murray J. Edelman, have focused on language as the key to politics in its broadest sense. Pocock concludes that only by attending to the language of historical political thinkers can we understand the history of political thought. He argues that language, not thought, is the political historian's proper and profitable subject.[53] The study of language, as opposed to the traditional study of political thought, gives the historian some grounding in traceable events, and releases him or her from the harmattan of ideas.[54]

Murray Edelman begins by converting the traditional political question "Why do men rebel?" into the more pertinent "Why *don't* people rebel?" Why, when the distribution of health, wealth, and happiness is so patently unfair, don't people rebel to change it? Edelman concludes that Gramsci's ephemeral "cultural hegemony" can be studied in its concrete form, as language. Vocabulary, syntax, and grammar, according to Edelman, "can help us understand . . . how we decide upon status, rewards, and controls."[55] Political symbols, which commonly appear in linguistic form, "justify established authorities and their policies while also rationalizing inequalities, deprivations, and ineffective courses of action."[56] Metaphorical language, in particular, establishes the central characteristics of political events or persons by creating assumptions about matters that are not seen.[57] As Edelman demonstrates in his study of American welfare policy, the logic of social hierarchies—including the hierarchies of profession—are embedded in the language used by the members of these hierarchies, by those at the bottom as well as those at the top. Because language is not merely another kind of activity, but is the archive of history, language is the "key to the universe of speaker and audience."[58] It is an integral part of every social structure and of the mental equipment of every person, binding people to each other and to their traditions, and integrating individual experience with social-historical precedent. Again, metaphorical language is particularly powerful: "Once accepted, a metaphorical view becomes the organizing conception into which the public thereafter arranges items of news that fit and in the light of which it interprets the news. In this way a particular view is reinforced and repeatedly seems to be validated for those whose attitude it expresses. It becomes self-perpetuating."[59] Just as a metaphor can be the organizing principle underlying a new scientific theory, metaphor is also found at the base of any political ideology. It lends coherence and social verisimilitude to all sorts of novel ideas, and is the basis for challenges to the status quo, as well as for its maintenance.

In the complex amalgam of social and epistemological activities subsumed under what historians study as "professionalization," language, and particularly metaphor, holds a central place. It is uniquely suited to resolving the contradiction between popularity and monopoly that lies at the heart of the project of professionalization, because it advertises without disclosing, and sells without delivering, the special knowledge that is the professional's commodity.

In the chapters that follow, I explore the historically particular political and epistemological uses to which an emerging professional community, American psychologists of the mental testing movement, put two metaphorical vocabularies—that of medicine and that of engineering. I will discuss alternative metaphors, including unsuccessful uses of medical language by other professionals, and relatively unsuccessful vocabularies within the school-psychology community. I will argue that the favored vocabularies of medicine and engineering did not arise "naturally" out of any superior rhetorical value embedded somehow in the words themselves, but were chosen systematically—though not always consciously—from a range of available alternatives, for specific biographical, social, and historical reasons.[60] I argue that the material accomplishments of early-twentieth-century medical and engineering practice created powerful models that psychologists emulated for particular practical reasons. Thus the historical realm of language and the historical realm of action are not separate, nor are they separable; language is a particular form of action, identifiable with social-historical consequences, and therefore part of the social landscape. At the same time, it is often distinguishable as a particular kind of human action as against other kinds. In the case that follows, I argue that medical and engineering language allowed a nascent profession to gain, though tenuously and partially, both popularity and monopoly, two requisites of professional power.

Psychology as a Science

The Science of human nature is of this description.
It falls far short of the standard of exactness now
realized in Astronomy; but there is no
reason that it should not be as much
a science as . . . Astronomy.
(John Stuart Mill,
A System of Logic, Ratiocinative and Inductive [1843])

I wished by treating psychology like a natural science
to help her to become one.
(William James, *Collected Essays* [1892])

T HE TERM *PSYCHOLOGY* dates at least from the seventeenth century, when it was used to divide the study of Man—Anthropology—into three disciplines: Psychology, the study of the soul; Somatology, the study of the body, and Hematology, the study of the blood.[1] It was the nineteenth century, however, that yielded the notion that the study of the "thoughts, feelings and actions of sentient beings" could be pursued in like manner to the study of inanimate and insensate phenomena.[2]

The very premise of a scientific psychological discipline was denied by positivist philosophers. Mill's and James's common conviction of the possibility of a psychological science was not shared by the French positivist Auguste Comte, whose works were first translated into English and made widely available as late as 1903.[3] Comte's dismissal of psychology as "an idle fancy, and a dream, when it is not an absurdity," stands retrospectively as the indictment against which twentieth-century American psychologists continually sought to defend themselves. The American measurement psychologists in particular struggled to rid themselves of such "soft" metaphysical characterizations, and their emphasis on practical application should be seen, in part, as a reaction against Comtean skepticism. Between 1890 and 1930, through divers efforts, they created a psychological enterprise that embodied both practical and scientific ideals: a quantitative psychology that, in their view, advanced knowledge of the human mind both for its own sake and for the purposes of practical social application.[4] Like other social scientists, as historian Dorothy Ross has observed, these psychologists "claimed to have established [their science] before they were in possession of any firm body of scientific knowledge."[5]

The intellectually prolific German physiologist and philosopher Wilhelm Wundt (1832–1920) is credited with being the first "philosophical psychologist spawned by experimental science."[6] Trained in medicine and in physiology, Wundt established the world's first experimental psychology laboratory at Leipzig in 1879. During a period when psychology was not as yet a well-established university course of study in the United States, Leipzig was the essential training ground for American scholars aspiring to the new scientific discipline.[7] With Wundt's experimental and physiological psychology came the most complete dissociation of psychology from metaphysics, and it was Wundt above all who inspired the Americans. As historian Daniel Robinson has argued, Wundt bequeathed the psychophysical method to twentieth-century psychology, but it should be added that the social structures and intellectual content of American medicine and engineering provided ample independent confirmation for this approach.[8]

Also essential to understanding the psychology of measurement in the United States is the influence of British polymath Sir Francis Galton. Galton, a cousin of biologist Charles Darwin, and son of Erasmus Darwin, was a scientist in the nineteenth-century style; his work ranged among the now-differentiated disciplines of criminology, anthropology, genetics, eugenics, physiology, psychology, and sociology. Galton coined the term *eugenics* to describe the scientific application of laws of inheritance to the improvement of the human race, and he is best remembered for his commitment to eugenics as a secular religion. However, equally important to the transformation of psychology from metaphysics was his emphasis on quantitative method, not only as proof of causation, but as insight into correlation. Correlation is the premise on which quantitative measures are based. In the words of statistician Karl Pearson, Galton's protegé and biographer, this emphasis "not only enormously widened the field to which quantitative and therefore mathematical methods can be applied, but it has at the same time modified our philosophy of science and even of life itself."[9] The American measurement psychologists were fond of comparing their own science with Galton's science of racial hygiene: psychometrics was to the prediction and control of the individual what eugenics was to the prediction and control of the race.[10]

It was James McKeen Cattell who brought the ideas of Wundt and Galton to the United States and introduced them into the university curriculum. G. Stanley Hall, who had completed his doctorate under William James and H. P. Bowditch at Harvard, was the first American to work at Wundt's laboratory; James McKeen Cattell in 1886 became Wundt's first American graduate. With William James, Hall and Cattell became the most influential mentors of the next generation of American psychologists, who created the subdiscipline of mental measurement.

By the end of the nineteenth century, practitioners of psychology in the United States were beginning to distinguish their inchoate discipline both from its matrix in philosophy and from the "superstitions" that surrounded it in mesmerism, spiritualism, and traditional religions. An emphasis on physiology, laboratory experimentation, and above all the quantitative method would demonstrate to potential clients, critics, and competitors alike that the "new" psychology, unlike its disciplinary forebears, was truly a science of the mind.

Following the examples of several other academic disciplines of American social science, psychologists in the late nineteenth century organized. The *American Journal of Psychology*, initiated through subscription in 1886 by Johns Hopkins professor G. Stanley Hall, appeared in October 1887; in 1891 Hall established a second professional journal, *The Pedagogical Seminary*. In 1892 Hall invited twenty-six men to join a new academic society, the American Psychological Association, institutionalizing at a new level the post–Civil War expansion of the discipline. By 1905 the Association had grown to 105 members; by 1920, over

300.[11] In Hall's judgment, expressed in 1894, psychology was "slowly rewriting the whole history of philosophy," promising a new era to succeed decades of evolutionary thought, the "psychological era of scientific thought." In this new age, Hall envisioned, all other sciences would bring their "ripest and best thoughts" to psychology, the "long hoped for, long delayed science of man."[12]

Hall had established the first psychological laboratory in the United States at The Johns Hopkins University in 1883, only four years after Wilhelm Wundt had opened the Leipzig laboratory. Over the next decade, nearly two dozen such laboratories were founded in the United States, most by scientists trained either by Hall at Hopkins (later, at Clark), by Wilhelm Wundt at Leipzig, or by William James at Harvard.[13]

As influential as Hall was in shaping the early interests of the measurement psychologists who developed mental tests, his open-mindedness toward Sigmund Freud's psychosexual theory and Hall's preoccupation with religion made some of his followers uncomfortable, for they wanted a purer science, free from the complications of religion, superstition, emotion, and sexuality. Although Hall inspired many of the early measurement psychologists, he initially did not approve of the measurement enterprise; his student at Clark University, Lewis Terman, recalled in fact that Hall had "strenuously opposed" such an endeavor. Terman concluded that Hall's opposition was due to his being "constitutionally incapable of appreciating the type of work mental testers attempted to do."[14]

With Wundt and Galton, French psychologist Alfred Binet was a primary influence from abroad on the development of mental testing in the United States. His commissioning in 1904 by the French government to devise a plan for diagnosing feeblemindedness among schoolchildren was the first such effort to use psychology practically to measure intelligence itself, rather than its physical correlates. This work led to the original Binet-Simon scale of intelligence, a classification by "mental age."[15]

As much an inspiration as Binet was to the Americans, his approach to mental measurement differed in fundamental ways from that of his followers in the United States, for Binet never embraced the large-scale quantitative emphasis that characterized the American field, nor its concomitant emulation of medicine and engineering. More particularly, Binet rejected the massive studies of the American psychologists in favor of a more personal approach, and favored orthopedic metaphors over epidemiological models. Binet's emphasis on small-scale studies, however, had led him in 1892 into a failed experiment in hypnosis that brought professional embarrassment to the eminent French researcher.[16] Binet's pained account of the corrupting influence of suggestion on his experimental technique spelled out the dangers of clinical experimentation on a small, personal scale. The Americans sought to avoid these difficulties by neutralizing what their German professors termed the "personal equation" through the amassing of data from large numbers of subjects. In a sense, the psychologists who attempted systems of measurement were endeavoring to escape their version of "Mannheim's paradox," in which their own insights into the workings of the human mind, which forced them to acknowledge their own intellectual frailties, tended to undermine their belief in the possibility of scientific knowledge *about* the human mind.[17] The American solution was to amass data in such quantities that the foibles of individual investigators became insignificant. What this method did not take into account was the potential for collective folly: it masked the social and political character of the psychologists' shared epistemology and allowed them to generalize confidently their own rather narrow experience.

Ironically in light of his skepticism about massive experimentation, it was Alfred Binet's work with medical student Theodore Simon that would give the American psychologists the broadest exercise for their numerical enthusiasms. Between the first publication of Henry Herbert Goddard's 1908 translation of the Binet-Simon intelligence scale and the entry of the United States into the Great War, more than 70,000 copies of the test were distributed in at least ten countries. By 1930 at least nine million adults and children had been tested by one of the Binet-Simon revisions.[18] Yet Binet himself had until his death in 1911 remained skeptical of large-scale studies, arguing consistently in favor of the personal approach.

It would be a mistake, however, to assume that internal methodological debates among philosophers and psychologists alone determined the Americans' quantitative emphasis to the new "Science of Man." The broader political culture of the Progressive Era in the United States lent enormous weight to quantitative method as a means of bridging the chasm between scientific research and practical application. Beginning in the early nineteenth century with the institution of a national census, numbers eventually became the *lingua franca* of American progressivism, giving expression to a political philosophy of idealistic compromise. The French political tradition of statistical collection, and British methodological advances in statistical correlation—in particular the work of Francis Galton's protegé Karl Pearson—as well as the development of quantitative methods in medicine, economics, eugenics, and sociology all lent power to numerical treatments of social issues.[19]

Progressivism in the United States was an illusion that worked, and statistics were one of its most effective tricks. Based on the hope of middle-class intellectuals that the abuses of nineteenth-century laissez-faire capitalism and the terrors of imported European socialism both could be overcome through the development and exploitation of human knowledge, progressivism as a political philosophy enshrined intelligence as a new natural resource.[20] In the wake of the closing of the western frontier in 1890, many intellectuals in the United States feared the end of American progress in the finitude of its natural resources.[21] Such fears spawned the early conservation movement and gave rise to the quintessentially progressive faith in scientific and technological advance as a surrogate for the exploitation of materials, land, and labor. Adherents to the progressive ideology recognized both the harsh injustices to the poor of laissez-faire capitalism and their own middle-class vulnerability to the solutions of socialism. The American economic "pie," they understood, had been unfairly distributed in the past, resulting in massive discontent that erupted in the violent strikes of the 1880s and 1890s.[22] The socialist solution, however, seemed equally unjust, as it would arbitrarily divide the "pie" into pitifully small pieces, distributed indiscriminately to the worthy and unworthy alike. The genius of progressivism

40

was its conviction that the exhaustion of natural resources, symbolized by the closing of the frontier, did not represent the end of American expansion. Rather, it offered an opportunity to continue expansion of a different frontier: the Frontier of Science. Through the intelligent application of science to human affairs, the American pie would be continually enlarged, so that the unfortunate masses, while receiving no larger *share* of the total good in American society, could receive a larger *amount* as more good was extracted from finite labor and materiel. What progressivism offered, the reason for its continued appeal well into the twentieth century, was a bigger pie altogether, allowing everyone a better life without any disconcerting redistribution of wealth.

"Efficiency" and "conservation," the twin incantations of progressive belief, embodied this ingenious solution to the intractable social problems besetting middle-class intellectuals about the turn of the century.[23] Both the correction of inefficiencies and the "elimination of waste" demanded measurement. Quantitative method represented these progressive intellectuals' attempts to take into account the experience of the less fortunate masses, while avoiding the corruptions of patronage and the harder political choices of economic redistribution, and nullifying—in theory—their own class interests. Coinciding as it did with the expansion of academic disciplines within the new land-grant universities, this social-scientific ethic capitalized on increasing numbers of graduate students whose labor produced the statistics on which progressive reforms could be founded.[24]

This progressive emphasis on research applied to social problems not only lent importance to quantitative method as a democratic technique, but elevated human intelligence as the key to human progress. To the Progressives, neither labor nor capital held real promise as the engine of civilization's advance in the new millennium; the mind, through science, would remake the world. This pervasive faith gave a strong mandate to psychologists interested in mental capacities, justifying their intellectual work in broad social terms and aligning them not with their cloistered academic predecessors in philosophy but with their new role models in the applied sciences of medicine and engineering.[25]

41

The rapid scholarly, institutional, and commercial successes of mental measurement techniques may be seen as a series of turns away from competing and foregoing schools of mental investigation, an avoidance of messy past associations with religion, spiritualism, and philosophy, and an adoption of methods already proved successful in the professions of medicine and engineering. The nineteenth-century traditions of introspective philosophy and a dominant Protestant religiosity had been challenged first by Darwinian evolutionary theory, which offered a biological explanation for the course of civilization and the development of mind. After the turn of the century, revolutions in psychological method followed several tacks: structuralism, relying on biological and physiological aspects of perception to account for mental life; functionalism, relying on the dynamic of adaptation to explain behavior; psychoanalysis, relying on language, dream imagery, and symbolism for clues to mental life; behaviorism, relying on habit, stimulus, and response to bypass questions of mental life in favor of observable behavior; and psychometrics, relying on collective statistics to standardize, order, and predict mental life. From one perspective, mental measurement can be seen as a compromise between its two closest competitors in early-twentieth-century mental investigation: psychoanalysis, which privileged the personal testimony of patients and adhered to a quasi-confessional, quasi-therapeutic model drawn from religious and medical practice, and behaviorism, which so reduced the personal experience of subjects as to blur the distinction between animal and human. Psychological measurement drew simultaneously from the highly personal, individualized methods of medical practice (thereby sharing some ground with psychoanalysis) and from the deliberately impersonal methods of engineering (thereby sharing ground with behaviorism). Finally, the new measurement psychology retained from nineteenth-century social Darwinism a fascination with hierarchy and the ostensible progress of civilization. In this it owed much to failed attempts of the nineteenth century to classify intelligence through physical measurements of cranial capacity and the like.[26] Placing individuals neatly into a hierarchical social order according to scientific standards of mental ability, for social purposes, was the ultimate goal of the new psychometrics.

As historian John Harley Warner has shown, a preoccupation with standards also characterized nineteenth-century medicine. As he has documented, a shift began in the 1850s in American medical thinking away from an individuated standard, referred to as the "natural" state of health in the individual patient, and toward a population standard, referred to as the "normal." Warner explains: "The hallmark of the new way of thinking about the goals of treatment was the reduction of signs of bodily order and disorder to objectively measured, quantified norms. [This change] . . . rendered the patient without special training incapable of interpreting the meaning of these signs in relation to his or her natural condition."[27] The diagnostic measurements that physicians increasingly used to assess a patient's state of health relative to the "norm" were temperature, respiration, and blood pressure, employing the thermometer, stethoscope, and sphygmomanometer, respectively. It was these same instruments that psychologists later referred to in comparing their measurement techniques to those of medicine, and from which example they pressed their search for mental "norms."

The same ideal prevailed in American engineering under the term *standards*; in fact, the National Bureau of Standards was established in 1902, before which time machine tooling and temperature calibration in the United States were dependent on German standards. As historian David F. Noble has argued, leading organizers of the engineering profession were instrumental in establishing a close articulation between public schools and private colleges in order to rationalize the selection and training of scientific talent around the turn of the century. The logic of engineering standards, as symbolized by the National Bureau of Standards and applied to the allocation of personnel, reached its fulfillment during World War I with the eager cooperation of the psychologists in the measurement movement.[28]

If any single engineering enterprise can be said to have captured this progressive spirit, in which the methods of science and the fruits of technology were brought to bear on human social and economic problems, it was the completion of the Panama Canal in August 1914. Claimed by both physicians and engineers as the ultimate demonstration of their professional achievement, the Canal represented not only ingenuity, but "American" ingenuity, and on a grand scale comparable to the building of the Egyptian pyramids.[29]

The husbanding of this resource, intelligence, became the self-appointed task of the nascent discipline of psychology. As the "revolt against formalism" swept through the academic disciplines, psychologists found themselves too closely identified with the formal, arcane and elite discipline of philosophy, and in need of demonstrating the practical side of their work.[30] By attaching themselves to the most conspicuous and tangible scientific and technological accomplishments of the age in medicine and engineering, they linked themselves to the engine of progressivism: a secular faith that human intelligence itself was a natural resource as fecund as land or labor and, when properly exploited and distributed, both more powerful and less easily exhausted than either.

Linked to the twin perceptions (among middle-class intellectuals) that land was running out and labor running amok at the end of the nineteenth century was a crisis in democratic theory: the population of the United States was growing, migrating, and diversifying at staggering rates, and the most conspicuous new citizens were markedly different from the yeoman image that had figured into early constitutional thinking. This early national archetype of a white, Protestant, middle-class male citizen was one that white, Protestant, middle-class men of the late nineteenth century were loathe to give up, so that the new diversity of the citizenry seemed to undermine the very possibility of democracy. In addition, the impoverished circumstances of most of the new migrants to the major population centers—Eastern European Jews, Southern Italians, and Southern African-Americans—left many of them with little or no education. Given the intimate philosophical connection between democracy and an educated citizenry, these people seemed to pose a profound challenge, if not an insuperable obstacle, to the survival of the United States as a political system.[31] To the comfortable middle class, labor unrest, social diseases, and political corruption all seemed associated with this foreign and backward class.[32]

This congeries of social problems ascribed to the "alien" new elements of the northern, urban populace represented both a challenge and an opportunity to those who would place intelligence at the center of their notion of progress. Depending on one's political orientation within the broad expanse of "progressive" ideology, this alien population was or was not educable into responsible citizenship. If it was not, immigration restriction and negative eugenics were dictated; if it was, educational reform was dictated.[33] In either case—and here is the genius of the measurement psychologists' appeal—a determination had to be made as to the "mental levels" of these prospective outcasts and citizens, in order to tell them apart.

Psychologists thus constructed intelligence and its standardized assessment as the driving wheel upon which the ideals, methods, and programs of progressivism depended: psychologists themselves became the engineers of a new machine of efficient democracy, powered by intelligence. It was a perpetual motion machine wherein technological innovation in psychology—driven by American ingenuity—produced and discovered, through psychology, more ingenuity. This ingenuity in turn produced the medical advances that psychologists emulated when the principles of engineering failed.

Education as a Profession

The Holy Father, he can send ye to hell, and the boss, he
can take away yer job er raise yer pay, but
the teacher, she can't do nothing.
(Child factory worker, 1913)

Among the social institutions where psychologists successfully implemented mental tests were the public schools. Although it may be argued that special schools for the feeble-minded, juvenile courts, and asylums adopted mental tests more readily and that the tests had an even greater impact on the organization and routines of these institutions, it was in the public schools that the tests reached the widest population and posed the greatest contemporary philosophical problems. It was their implementation in public schools, following the mass testing of army recruits during World War I, that stimulated the intense (but largely ineffectual) criticism of testing during the 1920s. Psychologist Lewis Madison Terman, who led the American testing movement (at least in the public eye), developed his techniques for mental testing largely in the context of public education, and it was in the schools that the wholesale psychological testing of intelligence flourished.[1] With their impressive scientific apparatus and technical vocabulary, psychologists seemed to offer educators new solutions to chronic pedagogical and administrative problems, just at a time when beleaguered educators were desperate for new ideas that would bolster their own professional claims. Teachers and school officials faced enormous practical difficulties during the Progressive Era, and their frustrations and failures in coping with these were having a serious impact on the status of education.[2]

Although test psychologists depended heavily on educators for their own professional livelihood, they did not view teaching as a profession worthy of emulation. During the Progressive Era teachers, like psychologists, were self-consciously attempting to become professional, and to acquire all of the attributes and privileges that, to them, professionalism entailed.[3] More often than not, psychologists and educators were in competition with one another for power and influence in educational policy and classroom procedure. In this competitive professional context, and in increasingly heterogeneous classrooms, psychologists sought to popularize their new mental tests.

As aspiring professionals, educators stood in pathetic contrast to physicians and engineers, their accomplishments, methods, and institutions ridiculed and attacked wherever medicine and engineering were celebrated. These judgments reflected the practical challenges facing educators. Newly organized school systems, swollen by new and diverse school populations, struggled to maintain a bare nineteenth-century standard of rote learning. As more and more pupils, particularly in cities, came to school from homes where English was not spoken, the traditional mass recitations that made up classroom routine became, by some accounts, a meaningless cacophony, without even the form of sense.[4] Historian of immigration Thomas Archdeacon writes that 18.2 million immigrants arrived in the United States between 1890 and 1920, compared with only 10 million between 1860 and 1890, and 4.7 million between 1830 and 1860.[5] Foreign-born and foreign-parented children brought different customs to the schools; internal migrations brought black families from southern farms to northern cities. Immigrant and native poverty, aggravated by the recent economic depressions and publicized by muckraking journalists and photographers, combined with the increasing enforcement of compulsory school laws and child labor laws to change radically the public perception as well as the experience of schooling.[6]

Schoolchildren and teachers in the largest cities experienced extreme overcrowding and chaotic diversity in the classroom. From 1899 to 1914 New York City school enrollments jumped 60 percent; in the middle of this period nearly three quarters of New York City schoolchildren had foreign-born fathers.[7] In smaller cities, too, most children came from immigrant families.

47

Of Duluth's 10,000 schoolchildren in 1908, 8000 had fathers born in either Sweden, Germany, or elsewhere in Europe; in Fall River, Massachusetts, 9000 of 14,000 schoolchildren came from British, Quebecois, or Portuguese families. In thirty-seven large and small cities surveyed in 1908, 58 percent of school-children came from immigrant homes; of these, 53 percent, or one third of all children surveyed, did not hear English spoken at home.[8]

The teaching force was nearly as diverse and as unaccus-tomed to American schooling as the pupils. Only about half of the public school teachers working in 1908 were native-born of native parents; almost 10 percent of all public school teach-ers were the daughters of Irish men.[9] In Worcester, Massa-chusetts, second-generation Irish teachers held more than a third of available teaching positions; in Shenandoah, Penn-sylvania, nearly half. Likewise, in Milwaukee and Cincinnati, German teachers made up more than one fifth of the public school teaching force. Second-generation Irish teachers were the single largest ethnic group working in the Boston, Buffalo, Detroit, Minneapolis, New Orleans, San Francisco, Philadel-phia, Pittsburg, New York, and Providence schools; German-fathered teachers ranked first in Baltimore, Cleveland, Kansas City, Los Angeles, Milwaukee, Newark, and St. Louis.[10]

Gender, as well as ethnicity, was a factor in the low status of education and in struggles for professional control.[11] An in-creasing proportion of schoolteachers in the late nineteenth century were women—some, mere girls.[12] In 1880 there were 126 female teachers for every 100 male teachers; by 1895, 205, and by 1905, there were 315 women teaching for every 100 men. In New York City the teaching force was 90 percent fe-male by 1908; in New Orleans, only four of nearly a thousand teachers were male. The few male teachers who remained in the schools in 1908 were, for the most part, survivors of an ear-lier generation; of the four in New Orleans, each had taught for more than twenty years.[13]

The employment patterns of female labor undermined an important aspect of professional identity in education: lifelong, permanent identification with a "calling." Women moved in and out of teaching. Many women taught at some time during their lives, but few taught for more than a few years. This pattern originated during the antebellum expansion of the common schools, and continued into the Progressive Era. Nationwide in 1908, over 20 percent of urban teachers had taught for fewer than five years; another 25 percent had taught five to nine years, and 20 percent, ten to fourteen years. Thus, only about half of all teachers had more than nine years' experience teaching. Only a third had more than fifteen years' experience, and in some cities—New York, New Orleans, and Omaha, for example—inexperience was even more pervasive.[14]

Salaries for the majority of teachers were extremely low. Women teachers generally could expect to earn one-third to one-half the salary of their male counterparts. This inequity encouraged school administrators to hire women in order to stretch already taut education dollars, a strategy administrators readily acknowledged.[15]

Very few teachers were graduates of teacher-training colleges, or "normal schools." To make matters worse, the general level of educational attainment had risen over the nineteenth century, so that graduation from grammar school, and even from high school, did not place the teacher much above the general population in educational attainment. Teachers suffered a decline in authority relative to that of the general population because they did not as a group maintain the relatively higher levels of education in the early twentieth century that they had enjoyed in the nineteenth.

Teaching at the turn of the century had none of the conventional attributes of a profession. Women's commitment to teaching as a career was low, if measured by their longevity in their jobs; teachers could claim as their own no specialized knowledge or training; salaries were low; and control of teachers' conduct was strict and resided outside the occupational community. The typical public school teacher of 1908 was a young, unmarried, second-generation immigrant woman with fewer than ten years' teaching experience and no professional training. It is hardly surprising that education inspired little respect as a profession. Moreover, organizational changes were already under way that would exacerbate the relative decline in teachers' cultural authority.

The consolidation of rural and urban schools into central-ized systems meant that previously independent, isolated, and homogeneous school populations became part of larger, inter-dependent communities. System superintendents (the job itself was an innovation) were confronted by new conflicts that previ-ously had been matters of consensus within narrower commu-nities. This new clash of values among previously isolated groups gave rise, in many aspects of life, to the "search for order" that characterized Progressive-Era reform. While it is difficult to show that education was somehow "worse" at the turn of the century than it had been thirty or forty years before, it is clear that newly perceived problems were emerging out of earlier consensus, largely because of demographic changes na-tionwide that affected the scale of school organization and the status of teachers relative to other professionals.[16] As compul-sory school attendance laws forced an increasing proportion of children into public schools, and as school expenditures rose, schools occupied an increasingly salient position in public policy at the local, state, and national levels.

A sense of professional crisis, rooted in daily classroom difficulties, led teachers to tolerate, if not always welcome, the new forms of educational testing offered by psychologists. The scientific trappings of the new mental tests, with their sophisti-cated statistical methods and medical-looking charts, helped teachers and administrators claim scientific status for their own profession in an era when virtually every social reform, from infant-feeding to automobile production, was subject to "scien-tific management."[17] However, as I argue in detail below, the particular medical and engineering language used by test psy-chologists had particular appeal to educators at this particular time, for social and historical reasons, whereas terms like *science* and *scientific method* were ubiquitous.[18]

Turn-of-the-century school administrators faced economic as well as pedagogical and professional problems, which led them to seek changes in school organization. In spite of econ-omy measures, such as the increased hiring of low-salaried fe-male teachers, school superintendents and taxpayers saw school expenditures rise even faster than enrollments during the late nineteenth century. In Portland, Oregon, for example, average daily school attendance rose from 10,387 in 1902 to 23,712 a decade later, more than doubling, but school expenditures during the same ten years rose from $420,879 to an astonishing $2,490,477—a sixfold increase.[19]

As if these social, financial, and administrative pressures were not enough, school officials were bedeviled by what they saw as professional interlopers who viewed schools as potential seedbeds of crime, poverty, and disease.[20] Medical professionals—doctors, dentists, and medical social workers—were particularly successful in gaining entry to schools, where they served, and were served by, the large concentrations of young subjects.[21] By entering the schools, these medical practitioners advanced their own professions at least as much as they advanced child health. This is not to say that their motives were necessarily selfish, only that both self-serving and altruistic interests dictated the same political strategy. These public health workers in the schools helped pave the way for psychologists.

HEALTH WORK IN THE SCHOOLS:
PRECURSOR TO MENTAL TESTING

The medical profession in the United States, following the European example, developed over the eighteenth and nineteenth centuries a sophisticated quantitative mentality that became one of its most powerful tools for the advancement of medical knowledge and political strength.[22] Statistical studies could justify the large, long-term public health reforms whose worth qualitative reporting, on a case-by-case basis, could never prove. These surveys, such as Irving Fisher's 1909 *Report on National Vitality*, represented a new kind of medical knowledge that was all the more powerful because its vast scale removed it from effective popular scrutiny.[23] At the same time, the scale of grand statistical studies dramatized their results so that policy recommendations based on such studies were inherently persuasive.

By the late nineteenth century, the prevention of disease had become an avowed aim of the medical profession, but in practice, organized medicine opposed many preventive reforms.[24] True professionals, some doctors argued, are those who devote themselves to eradicating the very conditions upon which their own livelihood depends. Although many organized physicians fiercely opposed the preventive schemes of public health physicians, many nonetheless used the language of "prevention" to bolster their professional claim to altruism.[25] During the first decades of the twentieth century, the public came to accept prevention as part of medical care. One Minnesota physician recalled in 1923 that even ten years before, parents seldom brought their children to him, "to make sure nothing is wrong." "Today," the doctor added, "I venture to say that the greatest part of the work a pediatrician has is in preventive medicine."[26] Medical reformers quickly recognized the importance of the child to any scheme of preventive medicine, and as quickly appreciated the convenience of public schools as research laboratories of child life. German and French physicians incorporated preventive health care for children into the schools in the late nineteenth century, and American reformers followed suit. American public schools, with their large immigrant populations, seemed to middle-class reformers veritable breeding grounds for disease. As one observer wrote in the 1888 *Journal of the American Medical Association*, the schoolroom was a "propaganda of contagion."[27]

Systematic medical inspection of public school children began in Boston in 1894.[28] By 1908 systems of medical inspection were operating in 102 American cities, 32 of these in Massachusetts alone.[29] Like political statistics, school medical inspections were a borrowed European tradition, dating from 1833 when French legislators charged municipal school committees with maintaining the sanitation of schoolhouses. In 1837 the women who supervised "maternal schools" (French kindergartens) were made responsible for the health of their pupils. By 1843, all public schools in France were to be visited annually by an inspecting physician, who was assumed to work *pro bono*. Enforcement of these laws was spotty, and few physicians complied. In Paris, school inspections began in earnest after 1879, when physicians were allocated salaries for school work. Thorough medical inspection of schoolchildren was not effective until about 1910, however, by which time the idea had spread across Europe and to the United States.[30]

In the United States, public health officials in New York, Chicago, and Philadelphia followed the Boston example, establishing school medical inspections in 1895, 1897, and 1898. Initially an extension of the preventive mandate of city health boards, medical inspection developed in three stages. In the nineteenth century, public sanitation officials (who were not necessarily physicians) inspected school buildings for safety and health hazards. They included schools in their inspections of public buildings, and recommendations for reforms were in the shape of architectural changes, particularly with regard to heating and ventilation. By 1894, public health officials joined sanitary inspectors in schools, and extended their oversight to include children as well as buildings and furnishings. By the early 1920s, at the height of educational progressivism, children in city schools were being given full medical and dental examinations routinely. In New York, Los Angeles, Buffalo, and other metropolitan areas, medical and dental treatment was also available to schoolchildren, at or near school, often at no charge.

Early inspection programs were cursory at best; they were designed solely to detect contagious diseases and parasites afflicting schoolchildren. As a rule, inspectors did not touch the children but had each child "pull down its own eyelids, open its mouth, show its hands and, in the case of girls, lift up her back hair."[31] An estimated 10 percent of schoolchildren were excluded from school on the basis of such examinations in five northeastern cities in 1907. The standard criteria for exclusion included evidence of scarlet fever, diphtheria, measles, mumps, chicken pox, whooping cough, smallpox, ringworm, scabies, impetigo, tuberculosis, and lice.[32]

Elaborate bureaucratic systems were developed to record and report the results of these medical inspections, but the strictures on actual treatment within school premises were tight, owing to active opposition by local physicians and parents.[33] School health officials complained that the most important work of treating disease and defect was left undone: the same children with the same illnesses showed up on reports year after year.[34]

Notwithstanding the exhaustive, if crude, statistical record-keeping that accompanied school hygiene programs, the information that school officials made available to parents was woefully inadequate. Consistent with a paternalistic philosophy of charitable aid, parental consent was not sought.[35] In 1906, outraged parents gave one group of school officials in lower Manhattan a memorable lesson in public relations and family rights. Acting independently, school doctors had begun performing tonsillectomies and adenoidectomies in the clinic at a Lower East Side public school, where most of the schoolchildren came from Italian immigrant homes. According to newspaper reports, a rumor circulated one morning that the children's throats were being cut at the school—that school officials were systematically murdering the children. "Frantic Italians," many reportedly armed with stiletto knives, "stormed" three school buildings, attacked teachers, and dragged their children from the schools. The schools were temporarily closed.[36]

Incidence of childhood diseases and defects did show a decline in the years before World War I, and school hygiene advocates were quick to claim the victory as their own. In New York City, the percentage of children needing treatment for disease (other than dental disease) dropped from 44.2 percent in 1909 to 30.1 percent in 1912. Even more dramatic was the apparent effect of school hygiene programs on the attitudes of parents toward obtaining medical care for their children. School hygiene workers in New York reported that of 30,000 pupils found to need eyeglasses in 1909, only about one fourth obtained them. By 1912, fully half of children needing glasses obtained these "luxury items."[37]

PROFESSIONAL DENTISTRY'S USE OF PUBLIC SCHOOLS

An interesting parallel with psychological testing can be seen in preventive dental-care programs in the schools. Both groups recognized in the public schools both a need for their services and an opportunity to popularize their professions. Moreover, the two enterprises—preventive dentistry and psychological testing—worked in tandem at critical junctures to promote one another. As comical as it may seem, serious reformers among both psychologists and dentists argued that the mental abilities of children were being destroyed by poor oral hygiene.[38]

Of all the diseases and defects found among schoolchildren, dental disease was by far the most prevalent, with an incidence upward of 80 percent. Coincidentally, large proportions of schoolchildren were "retarded" in their grades, failing to advance at a regular and satisfactory pace; many left school entirely in favor of factory work or life on the streets.[39] This prompted a few outspoken and ambitious dentists to attribute all school problems, even all social ills, to this single source.[40]

Isolated precedents notwithstanding, organized dentistry did not make a concerted effort to sell the gospel of oral hygiene to the larger public or to portray the school as the key agency through which to work a miracle in American dental health until 1909. In that year the National Dental Association appointed W. B. Ebersole to head its Oral Hygiene Committee. Ebersole's first step was to conduct an experiment in school dentistry in his hometown, Cleveland. It was essential, Ebersole concluded, to isolate oral disease from the other ailments associated with school failure, in order to determine whether a targeted program of dental education, prophylaxis, and treatment could radically improve students' educational performance.

Unfortunately, Ebersole's experiment was methodologically amateurish, to say the least. Although he gained permission from the Cleveland Board of Education to open dental clinics in four schools, he limited his experiment to the Marion School, the one school whose principal was devoutly committed to the use of schools for such experimental purposes. Located in a "downtown, congested, cosmopolitan and ghetto section," the Marion School was dominated by first- and second-generation immigrant children. From the initial inspection of their teeth, Ebersole selected the forty students with the very worst mouths. Eventually, he gained the participation of twenty-seven of them for all phases of the brief (fourteen-month) experiment. To do so, however, he had to promise each a five-dollar gold piece— an extraordinary prize at the time. Each child was carefully taught proper methods of toothbrushing and instructed to brush three times daily. Each child was also taught proper "mastication and insalivation" via a "test dinner" which they ate under the supervision of the school nurse. The nurse visited each child at home until she was satisfied that the children understood the prescribed techniques. Finally, each student had elaborate prophylactic, reparative, and restorative work performed in the school dental clinic, and was given an equally elaborate battery of physical, educational, and psychological tests to establish baseline data. Approximately half of the children had been held back at least one year in school, and 50 percent of them were two or more years behind their appropriate grade.[41]

The experimenters saw remarkable changes in the children during the course of the year, all of which they attributed to mouth hygiene. Sallow, muddy complexions turned bright and clear. "Fragile, delicate, and nervous" children became "sturdy and well." Twelve-year-old Gussie Hammerschlak, two years behind her school grade, was a "wild, gross, irritable and nervous girl" before the dental program began. "Her mouth was in such bad condition it was repulsive." Extensive dental repair using cocaine and anesthesia took months of appointments to complete and included twenty-two fillings in eleven teeth. When her mouth was finally put in a clean and healthy condition, Gussie became "quiet and ladylike," greatly improved in scholarship, behavior, health, and appearance. But the "banner pupil" was Morris Krause, the terror of the school yard. In her understated way, the school principal explained, "Morris had ideas peculiarly his own as to what a boy's duties and privileges were. These ideas were so much at variance with the conventional standards that difficulties arose, seemingly insurmountable at times. Since working with the class, he has been manly, tractable, and does not even seem to have the temptations that repeatedly assailed him and were almost the means of his downfall. The result obtained for Morris alone was worth all our effort."[42]

The Marion School experiment included one of the first applications of modern psychological tests to correlate mental with physical defects. Administration of the tests was not well supervised, however, and the planned testing of a control group was never implemented. Moreover, the school psychologist ignored the small size of the experimental group and reported results only in percentages. Because a few children scored enormous gains in health status and educational performance (gains that, in retrospect, probably call much of the baseline data into question), the reported results tended to exaggerate the effects of the experimental program. Nonetheless, these tests became the primary basis for organized dentistry's avid claim during the next decade that school dental programs could work educational miracles.

In hundreds of cities, children's dental care was established in school clinics. Most poor children thereby had access to complete dental care, at no or low cost; wealthier children benefited from diagnostic and hygienic services.[43] Preventive dental care went far beyond preventive medical care in the public schools, delivering actual treatment as well as diagnostic and hygienic services. In their need to create a clientele, dentists saw advantages to "giving away" their services to a specific population, hoping thus to establish remunerative provider-client relations with the families of treated children.[44]

The success of public-school dentistry, in establishing diagnostic and treatment outposts in schools, stands in stark contrast to the school physicians' almost purely diagnostic role. Organized dentists had little reason to oppose these public health activities, which helped popularize the very idea of patronizing dentists. Compared to medicine, dentistry was not yet a well-established profession at the turn of the century, and the importance of oral hygiene was not widely appreciated. Therefore, public-school dental clinics were for dentists a welcome means of popularizing the value of dentistry. Moreover, dental clinics in schools served only children, who were usually difficult and financially unrewarding patients. Dentists wanted to instill the habits of dental hygiene in children without having to treat children as part of their regular dental practices. Organized dentistry coyly averted its professional eyes from the "socializing influences" of publicly funded school dental clinics.[45]

In contrast, medicine at the turn of the century enjoyed relatively high prestige and widespread participation by clientele.

Regular physicians were still fighting challenges by homeo-
paths, who sought to demystify medical science. Understand-
ably, regular physicians opposed any measures, including in-
school medical treatment, that would further tip the balance
toward popularization of their exclusive medical knowledge.
As members of a more secure profession, doctors were concerned with monopolizing their knowledge; professionally less
secure, dentists still had to popularize theirs. Dentists in Buffalo, New York, went so far as to set up shop in a department
store window, where they operated *gratis* on indigent schoolchildren. By the 1920s the public school had become to dentistry what the hospital had long been to medicine—a place to
demonstrate charitable spirit and professional obligation; the
public school dental clinic was the profession's "service ideal"
manifest.[46]

Psychology was in a somewhat similar predicament before
World War I. Mental testing was not well respected, and psychologists in general were not respected as true professionals,
particularly by the physicians who controlled hospitals, asylums,
and many state schools for the feebleminded where test psychologists worked. Not content with testing people of low or
unusual abilities, the psychologists sought applications for their
tests among the general population. The ubiquitous calls for
"efficiency" in human affairs during the Progressive Era
seemed to them invitations, or at least opportunities, to develop
mental tests. But when they attempted to implement their new
science in factories and offices, they were confronted with
opposition from the subjects themselves and from union rep-
resentatives. As the German psychologist Hugo Münsterberg
explained in 1913, prisons, asylums, and schools made better
experimental settings.[47]

For beleaguered teachers and school officials, the incursion
of medical and dental personnel into the schools was a mixed
blessing. On one hand, statistics that showed schools to be nests
of contagion were embarrassing; but on the other, if children's
failure to learn was a result of ubiquitous medical "defects,"
who could blame the schools? Medical inspections thus advanced the interests of some school people as well as those of
doctors, dentists, and, in many cases, needy children.

From the point of view of school reformers, it was vastly easier and quicker to cure lice or remove adenoids than to improve teacher training, reduce class size, and rethink curricula. Generally, money for medical inspections and school clinics came from sources outside the school budget; medical personnel augmented the regular teaching staff, whereas curricular or administrative changes in school programs represented an added burden to overworked, underpaid teachers. Children's medical problems were tangible, widespread, and often curable. Doctors, even the public health doctors who worked in schools, brought with them the prestige of the medical profession that stemmed in part from the tangible and universal nature of disease. Medical intervention was dramatic, its results visible to school officials, taxpayers, parents, and children alike. Educational change was much less dramatic, and much less reassuring. Finally, school officials and parents could more easily agree on the value of treating children who suffered physically; consensus on educational problems was much more difficult to achieve.

Early advocates of medical incursions into the public schools justified their activities in terms of an earlier mandate for compulsory education. In this vein Lillian Wald, a leader of progressive social reform, wrote in 1905, "It is difficult to place a limit upon the service which medical inspection should perform. . . . If for safeguarding the state, mental training is made compulsory, is it not logical to conclude that physical development—the sound body as well as the sound mind—should so far as possible be demanded?"[48] Wald spoke the language of education to the educators whose cooperation she needed. Educators justified medical programs in the schools in terms of broad societal goals, rather than in narrow educational terms. Psychologist Lewis Terman referred obliquely to the widely publicized findings of the *Report on National Vitality: Its Wastes and Conservation* when he wrote in 1914: "The rapid development of health work in the schools is not to be regarded merely as an educational reform, but rather as the corollary of a widespread realization of the importance of preventive measures in the conservation of natural and human resources."[49] In each instance, reformers appealed to an authority broader than their own, using the language of their audience, and cast the innovations of medical inspection in the mold of better-established beliefs and practices.

School officials at the turn of the century were anxious for some system that would alleviate the overcrowding, failures, confusion, rebellion, and morbidity that blighted the schools. The progressive ideal of public health that grew out of late-nineteenth-century advances in medical science found fertile ground among these worried administrators. In spite of parents' sometimes violent objections, medical practices in the schools expanded through the prewar years to include free treatments and even minor surgery for schoolchildren. "School hygiene," as the medical inspection and treatment movement came to be called, seemed a dramatic preventive measure in the face of alarming and intransigent social and medical problems.

MEDICAL LANGUAGE IN EDUCATION AND PSYCHOLOGY

As early as 1880, female schoolteachers consciously tried to raise their own status by challenging the prevailing model of nineteenth-century education, the factory model. One such teacher, feminist leader Mary Abigail Dodge, argued that the logic of the factory metaphor in education imposed upon teachers the rank of mere operatives, and placed school superintendents above them as overseers. Dodge proposed a different metaphor that would guarantee teachers' professional autonomy: "Teachers ought to run the schools exactly as doctors run a hospital."[50]

In evoking this medical model in 1880, Mary Abigail Dodge anticipated by twenty years the model of profession that would captivate educational psychologists. But the medical analogy did not take hold among teachers. Why? In the context of nineteenth-century education, the suggestion that young female schoolteachers were anything like doctors must have seemed absurd, though not as farfetched as it would seem thirty years later when most women had been forced out of medical practice.[51] More importantly, medicine in 1880 was not the unified and prestigious profession it had become by 1910. Doctors did not yet enjoy the popular respect that new advances in bacteriology and public health would soon bring. As an ideal of profession, the 1880 medical model was a frail challenge to the factory model.[52] The medical metaphor never took hold among professionalizing teachers because historically and socially the comparison was implausible, and the literal referent weak.[53]

In contrast to nineteenth-century female schoolteachers, male psychologists in the early twentieth century were able to draw sufficient parallels between themselves and medical doctors for the medical metaphor to make sense to a wide public, including school people. Moreover, by the time the psychologists evoked the medical model, medicine itself had changed, and doctors were worthy of emulation.

The Biographical Referents of Metaphor

If I did not believe that psychology affected conduct
and could be applied in useful ways, I should regard
my occupation as nearer to that of the professional
chess-player or sword-swallower than to that of
the engineer or scientific physician.
(James McKeen Cattell,
"The Conceptions and Methods of Psychology" [1904])

THE PRIMARY LEXICON of intelligence testing is medical. Psychologists who measure intelligence speak as physicians, diagnosing, prescribing for, and treating their subjects, often in a clinical setting. So pervasive is medical language in the field of educational psychology that it has lost its metaphorical quality and has become accepted as literal. This was not always the case. Early in the development of the testing enterprise, medical language was a creative device that accomplished many things at once for the young psychologists who used it. Its interest to the historian lies not so much in particular uses of medical language by individual psychologists as in the wider patterns of usage within the community of psychological discourse. This usage helped define the social groups that made up the mental testing profession and its clientele. The semantic system by which individual test psychologists expressed their ideas also created their collective identity as scientific psychologists, defined their expertise, and defended both against charlatanism, encroachment, and criticism. Medical discourse was thus an essential activity in the formation of a psychological profession.[1]

The meaning of the psychologists' medical language is best interpreted historically, that is, with reference both to the personal histories of individual psychologists and to the contemporaneous medical practices to which these individuals referred. One of the reasons the psychologists in the testing movement so readily adopted medical language was that many of them had entertained the idea of becoming doctors themselves.[2] Nearly all of the leaders of the new quantitative psychology movement had been trained not in philosophy, which had nurtured the old introspective psychology, but in physiology. Several had at least tentative preparation for medical school. Moreover, most of the older scholars whose scientific work influenced the American psychologists—Münsterberg, Binet, James, Galton— held medical degrees or had studied medicine extensively.[3]

Contractions in the American system of medical education sharply raised the cost of pursuing a medical career at the turn of the century. The new scientific psychology, in contrast, was a relatively open field for young men interested in laboratory research. The young psychologists' early involvement with medicine, however, survived in their common medical vocabulary, which integrated them into a cohesive community of discourse upon which they founded their new profession.

As the new generation of American experimental psychologists began to shape their careers at the turn of the century, psychology was just emerging as a discipline distinct from philosophy. Only four American universities boasted separate psychology departments in 1904; by 1914, there were thirty-four. In Germany, the break had begun a generation earlier, and the German professors who inspired first Cattell, Hall, and Münsterberg and then their students Yerkes, Terman, Woodworth, Goddard, and Thorndike were trained as physiologists, not philosophers.[4]

Psychologist James McKeen Cattell, who published the first scholarly article on mental tests in 1890, and is widely credited with having founded the movement, had first entertained the idea of a career in medicine.[5] From 1886 to 1890 he vacillated between medicine and psychology, resisting the efforts of his concerned parents to push him toward the better-established and more secure field of medicine. Cattell defended his choice of psychology in a Christmas letter to his parents in 1890: "I am not anxious about securing a position. I think psychology is likely to be *the* science of the next thirty years—at all events the science in which the most progress will be made. I have, little as it is, done more for psychology than any American, and have no reason to doubt that I can easily stand among the first in the future."[6] For Cattell, medicine would have been the easier row to hoe. His parents were well enough situated to send him to medical school; his brother was a doctor. In 1890 medical schooling had not yet contracted along the lines it would by 1910; requirements were relatively lax and medical schools numerous. Cattell was the son of an eminent academic, the Reverend William Cassidy Cattell, president of Lafayette College in Pennsylvania, who spared no effort in advancing his children's careers. But psychology appealed to the younger Cattell precisely because its novelty and uncertainty provided opportunities for remarkable achievement. His father's position and educational activities had presented to Cattell unusual opportunities to study in Europe with German psychologist and physiologist Wilhelm Wundt, and Cattell understood his advantage over the American-trained students of psychology.[7] Cattell also became the conveyor to America of Francis Galton's work in mental measurement, first establishing at the University of Pennsylvania a systematic inventory of mental traits and subsequently developing the psychological laboratory at Columbia University.[8]

The next generation of American students, including Robert Yerkes and Robert Woodworth, would make their career decisions under quite different circumstances. Their turning from medicine as a career was involuntary; they never enjoyed the relatively free choice in the matter that Cattell had. The costs of a medical education—in tuition and in lost earnings—were much higher in 1900 than in 1890, while psychology still seemed an exciting alternative.[9] A similar overcrowding had occurred in nineteenth-century German universities, whereby physiologists were edged out of medical physiology and into psychology, a phenomenon sociologists have referred to as "role hybridization." This overcrowding in the field of physiology may have spawned the hybrid physiological psychology of Wilhelm Wundt at Leipzig. Wundt in turn influenced Cattell, G. Stanley Hall, Hugo Münsterberg, and William James, whose students—Thorndike, Woodworth, Terman, Goddard, and Yerkes—were the leaders of mental testing in America.[10]

Harvard psychologist Hugo Münsterberg emigrated to the United States in 1892; by the time of his premature death in 1916 he had become America's most renowned (and notorious) applied psychologist. Like many of his contemporaries in Germany, Münsterberg was a casualty of an overcrowded medical profession. Münsterberg held both a medical degree and a doctorate in psychology from Wundt's laboratory in Leipzig, where he met Cattell.[11] American interest in psychology contrasted sharply with that in Germany, owing in large part to Cattell's entrepreneurial activism in promoting the new profession. Münsterberg found his work much better appreciated in America than it had been in Germany. From his Harvard post, Münsterberg wrote to Cattell in 1898, "My elementary psychology course . . . has 360 students—what will this country do with all these psychologists?"[12] Among the Harvard crowd was Robert Yerkes, who would lead the army testing program from 1917 to 1921.

Münsterberg's influence in America was widespread, though he was discredited by allegations that he was a German spy during the war, an ordeal that contemporaries thought caused his early death in 1916.[13] During his lifetime, Münsterberg translated the principles of German industrial and scientific success into applied psychology, and publicized his work in popular magazines. In 1904 he organized the International Congress of Arts and Sciences, a showcase for his ideas that was held in conjunction with the St. Louis Louisiana Purchase Exposition. The congress included eminent academics, particularly social scientists, from all over the world. It featured a running demonstration of "anthropometric" tests of mental and physical powers. Visitors to the fair could pay to be tested, and the test results were then used by the psychologists and anthropologists for research. The focus of these measurements was a search for racial differences: as Robert Woodworth wrote from St. Louis to his mentor, Cattell, "We have not much more than begun on our 'primitive' material. I want also to get a hold of a good number of Japanese—and I can also get Syrians if desirable."[14] These crude mental tests were seen firsthand by hundreds of people, enhancing Münsterberg's reputation as a great popularizer of scientific ideas.[15] The German laboratory tradition had an extremely powerful influence on the young American psychologists, just as German scientific methods had influenced American medicine in the latter half of the nineteenth century. In both medicine and psychology, American researchers were dependent on the more sophisticated German machine-tool industry for nearly all of their precision instruments, a situation that did not begin to change until the U.S. government established its Bureau of Standards in 1902. The American psychologists' enthusiasm for German training, laboratory methods, and equipment allied them with their medical counterparts at the prestigious Johns Hopkins University.[16]

The scholar whose work most influenced the test psychologists was neither a German nor, to be exact, a psychologist. He was the British polymath Sir Francis Galton. Best remembered for founding and naming the hereditarian science of eugenics, Galton himself belonged to the illustrious Darwin family. Galton's scientific interests were extremely varied: he pioneered the forensic use of fingerprinting and the study of inherited tendencies among twins. Among his numerous inventions was the "Galton whistle," still used to measure auditory acuity. Galton was trained as a physician, and his medical work influenced his teaching in subtle ways. As his biographer Raymond Fancher has suggested, Galton's medical training was a reservoir of vivid anecdotes that he used in teaching his young American protegés.[17] In addition, Galton constructed his famous laboratory after a medical model, convinced that mental attributes were accessible to scientific study through their physical correlates.

Galton's "Anthropometric" laboratory in London attracted Americans—including Cattell and Goddard—to study the measurement of human physiological and mental capabilities. Anthropometry, nicknamed "brass-instrument" psychology, relied heavily on precision equipment that measured physiological responses to stimuli. Much of this technology, such as the spirometer, which measured lung capacity, and the sphygmomanometer, which measured blood pressure, was borrowed or adapted from medical laboratories. As historian Michael Sokal has shown, this cumbersome and delicate apparatus made such tests impracticable for institutional use.[18] Brass-instrument psy-

chology very likely impeded popular acceptance of mental testing, because its elaborate appearance gave testing an occult and
Frankensteinian air. As physician Adolph Meyer of the New
York State Commission on Lunacy wrote to Goddard, "The
chief thing to guard against is to pile up a lot of apparently very
scientific tests which in the eyes of the teacher and any com-
mon-sense individual would appear top-heavy, and therefore
bring discredit to the movement."[19] In addition, the equipment
was fragile, expensive, and difficult to procure from its German
manufacturers. Psychologists who used it complained of break-
age, malfunctions, and continual repairs.[20] But it was this dramatic, expensive, and unwieldy technology that Americans saw
at the St. Louis World's Fair in 1904, thanks to the entrepreneurial efforts of the German expatriate Hugo Münsterberg.[21]
One of Münsterberg's students at Harvard was Robert Mearns
Yerkes. Yerkes was a young man, anticipating a medical career
during a time when the medical profession was contracting se-
verely. Medical school tuitions were rising, and the number of
medical colleges falling, as new training requirements imposed
greater opportunity costs on prospective doctors. During the
1890s and 1900s, the standard academic year for medical students grew from four to eight or nine months; the length of
schooling required for the M.D. degree increased from two to
four years, to five to eight years beyond high school.[22] Most
nineteenth-century medical colleges had not required a high-
school diploma of their candidates.

Yerkes, who had placed himself among an academic elite by
taking a second bachelor's degree at Harvard, looked forward
to the scientific prestige and professional freedoms associated
with the medical degree. As he approached college graduation,
he saw those hopes evaporate. His immediate family was not
wealthy, and he depended on the favors of his mentors for
scholarship money. During the spring and summer of 1898, his
senior year at Harvard, Yerkes abandoned first his hopes to
study biology and then his alternate plans to study medicine. In
June he was turned down for a crucial biology scholarship; by
September, no medical scholarship had materialized. Though
he was not at all inclined toward self-pity, the strain of his financial worries is apparent in his diaries.[23] In despair he consulted

the new German professor of psychology Hugo Münsterberg, who advised Yerkes to "go at once into the laboratory."[24] Captivated by Münsterberg's familiar sociability, Yerkes plunged into psychological work with renewed enthusiasm. At the end of his first semester, on New Year's Eve, Yerkes reflected: "In the life . . . which psychology promises I sometimes think there will be too little opportunity to work for man and too great temptation to strive after fame."[25] This concern notwithstanding, Yerkes decided to press forward with comparative psychology, for there was "much work to be done," and "clouds of ignorance to penetrate."[26]

Years later, Yerkes recalled his deep disappointment at not pursuing a medical career, a product of his strong desire to "alleviate suffering." This wish, Yerkes acknowledged, stemmed from his witnessing at an early age the death of his young sister from scarlet fever.[27] Yerkes figuratively revived his forsaken hope of a medical career when he cast his psychological work in medical terms.

Yerkes's lifelong friend and colleague Lewis Madison Terman (1877–1956) came from a large Indiana farm family. His father was prosperous, Terman recalled, but in a family with fourteen children "prosperity is illusory."[28] Lewis Terman was the twelfth child, and the first of his family ever to attend college. As a high-school graduate he taught school in rural Johnson County, Indiana, in 1894–1895 and 1896–1897, and served as principal teacher at the high school there from 1898 to 1901. Terman received his A.B. from Central Normal College in 1898; then, like Yerkes at Harvard, he studied for a second, more prestigious A.B. at Indiana University from 1901 to 1902. After another stint teaching, he entered graduate school in psychology at Clark University, where he initially studied with G. Stanley Hall, leader of the child study movement. Against Hall's advice, Terman wrote his dissertation, "Genius and Stupidity," on mental ability and its measurement.[29]

Unlike Yerkes, Terman never attempted formal medical study. He pursued his interest in medicine within the context of his early career as a schoolteacher, joining the popular crusade for school hygiene.[30] Terman attributed his interest in preventive medicine to his own condition: he contracted tuberculosis in 1905 and was a semi-invalid for five years.[31] It was during the years of Terman's illness, and while he was working as a teacher, that the medical inspection movement took hold in public schools across the country. By 1911, nearly half the school population in the state of California, where Terman had moved for the sake of his health, was served by school medical inspection.[32] Terman's early publications are concentrated in the field of school hygiene, reflecting his immediate concerns: *The Teacher's Health* (1913), *The Hygiene of the School Child* (1914), and *Health Work in the Schools* (1914). Terman later described his personal stake in school hygiene: "There is an old saying that if you scratch a health reformer, you will find an invalid."[33] Although better known for his psychological work, Terman remained active in the school hygiene movement for twenty years, publishing numerous popular and scholarly articles in the field in addition to three major textbooks.[34] He used every opportunity to emphasize the connection between school hygiene and mental hygiene, arguing as early as 1911 for a broad "educational hygiene" that would supersede medical inspections and include such activities as "psycho-prophylaxis."[35]

During this time Terman felt himself to be on the fringe of the psychological profession, aware that "many of the old line psychologists regarded the whole test movement with scorn." He later recalled that during these early years, "I had the feeling I hardly counted as a psychologist, unless possibly among a few kindred souls like Gessell, Goddard, Kuhlman, Thorndike, Whipple and a few others."[36] Terman also recalled that he disliked the elaborate apparatus of contemporary "brass-instrument" psychology, which "doubtless had something to do" with his turning to "measurements of the kind that make no demands upon mechanical skill."[37]

For Lewis Terman, who came from a large rural family of limited education, psychology was a step up from schoolteaching as a career. For Yerkes, it seemed a step down, from biology and medicine. Each, however, came to psychology through medicine: Yerkes from academic premedical training in biology and physiology, and Terman from health-reform and preventive clinical activities in the schools.

Like Lewis Terman, Henry Herbert Goddard (1866–1957) studied psychology at Clark University under Hall. Goddard, inventor of the word *moron* and author of the notorious eugenical tract *The Kallikak Family* (1912), spent the best years of his psychological career as director of the research laboratory at the Vineland (New Jersey) Training School for Feebleminded Girls and Boys. As the first researcher in America to use the new tests of French physician Alfred Binet and his colleague Theodore Simon, Goddard was widely recognized as the foremost authority on the scientific study of feeblemindedness. In 1908 Goddard, with ample help from his assistant Elizabeth Kite, was the first to translate the Binet-Simon scale of intelligence. In 1897 Goddard had entered graduate study in psychology at Clark University, where he later met Lewis Terman. Like Terman, Goddard began working as a schoolteacher, rose to the rank of principal, and spent some years teaching at a normal school. Like Cattell, James, and Hall, Goddard went to Germany for training in physiology.

As director of the Vineland research laboratory from 1906 to 1918, Goddard's professional territory was in one sense much broader than those of university researchers like Terman, Thorndike, and Yerkes; his job placed him in a quasi-medical role in relation to the "boys and girls" at the colony, most of whom were grown men and women. To a much greater extent than in factory and public school settings, research at institutions for the feebleminded entailed great intervention in every aspect of subjects' lives, and thus potentially greater control over experimental work.[38] Goddard considered the Vineland Training School a "vast laboratory" for the study of the feebleminded. The setting of research in which Goddard worked was thus similar to a hospital clinic setting, in which physicians have ultimate authority and inmates are both medical patients and research subjects. Indeed, Goddard competed keenly with physicians for authority at Vineland and later at the Ohio Bureau of Juvenile Research.[39] One of Goddard's major reasons for leaving Vineland in 1918 was his expectation of extending the physiological aspects of his research on feeblemindedness and delinquency, a direction blocked by physicians at Vineland.[40] Competition with physicians also contributed to Goddard's leaving the Bureau of Juvenile Research for an academic post at Ohio State University in 1922.

Goddard's interest in the medical issues associated with care of the feebleminded can be traced at least as far back as 1907, a year after his beginning at Vineland. He traveled to Washington for the meetings of the School Hygiene Association; in 1910 he attended the Congrès International de la Hygiène Scolaire in Paris, and in 1913 he participated as a major speaker in Terman's special session on the Binet tests at the Fourth International Congress on School Hygiene in Buffalo, New York.[41]

Goddard openly rejected the Quaker tradition in which he had been raised; his mother's desertion of the family in favor of itinerant preaching had turned him thoroughly against most organized religion.[42] In particular, he opposed the doctrine of original sin, and described his work as an effort to explain degeneracy and delinquency without resort to that doctrine.[43] Goddard's psychology, like that of his colleagues Thorndike and Woodworth, was in part a means of coming to terms with the void left by his rejection of a more traditional faith. Medical language and quasi-medical professional behavior gave twentieth-century psychologists something of the same status in a secular, technical era that religious language and ministerial behavior had given nineteenth-century doctors in a moralistic age.[44]

Physiologist Robert Woodworth, a contemporary of Terman, Yerkes, and Goddard, also came to psychology through medicine. After early training in philosophy, followed by premedical work in physiology, Woodworth gravitated toward psychology in 1901 when he perceived that lack of a medical degree precluded his promotion to assistant professorship at the Bellevue Medical College in New York. He dryly confided to his mentor, James McKeen Cattell, that some "influential men" at Bellevue were opposed to promoting a "mere Ph.D." Regarding the apparently exceptional case of a colleague, Woodworth added, "Lusk is of course not an M.D., but they didn't know that when they made him professor."[45] Two years later, Cattell secured a lectureship for Woodworth in his psychology department at Columbia University.[46] Woodworth's experience was very much like that of German physiologists in the nineteenth century who moved into psychology when opportunities in medicine were scarce.[47] Woodworth also spent a good part of 1904 in St. Louis, testing with brass instruments the mental and physical capacities of visitors to the Louisiana Purchase Exposition, at Münsterberg's request.

Woodworth had been persuaded to come to Columbia University by one of Cattell's best students, Edward Lee Thorndike. Thorndike and Woodworth had been close friends as undergraduates at Harvard between 1895 and 1897, where Thorndike had conducted experiments in animal psychology under the guidance of William James.[48] Like Münsterberg, Binet, and Galton, James had training in medicine. James's sympathy for physiological experimentation in psychology led him to offer Thorndike the use of his home cellar for Thorndike's animal experiments. Best known for his work in learning theory and achievement testing, Thorndike contributed more than any of his contemporaries to the "scientific" study of education at Columbia University's Teachers College. Inspired by James's professed experimentalism and by Galton's versatile imagination, Thorndike advocated the application of quantitative psychological methods to all aspects of education. His outward enthusiasm for numbers ("Everything that exists, exists in some amount") belied Thorndike's sense that he had been inadequately trained in mathematics; his fondness for medical, engineering, and chemical analogies masked his admitted weakness in physiology and laboratory mechanics.[49] Like Lewis Terman, Thorndike attributed his interest in the new mental testing techniques in part to his "extreme ineptitude and distaste for using machinery and physical instruments."[50]

Thorndike had his widest influence among the students at Teachers College who followed his courses in educational measurement. His widely acclaimed first book, *An Introduction to the Theory of Mental and Social Measurements* (1904), spawned several generations of doctoral dissertations at Columbia, Stanford, Harvard, and other university schools of education. Thorndike tutored several of the educational researchers who led the school survey movement between 1909 and 1945, including George Strayer of Teachers College, Columbia, and

Ellwood Cubberley of Stanford University.[51] In these studies, which were often supported by municipal, state, or private philanthropic capital, doctoral candidates amassed fact upon statistical fact about every aspect of schooling in a given locale. After the World War, these surveys would become one of the primary mechanisms by which mental tests were introduced into schools.

For all of these young scholars—Yerkes, Terman, Goddard, Woodworth, and Thorndike—psychology offered apparently wider opportunities at less cost than were available in traditional professions. For Yerkes and Woodworth, psychology was the next best pursuit to a medical career. For Terman, Goddard, and Thorndike, psychology was better than schoolteaching, which had become overrun even in its professional association by "squabbling women."[52] Public education was in financial, theoretical, and administrative shambles, not at all a good career prospect for an able young man.

Through its alliance with medicine, psychology also helped these intellectuals reconcile their strong Protestant upbringing with their adult rejection of enthusiastic religion. As historian Dorothy Ross has documented, psychology became a kind of secular religion for a new generation of scientists who rejected the emotional enthusiasm of nineteenth-century Protestantism. In the two generations of psychologists whose careers straddled the turn of the century, many were the sons of Protestant ministers. James Cattell, Henry Goddard, L. L. Thurstone, Robert Woodworth, and Edward Thorndike were all preachers' sons. In a sense Lewis Terman belonged to the same enormous family, as a student (with Goddard) of the proselytizing G. Stanley Hall. But even as the younger psychologists rejected what they considered the emotional excess of contemporary Protestantism, they took as their professional inspiration a branch of science that was rooted in piety: medicine. Historically and linguistically, medicine, and particularly public health, was inextricably associated with ministry. Even as physicians sought to shed the mantle of religion in the twentieth century, "we are not God" remains an explanation of medical failure.[53]

With the exception of Yerkes, none of the test psychologists seems to have regretted his career choice, but all, to varying extents, expressed a lifelong professional identification with medicine in their metaphorical language. Like their predecessor and teacher James McKeen Cattell, the younger Yerkes, Terman, Goddard, Woodworth, and Thorndike envisaged psychology as a new kind of medicine, and themselves as a new breed of physicians. The medical metaphor would emerge as the prevailing mode of discourse used by psychologists in presenting themselves to their public.

Clinical psychology, as much of the new psychology was called, resulted from the coincidence of two distinct, widely separate changes in the social organization of medical practice. One was the briefly flourishing public health movement that extended to the schoolhouse and the schoolchild the progressive principles of preventive medicine. The school hygiene movement prepared schools for the subsequent incursions of clinical psychologists. A second change in the social organization of medicine was the displacement of many young scholars who, in an earlier generation, might have become physicians, but chose psychology instead as the next best career. These men saw their psychological work as a kind of medicine, but because they had no medical degrees, they found themselves increasingly shut out from physiological work in hospitals, an important economic base for medical research.

In establishing psychological "clinics," first in private asylums and state mental institutions and then in public schools, the new psychologists created institutions analogous to hospital clinics, realizing the medical metaphor that had inspired them.[54] They were able to do so not solely because they had imagined such clinics in medical terms, but because medical reformers had preceded them into the schools. The psychologists' collective self-image, projected in medical language, let them recognize the opportunities available to them in the schools. Their medical language also persuaded school administrators that they were worthy colleagues of the school nurses and physicians who had only recently established themselves in schools.

Once psychological clinics were established in public schools and began to function in ways analogous to hospital clinics, as both dispensaries and as teaching clinics for graduate students in psychology, the medical language that had anticipated their establishment took on a literal aspect, becoming less strikingly metaphorical. The same language that had described psychologists' hopes and expectations for their profession became descriptive of the status quo as those hopes were realized. So embedded in the language of late-twentieth-century psychology are words like *diagnosis*, *treatment*, *therapy*, *laity*, and *quackery* that they have ceased to function as generative metaphors and now reside quietly in the accepted literal vocabulary of the profession.

Historical Meanings of Medical Language

We may have experts who will be trained in schools as
large and well-equipped as our present schools
of medicine, and their profession may
become as useful and as honorable.
(James McKeen Cattell,
"The Conceptions and Methods of Psychology" [1904])

T HE SENSE OF the psychologists' past medical language must
be taken in context, that is, with reference to contemporaneous
medical practice. Without its historically specific referents,
medical metaphor has only the most crude and vague meaning,
and is easily misinterpreted according to commonsensical, ahistorical, or archetypal definitions of medical practice. The best
example of this potential problem is in the interpretation of
psychologists' frequent allusion to the IQ test as a clinical thermometer. In our late-twentieth-century experience, the clinical
thermometer is the mother's first resort in the home diagnosis
of illness; it is paired in advertising imagery with her dispensing
children's aspirin to a pathetic, feverish child in pajamas. The
clinical thermometer has become the symbol of popular home
health care and, by extension, of over-the-counter drugs. This
was not the case a century ago. On the contrary, the clinical
thermometer was a fairly recent addition to regular medical
practice; its reliability was not established until after 1880 when
the Yale Astronomical Laboratory began standardizing the calibration of thermometers, and it was not until the end of the
nineteenth century that thermometry provided physicians with
significant therapeutic guidance.[1] Despite the active and explicit efforts of the French emigré psychiatrist and educator
Edouard Seguin to popularize the home use of thermometry in
the United States in the 1860s and 1870s, the instrument remained in the hands of physicians. Interestingly, Seguin's work

on the education of "retarded" children, a concept he coined, influenced both the work of Alfred Binet and that of the Americans. Moreover, Seguin made arguments in favor of women's home use of thermometry as protection against unscrupulous or incompetent physicians that were identical to those that popularizers of the IQ test would later make in favor of teachers' use of that newly standardized diagnostic tool. Thus when Henry Herbert Goddard compared mental tests to thermometers in 1913, he referred to a practical new technology that was available only to professionals. He did not imply that tests should be used by parents for the home diagnosis of intelligence. Rather, he referred to a new, laboratory-validated instrument of precision that lifted medical diagnosis out of the realm of personal experience and into the realm of science.[2]

The meaning of a metaphor, then, is not immanent but historically specific. Although metaphors are commonly used to picture the future, the meaning of any particular metaphor can be derived only within the specific context of social experience to which its creators belong, and with reference to the past and current meanings attached to its literal referent. Only in its most basic sense (i.e., disease is bad and medicine is good) is the medical language of psychology in 1992 the same metaphor as the medical language of 1913.[3] In order to read the medical lexicon of intelligence testing, and through it understand the development of testing psychology, the historian must constantly inquire, in J.G.A. Pocock's words, "to what elements of the social experience the language in question can be shown to refer."[4]

In his 1904 speech at the International Congress of Arts and Sciences at St. Louis, James McKeen Cattell used a medical metaphor to project the ideal of a psychological profession, whose members would be specialists, trained in well-equipped laboratories, for prestigious work: a psychological profession "as useful and as honorable as the medical profession."[5] In evoking the medical model, Cattell revealed a bit of his own self-image, a vestige of his formerly planned medical career. At the same time he borrowed medicine's reputation as a practical and humane profession in painting a picture of the new psychology. The image impressed Lewis Terman, then a doctoral candidate

77

at Clark University. In his 1906 doctoral dissertation, published in G. Stanley Hall's journal *The Pedagogical Seminary*, Terman wrote: "The suggestion recently made by Cattell [seems] reasonable; namely, that there is destined to grow up a large body of psychological experts who will play a role in the future as important as that of the medical men at present."[6] This is one of the few instances where a metaphor can be traced directly from speaker to hearer within the community of new psychologists. The medical metaphor as of 1906 was still new to psychologists, and its full implications not yet elaborated by the people who adopted it. The subtle difference between Cattell's explication and Terman's recapitulation of the medical model, whereby Terman stressed the importance of psychological expertise as opposed to Cattell's emphasis on training, reflected the difference between their two generations. Cattell had to piece together an education in psychology, whereas Terman, entering graduate school thirteen years after Cattell, joined an established graduate program. Terman's emphasis on the importance of his new field also reveals in him a consummate ambition that kept him in the public eye for much of his career.

In a broad sense, the medical metaphor did not originate with Cattell; "doctoring" was already a common synonym for "fixing" or "ameliorating" in the nineteenth century, and was applied in contexts other than that of psychology. Beginning in the 1830s, for example, engineers who acted as industrial consultants in redesigning factories were called "mill doctors"; these experts were numerous by the 1880s.[7] Some of the more specific medical borrowings, however, date precisely from the period under study here, beginning roughly in 1890. For example, the *Oxford English Dictionary* cites 1888 as the first instance of the metaphorical use of the term *immune:* "But (to use the new medical barbarism) we are never 'immune' from the contagion."[8] The second instance cited in the *Oxford English Dictionary* is from psychologist Edward Lee Thorndike's textbook of 1904, *An Introduction to the Theory of Mental and Social Measurements*: "If the reader has been rendered immune to these errors . . . the purpose of this book has been fulfilled."[9] Thus it appears that the American measurement psychologists were among the first to expand a metaphorical vocabulary based on the new germ theories of disease. As Paul Starr has noted, "The search for legitimation by other agencies in society often promotes dependence upon the cultural authority of medicine."[10]

Disease metaphors have a much longer history in political discourse; they are one of the classic metaphors for representing good and evil. The very term *illness* derives from historical equations of disease with moral corruption, *ill* being an archaic synonym for *evil*. The word *illness* is an artifact of obsolete medical interpretations of bodily disease, which were based on moral theology; its moral connotations also survive alongside modern, secular, medical theories.[11] When psychologists used medical language, casting themselves as doctors and their work as therapy, they evoked the moral tradition of political discourse according to which health is equated with all that is good, and illness with all that is evil.[12]

While it is possible, then, to trace the medical metaphor in psychology directly from Cattell to Terman, both men were also participating in an older and more general discourse in which the "body politic" was compared to the human body. Nonetheless, the would-be doctors who elaborated the metaphor in service of the new psychology created a community of discourse that was distinctive, if not altogether unique. Their language had a consistency and system to it that branded each native speaker as a member of the psychological community. This system of discourse overlapped and intersected the discourse of other related fields, notably the contemporary discussion on eugenics.[13]

THE WEAK AND THE STRONG: MEDICAL LANGUAGE, PSYCHOLOGY, AND EUGENICS

Preceding Terman at Clark University was another student of G. Stanley Hall, George Dawson. Dawson's interest in psychology hinged on questions of heredity and criminality. In a paper published in Hall's journal *Pedagogical Seminary*, Dawson argued for a medical solution to the problem of delinquency and degeneracy: "Society has not yet learned to supplement cure with prevention. It quarantines its communities or families infected by disease; it takes advantage of every known prophylactic to prevent the onslaught of small-pox or yellow-fever, but it throws no quarantine about its plague-spots of vice and crime; it destroys no germs of immorality through disinfection." Dawson hoped that science would become "the handmaiden of righteousness" whereby civilization would "redeem itself from the morbid conditions which produce its defective and delinquent classes."[14] In Dawson's metaphor, the germ that infected society was the reproductive germ plasm of defective individuals; he meant to "disinfect" these people by sterilizing them, or "quarantine" them by institutionalizing them.[15] When this philosophy of prevention was turned to practice at the Ohio Bureau of Juvenile Research, for example, it resulted in early intervention by the state into matters of potential juvenile delinquency. As Henry Herbert Goddard proudly noted in 1919, Ohio law allowed the Bureau to receive for testing "any child from any person having legal guardianship": *This is indeed progress* for it looks not to cure but to prevention. Already there are being brought in many children who are a little peculiar, a little unusually troublesome at home or at school; and their cases are diagnosed and treatment recommended, without waiting for them to commit a misdemeanor and get a court record."[16]

Goddard and Dawson used what I call the "strong" medical metaphor, in which contagion is the primary image and death its dire consequence. In this strong version, writers tend to view people as germs, and tend to obliterate individual human rights in the name of public health. In the "weak" version of the medical metaphor, writers tend to view people as patients, and emphasize therapy over prevention. Both the "strong" and the "weak" versions of the medical metaphor have invidious consequences for the people cast in the subordinate role, but the strong metaphor has much more extreme consequences, in that subordinates are denied their status as human beings and become themselves disease organisms. In general, the strong metaphor generates and legitimates totalitarian social policy, whereas the weak metaphor generates and legitimates liberal-capitalist policies, although the two versions are often confounded. Activists in the eugenics movement who were doctors or biologists tended to favor the strong metaphor; psychologists and educators who were sympathetic to—but generally less active in—eugenical reform favored the weaker version. With two exceptions (Edward Lee Thorndike and Truman Lee Kelley) the leaders of the mental testing movement renounced eugenics in the late 1930s, when it no longer furthered the cause of testing. As a social policy that seemed scientifically based and promised "prevention" over "cure," eugenics was not only consistent with progressive thought, it was the epitome of the era's naive scientism.[17]

Walter E. Fernald, superintendent of the Massachusetts School for the Feeble-Minded, was America's foremost expert on the problems of feeblemindedness, and an associate of Goddard. A medical doctor trained in psychiatry, Fernald was among the most active proponents of eugenics in the United States. Fernald spoke of feeblemindedness in medical terms, using the strong metaphor that equated people with disease. He argued that feeblemindedness among women was a contagion, because women reproduce. "A single feeble-minded girl," he reasoned, "among a group of boys becomes a plague spot the consequences of which are frightful."[18] When people are equated with disease germs, as in Fernald's strong language, it begins to seem not only possible but desirable to eliminate them entirely.[19]

Among the inventors of intelligence tests, the weak medical metaphor prevailed. The psychologists likened schoolchildren, immigrants, the feebleminded, and the lower classes to patients, themselves to medical doctors, and educational and social problems to diseases. The intelligence test was a "thermometer," its interpretation, "diagnosis," and concomitant educational policies, "treatments." Any single metonymic term in this metaphorical system evoked the entire system, much as a single numeral implies a numerical system, or a word ("Bonjour!") represents an entire language.[20] The strong and weak versions of the medical metaphor in the early twentieth century evoked the same system of contemporary medicine, but assigned different roles to people, according to the analogy. The contrast between the two in terms of their implications for social policy is striking.

Fernald's plan to "quarantine" and "disinfect" the feebleminded contrasts sharply with the recommendations of French psychologist Alfred Binet. Two years before his death in 1911,

Binet, the originator of the classic intelligence scale, argued that it was society's first duty to teach the feebleminded how to learn: "We have therefore devised . . . what we call exercises of mental orthopedics. The word is expressive and has come into favor. One can guess its meaning. In the same way that physical orthopedics straightens a crooked back, mental orthopedics strengthens, cultivates and fortifies attention, memory, perception, judgment and will."[21] Binet used the term *mental orthopedics* to evoke a whole system of meaning, founded on a humane, ameliorative approach to medicine. In addition, "orthopedics" was a medical specialty most valuable when patients were young, so that the metaphor implied that the feebleminded could be reached, and treated successfully, if reached at a young age. Orthopedics was a dramatic therapy, making the metaphor a vivid one. (In educational and social-work publications, orthopedic work among the poor was a favorite subject, usually embellished by "before-and-after" photographs.) The orthopedic metaphor was characteristic of Binet in that it implied a deep optimism and great empathy for sufferers. American followers of Binet, among them Goddard, who in 1909 first translated Binet's work into English, and Terman, who in 1916 published the Stanford American revision of the Binet-Simon intelligence scale, admired this quality in Binet and for the most part adopted his "weak" version of the medical metaphor. As the Americans often noted, Binet's death in 1911 deprived them of the leader who might have influenced more American educators to adopt intelligence testing before the Great War. Binet's death also quieted an eloquent speaker of humane medical language.

THE BIAS OF DIAGNOSTIC ERROR:
FEEBLEMINDEDNESS AS CONTAGION

In medicine, the availability of new diagnostic technology influences the kinds of errors practitioners are likely to make. Historian of medicine Stanley Joel Reiser has argued that where it is possible to diagnose a medical condition that poses, or seems to pose, a major risk to public health, the bias of diagnostic error takes a conservative turn.[22] Doctors have always tried to minimize costly mistakes, but when the possibility of serious contagion has arisen, they have been caught in a difficult professional dilemma. The consequences of a false positive diagnosis fell hard on the patient's family: "forced isolation, household quarantine, and the disruption of business and social relations." The consequences of a false negative diagnosis could be disastrous for the physician, let alone the wider community; if an epidemic resulted, the doctor could be prosecuted by public officials. Scientific laboratory testing relieved the physician of this burdensome diagnostic responsibility, protecting the physician particularly from the onus of a false positive diagnosis in cases of diphtheria, for example. With laboratory tests for contagious diseases, physicians no longer based their quarantine orders on mere personal opinions, and thus could not be held personally responsible for the social disruptions suffered by the family of the sick person.[23]

In the case of mental testing, directors of institutions for the feebleminded, who typically viewed feeblemindedness as a contagion, tended to bias their diagnoses toward "quarantine," or institutionalization. To these officials, the consequences of a false negative diagnosis seemed much worse than those of a false positive. So strong was this conviction among some directors that even the scientific Binet test was not assurance enough of correct diagnosis; its availability strengthened the conservative bias of diagnostic error by depersonalizing the positive diagnosis of feeblemindedness. With the Binet test, such a diagnosis no longer rested upon the personal opinion of family, friends, teacher, or physician.[24] At the same time, the medical model, according to which the Binet test was likened to the Wasserman or other medical tests, tended to strengthen practitioners' conviction that mental deficiency was a contagion, making the consequences of a false positive diagnosis of mental health all the more dangerous.

Such was the concern of Dr. A. C. Rogers, the medical superintendent of the Minnesota School for the Feebleminded. Rogers wrote to his New Jersey colleague Goddard in 1911, alarmed that one Dr. Chamberlain in Minnesota was ready to release inmates merely on the basis of normal Binet scores. Rogers warned Goddard that Chamberlain "has adopted all of our tentative work *in toto*. . . . he has a list of children that he is ready to discharge because the Binet test makes them out normal."[25] In his reply to Rogers, Goddard questioned not the tests themselves but Dr. Chamberlain's use and interpretation of them. Goddard worried especially that the tests might be used in institutions, "with the possible result that some will go out who ought to remain in." Rogers agreed: "Nothing would bring greater discredit upon our work than ill-advised and hasty pseudo-scientific work."[26]

THE BEST DEFENSE

Before 1908, when Goddard published his American translation of the Binet-Simon intelligence scale, psychologists worried very little about overpopularizing their work. By 1913, when the scale made its professional debut as the subject of a special session of the Fourth International Congress on School Hygiene, psychologists often were warning each other and their public against indiscriminate and amateurish use of the tests. As useful as medical metaphors were in explaining mental tests to the lay public, these metaphors could succeed too well, exaggerating psychologists' claims in ways that endangered their profession. Such was the fear of psychologist J. E. Wallace Wallin, founder of the University of Pittsburgh Psychological Clinic. The Binet scale, Wallin wrote, "has recently been victimized by the indiscriminate exploiter. It has been hailed by popular writers in the daily and periodical press, and even by scientific workers, as a wonderful X-ray machine, which enables us to dissect the mental and moral mechanics of any normal or abnormal individual."[27] The tests must be safeguarded, Wallin urged, "from uncritical exploitation and mystification, and rescued from the educational fakers [*sic*] and medical quacks."[28] In Wallin's view (which many of his colleagues shared) medical doctors who administered psychological tests were by definition incompetent quacks. The psychologists situated themselves between uncritical educators and pretentious physicians as the true examiners of mental efficiency.

Wallin's published attacks on the Binet tests, and his generally offensive personality, earned him the disdain of his colleagues. His was one of very few critiques of the testing movement to come from within psychological circles, and by attacking the medical metaphor directly he "broke faith" with his colleagues. It is difficult to know which came first, his colleagues' dislike or his defensive, belligerent manner; regardless, Wallin criticized the very vocabulary of mental testing and thereby placed himself socially apart from his peers. Wallin himself was prone to using a highly technical medical jargon in discussing mental measurement, inventing hybrid terms like *orthophrenics*, *euthenics*, and *oligaphrenist*. Some of these, such as *mental orthopedics*, Wallin borrowed directly from Binet, and his fondness for such language marked him as a kind of fundamentalist follower of Binet. Wallin objected not to the Binet test per se but to its corruption at the hands of American psychologists and popular scientific writers. In an effort to rise above this rabble, Wallin chose highly technical-sounding medical words that allied him more closely with medicine than with psychology. In his autobiography, he complained bitterly that his lack of a medical degree forced him to endure second-class treatment at the hands of directors of institutions in which he tried to conduct research.[29]

Wallin's overuse of medical neologisms marked him as a renegade. Like obsolete and cumbersome laboratory apparatus, obscure language threatened to upset the delicate balance between the popularization and professional monopoly of psychological knowledge. Doubtless such overly technical language made his presumptions to medical knowledge all the more offensive to physicians with whom he worked.

Wallin was always on the attack, quick to denigrate those who failed to recognize the merit of his work. The Fourth International Congress on School Hygiene in 1913 was a convocation of medical doctors, educators, psychologists, and social workers, the first such congress to include mental tests among its subjects. At the conference, Wallin berated educators for their backwardness in adopting scientific measurements: "It is only within the last few years that the laity . . . have so much as suspected . . . that there is a sphere of corrective pedagogics and psycho-educational therapeutics paralleling the sphere of dento-medical care and surgical removal or correction of physical handicaps."[30]

Wallin continued to criticize the published American version of the Binet scale, which Goddard had produced. He incurred the irritation and anger of his colleagues who viewed the test as the single instrument most likely to put psychology on a scientific basis. In his 1914 book *The Function of the Psychological Clinic* Wallin attacked the Binet-Goddard scale for classifying too many children as feebleminded.[31] In a reply to Wallin, Goddard's protegé at the Vineland Training School, Edgar A. Doll, remarked on how similar Wallin's charge was to earlier criticisms of school medical inspection. "This looks like a history of medical inspection," Doll wrote. "The doctors found too much physical defect, and were therefore condemned. The criticism now is that not enough defects are detected!" He wondered, "May not psychological inspection be going through the same stages?"[32] By comparing Wallin to retrogressive critics of school hygiene, Doll could refute Wallin without mustering a concrete argument in defense of the tests. By removing the debate to metaphor, Doll discredited Wallin without having to prove him wrong, thereby preserving the reputation of the American Binet scale, in which he, as Goddard's protegé, had a stake.

Doll was by no means alone in deflecting criticism by evoking medical analogies. Lewis Terman thought very little of his own critics. With characteristic sarcasm, Terman in 1916 defended his Stanford Revision of the Binet scale by insulting his opponents: "It is only natural that those who are unfamiliar with the methods of psychology should occasionally question [the tests'] validity or worth, just as there are many excellent people who do not 'believe in' vaccination against typhoid or smallpox, operations for appendicitis, etc."[33] Terman was a master of the medical lexicon, packing many meanings into a single phrase. By equating his critics with those "excellent people" who opposed modern medicine, Terman took advantage of popular disdain for Christian Science and other ostensibly antiprogressive faiths. At the same time, he implied that the Stanford-Binet intelligence test was as scientific, as reliable, and as important as vaccination against contagious disease. According to this logic, the test was a preventive against social ills as well as a certificate of personal health. By evoking typhoid and smallpox—in 1916 still threats to public health in the United States—Terman implied that opponents to mental testing risked death itself in their folly.[34] The metaphor is packed with exaggerated claims about the importance of tests and the social risks of opposing them, but because these claims are never stated literally they are protected from exposure as absurd.

Metaphor is effective in carrying emotional force without being readily subject to logical critique. With his medical language, Terman conjured the entire social system of medicine, and all of the powerful emotional force of sickness and health, using the cultural authority of medicine in political arguments about testing.[35] In referring obliquely to Christian Science, he evoked not only a fashionable distaste for that particular creed, but two entire worlds: the progressive world of light and modern science, and a backward world of darkness and superstition. The conflict was a generational split as well as an ideological one; as the cultural authority of religion declined, the status of science rose.[36] Like many self-styled Progressives, Terman had little professional use for the traditional nineteenth-century authority of religion, and preferred instead to stake his future, and that of the nation, on science. Medicine, with its roots in moral philosophy and its branches in modern clinical research, was the dramatic realization of that faith in science.[37]

TERRITORIAL DISPUTES

As much as psychologists liked to "play doctor" linguistically, they were not protected from competition from real doctors in institutional settings, including public schools. Competition between doctors and psychologists for the authority to conduct mental examinations of schoolchildren was a major preoccupation of the test psychologists. As they cast other conflicts in medical terms, the psychologists compared mental tests to recently developed medical tests in order to establish their own province of expertise and defend it against encroachment by physicians.

One such territorial dispute appeared as a controversy over technical terminology. At the annual meeting of the American Association for the Study of the Feebleminded in 1910, American and British psychologists leading the study of mental subnormality convened a special session to consider a serious problem of medical terminology. British psychologists and medical doctors were in the habit of using a generic term, *mental deficiency*, to describe their entire field of study, and applied the more specific term *feebleminded* to a particular marginal condition of mental deficiency. The Americans, on the other hand, used the term *feebleminded* to refer to their entire professional subject, and had no standard terminology for various degrees and conditions. This divergence led to semantic confusion when British and American experts met or corresponded. Either the British must have a new generic term or both professional groups must agree on a new specific term for borderline deficiency.

As the nation's acknowledged expert in the study and care of the feebleminded, Henry Herbert Goddard was well situated to propose new professional terminology. Arguing before his colleagues that the suggestion from the floor, *fool*, should be eschewed as overly harsh, Goddard proposed a neologism, derived from the Greek word for "slow." The term would refer specifically to borderline feeblemindedness or mental deficiency, thus obviating the need for either British or American professionals to adopt the other group's generic term. The assembled academy voted in favor of adopting Goddard's new word, *moron*.

This would have been the end of the matter, had not Dr. A. C. Rogers taken exception to the decision. As the director of the *other* institution for the feebleminded, the Minnesota School for the Feebleminded and Colony for Epileptics in Fairbault, Dr. Rogers had professional reasons for not wishing to confer upon Goddard, his rival and a mere Ph.D., the prestige of coining such an important new term. After consulting Professor Hutchinson of the University of Minnesota Greek Department, Rogers wrote to Goddard in November of 1910, suggesting that Rogers' own proposal, *aphron*, was etymologically superior to Goddard's *moron*. Goddard politely responded that he preferred *moron*, and in any case, the Association had already voted. Dr. Rogers was not appeased. He wrote again to Goddard, saying that he had received a letter from another physician, who criticized the term *moron* on grounds that it meant "mulberry" in modern Greek. In February 1911, Rogers again consulted Professor Hutchinson of the Greek Department, and again sent his criticisms to Goddard. Goddard, known as a gentle man, at last lost his temper: "Personally, I must confess I do not see any good in discussing it. As far as I am concerned I would be perfectly willing to call them *stubs* or anything else. The fact of the matter is that the whole group will determine the meaning of the word and it does not matter whether we take Greek, German, or French. Our word is a good Greek word and correct etyologically [*sic*] and I don't see any use of fussing about it."[38] Dr. Rogers apparently did not reply, and *moron* prevailed.[39]

This story illustrates the importance of language to profession, at several levels. It reveals the self-conscious recognition, on the parts of national and disciplinary communities, of how terminology matters to them socially as well as intellectually. More specifically, this story dramatizes how physicians could claim that their own classical scientific training distinguished them from psychologists in the contested terrain of mental disease and defect. The exchange also illustrates an early internal debate about the nature of mental deficit as measured by the new tests: *aphron* meant "one who is weak," while *moron* meant "one who is slow." Lastly, the naive paternalism of Henry Herbert Goddard is enshrined in his rejection of the vulgar and cruel *fool* in favor of the scientific-sounding neologism *moron*.[40]

In 1916 the psychologist for the New York Public Education Association, Elizabeth Irwin, rendered in medical terms the psychologists' territorial dispute with doctors. In an article for Goddard's *Training School Bulletin* Irwin noted that mental "diagnosis" until recently had pertained only to disease, and had rested largely on opinion rather than fact. Now—in 1916— scientifically established mental tests allowed psychologists to obtain objective proof of mental normalcy. "Opinion," Irwin argued, "has no place in modern diagnosis." But psychological testing, no less than medical testing, demanded of the tester special competence and scientific accuracy. A psychologist, Irwin declared, "is in no way qualified to use the Wasserman test [for syphilis] unless he should by chance also be trained in this entirely separate science [of medicine]." By extension, she argued, "the physician, unless he is also a trained psychologist, has not the qualifications to make a psychological examination and pronounce a child either normal or defective." Irwin admitted that a physician was a useful, though not essential, part of a psychological clinic's staff, and urged cooperation among psychologists and physicians. But she implied that doctors' encroachment in the administration of mental tests was a dangerous extension of their authority into a realm in which they were not competent. The consequences of such encroachment would be as drastic, she warned, as if laypersons were to practice medicine. While the medical metaphor emphasized the similar professional status of psychologists and physicians, Irwin's particular comparison of the Binet test with the Wasserman test defended the former against actual use by real doctors.[41] At the same time, the Wasserman analogy radically dramatized the life-and-death urgency expressed by psychologists in their equating social hygiene with mental hygiene.

There is some irony in the psychologists' use of medical language against medical practitioners, but this contradiction is obscured by the emotional power inherent in the logic of the metaphor. This effect is possible because metaphor softens contradictions by removing discourse from one logical category—in this case, the category of educational policy—and placing it in another—in this case, medicine.[42] The "Wasserman" metaphor makes many statements at once, about the value of mental testing, the training and competence of testing experts, the reliability and social importance of a particular mental test, and the exclusivity of psychologists' expertise. It accomplishes all of these rhetorical tasks at once, while at the same time diverting attention away from other problems that pertain not to medicine but to the evaluation of mental ability and the education of children.[43]

The "Wasserman" analogy is interesting as a marker of both political commitments and institutional affiliations. It reflects the eugenical concerns of Irwin and Goddard—concerns broadly shared during the Progressive Era, and of particular significance to the mental testing movement. As a metonym for the "social evil," venereal disease, the Wasserman-test analogy emphasized the gravity of psychologists' business by linking the novel enterprise of mental testing to popular, topical fears of disfiguring disease and stigmatized death.[44] At the same time, however, the analogy reinforced the association between mental testing and mental abnormality (syphilis was popularly viewed as a leading cause of insanity) that psychologists like Lewis Terman hoped to erase. For Terman, who foresaw the implementation of mass testing programs in public schools, any popular association of mental testing with mental disease or deficiency was counterproductive in that it exacerbated the already difficult task of persuading parents that their "normal" children should be routinely tested.[45] According to historian Elizabeth Lunbeck, psychiatrists commonly compared mental tests to the Wasserman test for syphilis; psychologists working outside asylum settings did not favor this particular medical metaphor.[46]

Psychologists adopted other analogies to blood tests that had, in contrast to the blood test for syphilis, a more positive valence. Ellwood P. Cubberley evoked the blood count in his introduction to Lewis Terman's 1916 text for schoolteachers, *The Measurement of Intelligence*. Cubberley, the professor of educational administration who had brought Terman to Stanford in 1910, edited a Houghton Mifflin series on mental measurement, of which the Terman book was the best-seller. The "bible" of mental testing, *The Measurement of Intelligence* remained in print until 1952.[47] "It is the confident prediction of many students of the subject," Cubberley wrote, "that, before long, intelligence testing will become as much a matter of necessary routine in school room procedure as a blood count now is in physical diagnosis."[48]

Psychologists involved in mental testing adopted medical language more often when explaining their work to nonpsychologists, especially schoolteachers, than when communicating with each other. Typical is the 1904 report of Edward Lee Thorndike to the principal of Public School #77 in New York City, Miss Julia Richman.[49] Thorndike had taken "extensive physical and mental measurements" of thirty "exceptional" girls and two hundred "ordinary" children in the school.[50] Thorndike observed that where children exhibited specialized defects, for example, deafness, epilepsy, dyslexia, poor vision, kleptomania, or "morbid sexual traits," "diagnosis and treatment" were relatively easily accomplished. When children simply did not learn, however, "these cases are less easily diagnosed" and "very rarely given proper treatment." The children with special defects, Thorndike urged, should be sent to a special school or "educational hospital," to remove from teachers their "tremendous burden." Even the finest principal would make grave errors in "diagnosis," Thorndike alleged, by mistaking immaturity for incapacity, or failure in arithmetic for "general weakness." "These dangers," he concluded, "can be avoided most easily, of course, by an expert's examination of the children before their assignment to a special class and thereafter at yearly or half yearly intervals." At the very least, he advised, someone should make a "rough differential diagnosis" among kinds of mental defect and weakness among the children. With proper training, a superintendent or principal might learn to do this crude analysis; Thorndike even suggested that Principal Richman encourage the "intellectual and social association of teachers engaged in this work, so that friendly rivalry, a professional spirit and the zeal of the expert may be awakened." In his own professional zeal, and his early enthusiasm to popularize the new psychology, Thorndike minimized the exclusive character of psychological knowledge, a position from which he would later retreat.[51] Perhaps he recognized that Principal Richman, who had just been appointed New York's first female district superintendent, would not likely value the expertise of an unproved outsider over that of her teachers.

As Thorndike and his colleagues grew older and their profession matured, they increasingly asserted their own authority over that of teachers. Their medical language became more assertive, even arrogant. Nine years after making his liberal recommendations to Julia Richman, Thorndike wrote an article for *Science* magazine, entitled "Educational Diagnosis," in which he denigrated teachers' ability to judge mental levels.

Like most of his colleagues, over the years Thorndike became more insistent on the territorial imperatives of the psychological profession.

OBJECTIVE DIAGNOSIS

Psychologists used medical metaphors to evade a crucial criticism of the Binet test: that its results were not always consonant with school grades and other qualitative judgments of mental ability. Promoters of standardized tests claimed that the discrepancy was due to the superiority of mental tests to old-fashioned grades and examinations, arguing that the new tests were not marred by subjective opinion.

Like the newer diagnostic instruments in medicine, standardized intelligence tests removed the onus of objective diagnosis from the individual practitioner and placed it on a mechanical instrument whose reliability was founded on scientific consensus. Proponents of new medical technologies argued that such medical instruments as the sphygmomanometer, the electrocardiograph, and the x-ray machine delivered objective results that were subject to group interpretation, thus reducing diagnostic reliance on the personal experience and skills of the individual doctor.[52] As Stanley Joel Reiser has explained, the growing reputation of such instruments was in part due to their "requiring minimal skill to produce good results," and the consequent tendency of medical instruments to equalize the abilities of different physicians. Significantly, these medical innovations also reduced or eliminated the physician's reliance on symptoms as reported by the patient.[53]

These considerations also pertained to the new educational instruments, standardized mental tests. Psychologists were so confident in the objective accuracy of the tests that they attributed any problems in test use to the poor training of the user. This claim contradicts the alleged superiority of mental tests over teacher opinion as measurement of a child's abilities, but the medical metaphor tended to obscure this contradiction. On the one hand, psychologists claimed that "the tests show facts; all opinion and guess work is eliminated."[54] On the other, they cautioned that anyone who is "not self-controlled" or is "lacking in poise" would fail in administering standardized tests, since "undue emotionalism of any sort is incompatible with scientific accuracy."[55] As Thorndike explained in his article "Educational Diagnosis," "the results of two hours' tests . . . gives [sic] a better diagnosis of [a person's] general intellectual ability than the result of the judgments of two teachers . . . who have observed him in the ordinary course of life each for a thousand hours."[56]

While proponents of mental testing claimed its victories as their own, they quickly disowned any errors that might be attributed to the new technology: "Such criticisms as have been made [of the Binet tests] are of much the same kind as might be made against a fine surgical instrument which in the hands of an unskilled surgeon failed to do good work."[57] This analogy between the Binet scale and a "fine surgical instrument"—a scalpel, for instance—implies that the manufacturing of intelligence tests was a value-free, technical problem, an *engineering* problem, and that the merits of the test are self-evident, verifiable, and wholly dependent on the skill of its employer. It also implies that the Binet test was rigidly objective: that although inept practitioners might misuse it, the instrument itself was not compromised by misuse.[58] Though the test authors claimed that the new standardized tests gave accurate results by eliminating personal bias and whim from the classroom assessment of mental abilities, they also blamed the untrained practitioner for any bias that might affect test results, and lambasted the critic who dared to suggest that the tests were imperfect. The argument was tautological: the tests were designed by psychologists to be superior to traditional assessments and were "more accurate" than teacher opinion and therefore should supplant it, but the psychologists were not to be held accountable if incompetent teachers used the tests badly with poor results. In this spirit Goddard wrote that the Binet test was not only valuable, but "of such remarkable accuracy that it supercedes everything else." From the exalted position of the medical doctor, rather than from the questionable vantage point of the new psychologist, Goddard condescended to his critics. By evoking medical analogies, he and his colleagues claimed a degree of specialized, practical psychological knowledge that they did not yet possess. They further delineated their profession's social role in relation to the "lay" public by defining opposition, *ipso facto*, as ignorance. By 1913, Goddard believed, those familiar with the tests had "become so entirely confident of their supreme merit, that the criticisms that arise from time to time only arouse a smile and a feeling akin to that which the physician would have for one who might launch a tirade against the clinical thermometer."[59]

Human Engineering

Education is one form of human engineering and will
profit by measurements of human nature and
achievement as mechanical and electrical
engineering have profited by using the
foot-pound, calorie, volt and ampere.
(Edward Lee Thorndike,
"Measurement in Education" [1922])

Just as psychologists drew their medical language from their
personal and professional experiences with physicians, they
drew engineering language in part from their direct contacts
with engineers, and in part from the general contemporary
ethos of engineering. Though few of the test psychologists aspired to become engineers (and the elaboration of engineering
language in psychology was correspondingly weak as compared
with medical language), their involvement with engineers after
about 1910 was extensive. Some of the most celebrated public
figures of the period were engineers: Herbert Spencer, Charles
Steinmetz, Michael Pupin, Morris L. Cooke. Schools of engineering grew, and the cumulative number of engineering
graduates multiplied tenfold between 1890 and 1900. Professional associations multiplied, from the first American Society
of Civil Engineers in 1852 to over thirty such organizations by
1930.[1]

The social relations between psychologists and industrial engineers were reciprocal: just when engineers discovered that
psychology could make them "engineers of men," psychologists
discovered that their work was a form of "human engineering."
Engineering language, like medical language, was an essential
part of the professionalization of measurement psychology. It
became particularly prevalent during the Great War.

The logic of engineering metaphor more often complemented than contradicted the medical language that had carried the mental testing movement thus far. Moreover, engineering language had a fresh ring to it, especially after its *new*
popularization in 1911 by Frederick Winslow Taylor; by 1917,
medical language was no longer as dynamic a generative metaphor as it once had been, but was well incorporated into psychology's literal vocabulary.[2] In contrast, psychologists as late as
1924 proposed engineering metaphors as novel insights into
the social and intellectual promise of quantitative psychology.
Medical language, temporarily eclipsed by the dazzle of efficiency, would wax again after the Great War.

Like medical language, engineering language had precedents in educational discourse. Nineteenth-century educators
had favored an industrial model of schooling, likening schools
to factories. This factory analogy was one basis for the dialect of
efficiency that school officials adopted in the Progressive Era,
when psychologists took on the role of consulting engineers.
Like the medical metaphor, the factory model had a weak and
a strong version. In the weak version, schools were factories
and children were little workers; in the strong version, schools
were factories and children were raw material, to be transformed into finished products. But as historians Carl Kaestle
and David Tyack have eloquently observed, the creators of the
factory analogy did not necessarily see the woeful implications
of the analogy that are evident to late-twentieth-century observers. Nineteenth-century educators worried less than we do
today about the stultifying implications of an industrial model
for education.[3]

EFFICIENCY

To the liberal thinkers who embraced it, "efficiency" promised
greater economic and social equity without forcing a drastic redistribution of the nation's resources. As Samuel Haber writes,
"Efficiency provided a standpoint from which those who had
declared allegiance to democracy could resist the leveling ten-

dencies of the principle of equality."[4] For the new psychologists, "efficiency" countered the costly implications of the medical metaphor: individual "diagnosis" and "treatment" was prohibitively expensive. More essentially, "efficiency" gave place to expertise and rationalized a meritocratic educational system founded on the new mental tests.

By 1905 many American public-school educators spoke a language of efficiency, in which mental powers were seen as a finite natural resource, and education as the technical problem of its use.[5] By 1909, "conservation" had entered educators' vocabulary, and by 1912, "scientific management." All three terms were part of a general mechanistic analogy, not unique to educational discourse, in which human society was likened to a vast machinery, and the mind to a mechanism. This ancient metaphor had gained new urgency after the official closing of the American frontier placed sharp limits on the nation's natural resources.[6] Like medical metaphor, the mechanistic language of efficiency can be traced infinitely backward in the discourse of Western political philosophy, but it is the topical referents that are most interesting. This technical vocabulary utterly dominated public policy in America during the Progressive Era.[7] As the engineering profession had claimed since the 1920s, and philologist H. L. Mencken noted soon after, anyone who aspired to a higher calling might adopt the honorific title "engineer."[8]

By reducing waste in education, the proponents of scientific management in the schools hoped to improve education without increasing expenditures. Administrators hoped to resolve incipient labor problems at both ends of the educational production line, so to speak: greater efficiency would produce happier workers (teachers) and better products (children, future workers). One spokesman of the new efficiency suggested to his audience of school superintendents in 1915, "It is proper to say that the schools are like factories turning out graduates, which, in turn, become employees of the business houses and may be considered the raw material of business."[9] Using a similar construct, the president of the Carnegie Foundation, Henry Suzzalo, saw higher education as a "system of getting brains for the public purpose." Schools had a "sanction in public efficiency as well as in equality of personal opportunity," Suzzalo proclaimed; moreover, the "processing of human beings through intellectual experiences" was "far more important than the processing of material things."[10]

THE LANGUAGE OF ENGINEERING AND ITS SOCIAL CONTEXT

In the early part of the twentieth century, as their profession emerged from its beginnings in shop culture, engineers typically became the salaried employees of large corporations, and corporate managers were increasingly recruited from the ranks of college-trained engineers. As the social positions of engineers within industry changed, the nineteenth-century factory metaphor and the twentieth-century business management metaphor converged in the form of "scientific management." By 1905 the distinction was already blurred; by 1919 the two were not only compatible, they were virtually inseparable. The independent consulting engineer had become a rare bird, except in his profession's collective imagination.[11] The engineering language spoken by educators, psychologists, and indeed many other professionalizing groups broadened concomitantly, keeping approximate pace with these social changes.

As early as 1904, James McKeen Cattell outlined the analogy between his new science of psychology and the much-celebrated science of engineering.[12] "The extraordinary growth of the material sciences with their applications during the nineteenth century requires as its complement a corresponding development of psychology," he wrote in *Popular Science Monthly*. He illustrated his point with an engineering problem: "It would under existing conditions be intolerable to erect a building without regard to the quality and strength of materials; yet we often do much this thing in selecting men for their work and adjusting them to it."[13] Cattell's suggestion did not gain immediate support even among his protegés. Cattell's star pupil at Columbia University, Edward Lee Thorndike, took exception to the implications of an engineering model for psychological measurement in the realm of education. In his 1904 textbook *Introduction to the Theory of Mental and Social Measurements*

Thorndike argued that although "the attraction of children to certain studies can be measured," such psychological phenomena could not be measured with the ease with which electromagnetism could be measured; and though the fluctuations of the stock market are "due to law," the law is not so simple as that governing the fluctuations of mercury in a thermometer.[14] Thorndike soon abandoned these caveats, as the engineering model was widely adopted by popular and scholarly writers on education and psychology.

Engineering metaphors also provided progressive reformers with a useful framework for criticizing public education. Physician turned educator Joseph Mayer Rice, whose harshly critical exposé of the public schools appeared in the *Forum* from 1895 to 1903, began to publish under titles like *Scientific Management in Education* and "Why Our Improved Educational Machinery Fails to Yield a Better Product."[15] Rice argued that education, like engineering, must be governed by the laws of nature, discoverable through scientific investigation. Through obedience to these laws, the nation's schools could eliminate waste and "generate more and more power with a given amount of raw material," the Progressives' utopian aim.[16]

Concern for the efficient use of raw human talent was hardly limited to educational reformers such as Rice; the American system of common schooling was still fairly new and confronting an enormous challenge presented by the diversity of the student population.[17] In an epoch of industrial strikes, depressions, and riots, peaceable reformers, most of them uninterested in radical social transformation, looked hopefully to education, and to a better division of labor, for amelioration. Thus the schools were under political pressure in two parallel ways: they were seen as potential solutions to the broad social problems of democratic capitalism, and they suffered in microcosm and by analogy from the very same difficulties. Scientific management, and its watchword of efficiency, answered both. In the broader context, the proponents of scientific management in industry themselves adopted "teaching" as their favorite analogy for their own program, enhancing the social importance of education. In the narrower school context, economic pressures and cultural diversity within the schools and a burgeoning union movement among teachers seemed to recapitulate the labor problems of industry.

Just as medical analogies suffused early Progressive-Era social reform, and were not in their general form unique to psychology, engineering analogies were neither completely new nor wholly specific to the war effort. Nor were they rigidly tied to specific feats of engineering—the Panama Canal, the Brooklyn Bridge, the new skyscrapers. As historian Cecelia Tichi and others have shown, social "engineering" provided forward-looking reformers with an expressly practical, secular yet socially conscious model for their efforts.[18] The engineering vocabulary so popular between 1880 and 1930 appealed not only to actual industrialists but to those who would make technological know-how serve social ideals.

Among the more articulate of these reformers was the utopian novelist Edward Bellamy, whose best-selling visionary tract *Looking Backward 2000–1887* inspired voluntary societies organized to put Bellamy's principles of nationalism into practice. *Looking Backward*, which was followed in 1897 by a sequel, *Equality*, has remained in print continuously for over a century. Although Bellamy is not quoted directly in the educational or psychological literature, his emphasis on happiness as the result of fit employment echoes throughout both the industrial and the educational scientific-management discourse.[19]

A key point in Bellamy's system of nationalism, which is powered by an industrial "army," is "that a man's natural endowment, mental and physical, determine what he can work at most profitably to the nation and most satisfactorily to himself."[20] Bellamy's critique of late-nineteenth-century American industrial education and training is telling. Dr. Leete, a fictional inhabitant of Boston in the year 2000, discusses the great tragedy of the nineteenth century to time traveler Julian West, a visitor from the year 1887. Later, alone, West muses, "The failure of my age in any systematic or effective way to develop and utilize the natural aptitudes of men for the industries and intellectual avocations is one of the great wastes, as well as the most common causes of unhappiness of that time."[21] Henry Herbert Goddard expressed the same concern in *Human Efficiency and Levels of Intelligence*, first delivered as a lecture series at Princeton University in 1919: "A man who is doing work well within the capacity of his intelligence and yet that calls forth all his ability is apt to be happy and contented and it is very difficult to disturb any such person by any kind of agitation."[22] Without applied techniques of mental measurement, the unfit worker in the wrong job "usually drifts into the ranks of 'casuals,' constantly moving from job to job, chronically 'out of work,' the ready dupe of agitators and the prophets of social unrest and revolution; disheartened, anti-social, perennially unhappy; the most expensive sort of an employee in any position no matter how small the wage—yet a human being, and as such entitled to liberty and the pursuit of happiness!"[23] Harmonizing with more academic voices of the "intellectual gospel"—those of John Dewey, William James, and G. Stanley Hall—Bellamy's more explicit meritocratic socialism popularized the corporatist vision, if not the same political agenda, later adopted by psychologists Goddard, Yerkes, Thorndike, and Terman.[24] Bellamy's popular formulation of the ideal relation between individual aptitude and social usefulness, with its explicit reliance on advanced technology to test "aptitude" and "fitness," underlay the optimism with which the psychologists of the next generation propounded their reformist technic.[25]

After 1890, variations on the engineering metaphor vied for place in educators' professional language.[26] Though educators sometimes explicitly rejected the engineering analogy, which threatened teachers' professional status by likening them to manual laborers and factory workers, they could not afford to reject altogether the efficiency philosophy that educational muckraker Joseph Mayer Rice and others represented in engineering terms.[27]

In 1905 the secretary of the Massachusetts State Board of Education, George Martin, thus expressly preferred a business management metaphor to the engineering analogy. Martin argued that although an engineer could measure a laborer's efforts "by means of a stop-watch," the person who expects to apply similar measurements to the education of children "is a fool." Martin then proposed a better model for educators than the efficiency engineer: the business manager. The business manager, Martin argued, ensured efficiency through two "modern business methods: "laboratory testing of materials," and knowledge of "conditions for most rapid procedure, the object being . . . to attain that seemingly contradictory combination—high wages and low labor cost." Martin's business analogy, far from negating the engineering model, incorporated the rudimentary principles of scientific management that Martin claimed to oppose.[28] His discomfort with engineering analogies apparently stemmed from the possibility that outside experts, "educational engineers," would be brought in to the schools as consultants, threatening the fragile professional autonomy of teachers and superintendents. This outside-expert or consultant status was exactly the role many educational psychologists explicitly sought in evoking the modern efficiency engineer. The business-management model, alternatively, incorporated the new expertise of efficiency engineers while suggesting that administrative roles would continue to be filled according to a traditional policy of "promotion from within." As Martin elaborated it, this metaphor also implied a subtle attention to the differences among children. Proponents of the engineering metaphor, Martin argued, paid no attention to "the fact that in a group of five-year-old children there are as great differences as between sea-island, upland, and Egyptian cotton."[29] Thus, in a roundabout fashion, Secretary Martin arrived at a metaphor almost indistinguishable from the one he had sought to refute, asserting the strong industrial metaphor (children as raw material) over the weak (children as workers).

The strong versions of both the engineering metaphor and the business metaphor equated children with the raw materials of industry and viewed education as a technical problem.[30] The confusing, interchangeable use of business-management, engineering, and conservation terms by educators and psychologists is in large part a concomitant of the rapidly changing social relationships among business managers, engineers, and conservationists during the Progressive Era.[31]

One of the most consistent advocates of the industrial-production model for education during the Progressive Era was Franklin Bobbitt, professor of educational administration at the University of Chicago. Bobbitt, best known for his postwar work in curriculum design, cast virtually all of his professional advice to educators in engineering terms. Waste in any form appalled him; one of his earliest crusades promoted efficient use of "the school plant": "That an expensive plant should lie idle during all of Saturday and Sunday while 'street and alley time' is undoing the good work of the schools is a further thorn in the flesh of the clear-sighted educational engineer."[32] By eliminating traditional school holidays and running the school "plant" on weekends, Bobbitt proposed to increase the returns on every educational dollar spent. In his postwar work, he extended engineering principles to curriculum design, making inventories of social skills the bases for scientific curricula.

Fiscal matters were only part of the progressive administrator's concern. Proponents of scientific management in the schools saw it as a solution to widespread labor unrest and creeping socialism, not only among teachers threatening to unionize, but among schoolchildren as future citizens and potential malcontents. In 1913 one education writer described the national climate as one of "turbulent unrest," listing mill workers' protests in Lawrence, Massachusetts, and Passaic, New Jersey; coal miners' strikes in Pennsylvania and California; and the rising tide of socialism in Germany, France, and England as causes for alarm. Taking to heart Frederick Taylor's second principle of scientific management, "Harmony, not discord," the author proposed that social unrest could be quelled by the more efficient management of school affairs. "Nowhere is efficiency of management quite so fundamental as where such vital interests as the educational and social welfare of human beings are concerned," he affirmed. "The conservation of the time and effort of the young is, after all, the highest type of conservation."[33]

The linguistic relationship between engineering and education was reciprocal; efficiency engineers adopted the language of education for the same reasons educators and psychologists adopted the language of engineering: by evoking another profession as its model, each professional group emphasized certain desirable attributes in its own collective self-image and minimized other attributes. Thus Frederick Taylor and his colleagues used a teaching analogy to mitigate the authoritarian and antilabor implications of scientific management. In a phrase remarkably parallel to one used by Cattell in 1904, Taylor explained why shop tasks should be precisely defined: "No efficient teacher would think of giving a class of students an indefinite lesson to learn." In Taylor's words, "all of us are grown-up children" and, like a child, the "average workman" would perform most efficiently and to his own greatest satisfaction if tasks were patiently explained by a "teacher," or "functional foreman." Responding to organized labor's criticism of his plan as an undue narrowing of industrial training, Taylor called the "education" of the workman under scientific management "almost identical" to the training of the modern surgeon. Taylor argued that a "narrowing" of surgical training was inevitable under modern conditions, relative to the broad training of the "frontier" surgeon who had played the role of "surgeon, architect, builder, farmer, soldier and doctor."[34] Taylor used educational metaphors throughout his famous *Principles of Scientific Management*, and his followers Lillian and Frank Gilbreth preserved the analogy. Using a teaching analogy, the Gilbreths defended the division of authority under scientific management. The workman does not "'serve eight masters' . . .[;] he receives help from eight different foremen or teachers."[35] Educational language emphasized the humanitarian and paternalistic aspects of scientific management, while reconstructing the meaning of Taylor's de-skilling division of labor.[36]

Prior to World War I, psychologists drew heavily on educators' engineering analogies when they wrote of psychology's practical applications to education. In his 1911 text *Introduction to Psychology*, Robert Yerkes deplored the tradition-bound and unscientific state of public education. Schooling was the product, Yerkes declared, "of more or less happy guesses," and was not based, as it should be, "upon definite knowledge of the laws of mind." In constructing this dichotomy, Yerkes echoed the first principle of scientific management: "Science, not rule of thumb." Trial and error could be dangerous, as well as inefficient: "We laugh sadly when anyone is foolhardy or stupid enough to attempt to use electricity in utter ignorance of its properties," Yerkes wrote; but even more pathetic was the person who struggled through life "in ignorance of his psychological characteristics and possibilities."[37] The metaphor implied that the psychologist, like the electrical engineer, was on the cutting edge of applied science; to ignore his expertise was to court disaster.

In the introductory pages of *The Measurement of Intelligence* Terman explained how the "trial and error" methods of education could and should be replaced by scientific method. "Tests and forethought must take the place of failure and patchwork," Terman urged. Recalling Cattell's vocabulary from 1904, he explained: "Before an engineer constructs a railroad bridge or a trestle, he studies the materials to be used, and learns by means of tests exactly the amount of strain per unit size his materials will be able to stand. He does not work empirically, and count upon patching up the mistakes that may later appear under strain of actual use."[38] The "educational engineer," Terman concluded, should emulate this example: "It is time to leave off guessing and to acquire a scientific knowledge of the material with which we have to deal."[39] In his version of the engineering metaphor, Terman equated children with the raw material of the social structure; the "strain of actual use" referred to the useful life of each child. Without a system of mental measurements, the social structure—like a poorly constructed bridge—was in danger of total collapse. This trite analogy between society and a bridge becomes hackneyed with repetition, but the consistency with which it is evoked to illustrate key points of the psychologists' ideology makes it significant. The image is a kind of shorthand for a whole set of assumptions about human talent and the special role of the psychologist in evaluating that talent for the good of society. Moreover, it is important to recognize that in an age before air and space travel, bridges embodied some of the most difficult engineering challenges known, so that new bridge-building techniques, new materials of greater tensile strength, represented exciting new possibilities for transportation, commerce, and communication. Conversely, bridge failure could mean social and economic paralysis. The analogy was at the time less trite than it now reads.[40]

Though they shared an enthusiasm for engineering and medical language, psychologists could not agree among themselves on a suitable definition of intelligence; this difficulty worried them, and sustained their critics. Science demanded accuracy, and definition of terms and objects of study was fundamental. Unperturbed, Terman used an electrical engineering example to argue that psychologists did not have to define intelligence in order to measure it and to recommend its use: "To demand, as critics of the Binet method have sometimes done, that one who would measure intelligence should first present a complete definition of it, is quite unreasonable. As Stern points out, electrical currents were measured long before their nature was well understood."[41] By equating intelligence with electricity, psychologists not only evaded the definition issue, but reinforced the idea that intelligence was an objective phenomenon, if still mysterious and intangible. It existed, the metaphor implied, "out there in nature," in the province of scientists like themselves, and not in the messy political world of human affairs, where tradition, culture, superstition, rule of thumb, opinion, and guesswork held sway. Intelligence, according to the logic of the metaphor, was no more subjective than the glimmer of a light bulb. Even if its properties remained somewhat mysterious, intelligence was not in any sense a social construct, but a natural phenomenon: mysterious, but beyond politics. The electrical version of the engineering metaphor also had a distinct advantage over other versions: the electrical engineering profession was considerably more "scientific" than mechanical or civil engineering, having developed from the beginning in the laboratory setting. In addition, after the 1893 Chicago World's Fair, electricity itself had come to signify anything modern or exciting.[42]

It was but a short step from the intensely practical emphasis of engineering to its commercial importance, and this too made engineering analogies more appropriate to some rhetorical purposes than were medical analogies. Onward Bates, the president of the American Society of Civil Engineers, reassured his audience in 1909, "It should not be considered unprofessional for an engineer to be a capitalist." As their correspondence with test publishers reveals, the psychologists were similarly inclined toward capitalism.[43] The engineering metaphor, in both its "civil" and its "electrical" versions, justified psychology as an applied science, utterly divorced from its speculative origins in philosophy. In generating the comparison between themselves and engineers, psychologists capitalized on the hard-won reputation of the engineer as a practical man of affairs, whose constant concern was "Does it pay?" In sometimes specifying electrical engineering over civil or mechanical engineering, psychologists chose a professional model that was more firmly rooted in the tradition of laboratory science, rather than mechanical "rule of thumb," and which captured all of the boundless possibilities that excited them in their own work.[44] In echoing the vocabulary of scientific management that was current among school administrators, they smoothed their way into the institutions where they ultimately had their greatest impact on the largest number of "normal" children. For as long as their subjects were the poor, the handicapped, the foreign, and the criminal, the psychologists would never achieve the professional esteem that they sought. The language of efficiency mitigated the financial concerns of school administrators adopting the new psychological technology. Finally, by incorporating engineering and management principles into their language, psychologists created a positive model for the commercialization of the testing technology, just as James McKeen Cattell had urged the profession to do. They did not wish to risk the genteel poverty of so many in the classical professions.[45]

The Great War

Pencils up! Forward March!
To the great victory of Psychologee in the Army.
("March of the Psychos," *Camplife Chickamauga*
army newsletter [1918])

AMERICA'S ENTRY into the Great War came at a time when psychologists were actively seeking additional research funds in order to develop mental tests that would be useful in large institutions, including the public schools. Two groups of psychologists, whose work had intersected only minimally before the war, came into direct contact and sharp conflict with one another during the war. One group, led by Robert Yerkes and including Lewis Terman, Henry Herbert Goddard, Robert Woodworth, and others, formed the Psychology Committee of the National Research Council.[1] Yerkes's group were commissioned in the Sanitary Corps and devoted themselves to measuring the intelligence of army recruits—1.7 million by the war's end. The other group, led by Walter Dill Scott and including Walter Bingham, Edward Lee Thorndike, and L. L. Thurstone, was called the Committee on Classification of Personnel (hereafter, CCP). Members of the CCP devoted themselves to evaluating trade aptitudes among army personnel. Most of the CCP members came to the army with extensive experience in industrial psychology, including close working relationships with engineers. Scott's group, who had no military status except as civilian consultants, were far more successful than Yerkes's group in communicating with army officials and in seeing their methods adopted in the permanent army. Scott and his colleagues spoke an argot of efficiency, an engineering language firmly tied to their industrial consulting experience, that appealed to army officials and to the nation's industrial leaders, who were vitally concerned with manpower allocation during the war.

Given the wartime success of Scott's CCP, it is not surprising to find Yerkes, Terman, Thorndike, and Goddard all supplementing their medical vocabulary with engineering terms. The engineering model was enhanced further during the war by the very results of the army testing program, which showed officers of the Engineering Corps to be intellectually superior to all other occupational groups, including army physicians.[2] Medical affiliation proved almost an embarrassment in light of the test results. After the war, medical language revived, and psychologists have since compared themselves alternately to doctors and to engineers.

The first commercial group tests were published in 1919, and by 1929 several million tests were being administered in schools each year.[3] As testing gained a place in public-school practice, critics became more insistent, focusing on the corporate ethos of social engineering that emerged from the army testing program. This time, critics attacked the psychologists as "quacks," whose misplaced enthusiasm for efficiency was undermining the democratic principles served by public education. Psychologists answered the charge by comparing themselves to physicians.

HUMAN ENGINEERING DURING THE WAR

The coming of World War I brought psychologists from the new field of educational testing into direct contact with their colleagues in industrial psychology. Yerkes, Terman, and Goddard saw great strides being made by psychologists like Walter Dill Scott, Walter Bingham, Edward Lee Thorndike, and Elsie O. Bregman in the integration of psychology into industrial management practices.[4] They saw efficiency experts, notably Lillian Moller Gilbreth, turn from managing machines to managing men.[5] In contrast to meagerly supported research on educational testing, personnel testing for industry enjoyed the financial and political support of major engineering, manufacturing, and retail firms, even before the war. Moreover, the educational leaders of rapidly expanding engineering colleges recognized as early as 1910 a need for systematic personnel testing that would integrate education with industry for greater national efficiency.[6]

The war years brought together psychologists who worked on intelligence tests and modeled themselves primarily after doctors, and psychologists who worked on trade tests and modeled themselves after engineers. However, as the previous chapter makes clear, school officials too had adopted factory analogies, and the progressive, quantitative vocabulary of efficiency was easily understood by industrial psychologists and educational test advocates alike. This wartime partnership was not a happy one, but the psychologists came away with a new sense of the practical usefulness of their work, and with a refreshed vocabulary to promote it, a vocabulary based on engineering and industrial production metaphors.[7] Most importantly, the war provided psychologists with the "industrial army" to be duly tested and mustered into jobs befitting each soldier, realizing and extending Edward Bellamy's vision.

The First World War brought new opportunities and new problems to the psychologists of the mental testing movement. As several historians have shown in great detail, psychology probably benefited more from the war than the war effort did from psychology.[8] Within days of the war declaration on April 6, 1917, psychologists organized themselves into committees to consider ways in which they could serve their country professionally.

Robert Yerkes, by this time a Harvard professor, was president of the American Psychological Association when the United States entered the war. He organized the Committee on Methods of Psychological Examining of Recruits and submitted to Secretary of War Newton Baker an outline for a testing program in the army, entitled "Plan for the Psychological Examination of Recruits to Eliminate the Mentally Unfit." He hoped to see his psychological experts commissioned in the Medical Reserve Corps, "in order that psychological work may be conducted with proper decorum and with due respect of private for examiner."[9] Instead, the army appointed Yerkes's team of psychologists to the Sanitary Corps, much to Yerkes's dismay.[10] For Yerkes, the decision marked the beginning of a frustrating five years of army service, during which he spent most of his time arguing for the opportunity to do psychological work, and little time doing it.[11]

Psychologist Walter Dill Scott and his colleague Walter Bingham at the Carnegie Institute of Technology entered the war effort with considerable experience in applied psychology. Scott was well established as an expert in the psychology of advertising, an applied new branch of J. B. Watson's behaviorism; in large part owing to Scott's efforts, Bingham was the director of the new Bureau of Salesmanship Research at the Carnegie Institute of Technology.[12] Following the lead of Harvard's controversial Hugo Münsterberg, Bingham, Scott, and Edward Lee Thorndike of Columbia before the war had developed personnel tests for corporations including American Tobacco, Westinghouse, Western Electric, National Lead Company, Metropolitan Life Insurance Company, United States Steel, and Packard Motor Car.[13] Bingham and Scott had also worked with the managers and educational directors of major corporations, including the Winchester Repeating Arms Company and the United States Rubber Company, as part of their work with the Bureau of Salesmanship Research.[14] Scott and Bingham, and to a lesser extent Thorndike, brought their familiarity with "the practical world of affairs" to bear on their designs for a wartime psychology. As honorary members of the corporate business community, these psychologists were much better able than were academics like Robert Yerkes to sell their ideas to men like Secretary of War Newton Baker and his secretary, Frederick Keppel, and to their advisors in industry.[15]

The war provided psychologists with an unprecedented opportunity to develop and test a group examination of intelligence, an expensive project that had hitherto eluded them.[16] Only a week before Congress declared war, Terman and Yerkes were vying for funds from the Rockefeller Foundation's General Education Board. Each wanted the funding to develop an efficient test that would be more appropriate for institutional and educational use than was the two-hour individual Binet exam.[17] The war turned Yerkes's and Terman's competitive relationship into a collaborative one.[18] It temporarily unified psychologists in the public eye, though it exacerbated tensions within the emerging profession.[19] The war provided

psychologists not only with funding and 1.7 million test subjects, but with a legitimacy founded on patriotism that
enormously elevated the status of psychology.

RENOWN AND RIDICULE

With this new renown came new problems; the delicate professional balance between popularity and monopoly was upset by
the celebrity of the army tests. In January 1918 Robert Yerkes
wrote in his diary, "we are now far too much in the public eye
for the good of our own work and comfort." He feared that
publicity would reveal the psychologists' methods to the enemy:
"American publicity is ridiculously overworked," he worried.[20]
The explosion of publicity that accompanied the psychologists'
war efforts made them uneasy, and fostered their increased attention to matters of professional secrecy and monopoly. Already in 1916 the American Psychological Association had
voted to restrict the administration of mental tests to qualified
psychologists; the wartime publicity, though welcome in general terms, made such controls both more urgent and more
difficult to effect.[21] Yerkes, always more cautious in regard to
publicity than his colleague Terman, found the limelight uncomfortable.[22]

Yerkes did by turns fall into the spirit of army work, and
marveled at the psychologists' adaptation to army routine. "It
was a great experience," he mused, "to see a company of fifty
psychologists marching in perfect formation at Retreat."[23] His
concerns about the status of psychologists in the army were well
founded nonetheless. When mass testing of army recruits
began in earnest in April 1918, enlisted men formed their own
less-than-respectful opinions of Yerkes's enterprise. The following dirge appeared in an army post newspaper, *Camplife
Chickamauga*:

"MARCH OF THE PSYCHOS"
(Air: Chopin's Funeral March)

The valiant, bespectacled psychos are we
Prepared to assign every man his degree

113

Add the place he's best fitted for in the armee
By psychologee, psychologee.

Bill Kaiser will shake in his throne 'cross the sea
When he feels the earthquake of our efficiency
Pencils up! Forward march! To the great victory
Of Psychologee in the Army.[24]

Aware of their tenuous position in the military establishment, Yerkes and his staff continually revised their procedures under pressure from army officers and men in an effort to make their work more efficient and "more military in appearance."[25] They incorporated military language ("'Attention!' means 'Pencils up!'") into the test routine, and the vestiges of this language are still found in the administrative routines of such standardized group tests as the S.A.T.[26]

In his efforts to mitigate criticism and enhance cooperation among psychologists, Yerkes also adopted the industrial engineering vocabulary of Walter Dill Scott, Walter Bingham, and the other industrial psychologists whose relationship with the military command was much more satisfactory than his own. In his diary he admonished himself, "I must do some more skillful human engineering in order to assure the safe and rapid development and expansion of our work."[27] By the end of the war, Yerkes had come to believe that "the scientist who cannot justify his work by application is in a measure unworthy of his opportunities."[28]

The mobilized psychologists also endured ridicule in congressional testimony. At a September 1918 hearing on intelligence testing in the army, Illinois senator Lawrence Sherman parodied the psychologists' medical claims by comparing them not to doctors but to magicians: "Everything will be discovered. . . . Psychologists with x-ray vision drop different colored handkerchiefs on a table, spill a half-pint of navy beans, ask you in sepulchral tones what disease Sir Walter Raleigh died of, and demand the number of legumes without counting! Your memory, perceptive faculties, concentration and other mental giblets are tagged and you are pigeonholed for future reference."[29]

Throughout their army years, the mental test psychologists—

particularly Yerkes and his group in the Sanitary Corps—retained a sense of alienation from army routine and ideology. Although they adopted some of the mannerisms of their military superiors, they never truly became a part of the military service. Military language, uniforms, and behavior did not displace the medical vocabulary that had inspired psychologists through the early years of their profession. Nor did psychologists' wartime enthusiasm for engineering language supplant the medical model. Instead, medical and engineering language survived side by side, complementing and reinforcing each other as psychologists presented their new techniques to the postwar world.

POSTWAR DEVELOPMENTS

As the war machinery ground to a halt, psychologists congratulated one another on their unprecedented feat of "mental engineering." Their jubilance rang with engineering terms. Yerkes, who expressed great relief at the end of his war service, expected the army work to guarantee a permanent place for mental engineering in education and industry. In two popular magazine articles, his colleague Raymond Dodge, another army psychologist, credited Walter Dill Scott's Committee on Classification of Personnel with conserving the manpower of the United States. By "mobilizing knowledge," psychologists had accomplished "the greatest single piece of mental engineering" ever attempted in this country.[30]

In spite of grave difficulties in working with each other during the war, psychologists came out of the army experience with hearty enthusiasm for the benefits of cooperation.[31] "Cooperation" had been one of the first principles of scientific management, a system designed to place every worker in the "function for which he is best suited."[32] The corporate mentality fostered by the war became the object of barbed humor in a doggerel verse circulated among psychologists, the primary target of which was Robert Yerkes, chief "organizer." The song was called "The National Reachers Council" [sic], and the chorus ("Pas de deux") went like this:

Organize, oh, organize!
That's the way they all got wise.
Newton, Fauss, and Socrates,
Carty, Dunn, and Robyerkes,
All have shown the way to rise;
Which is, by heck, to organize![33]

SELLING THE ARMY TESTS

Soon after the war, book publishing companies began to issue versions of the army tests for use in the public schools. Lewis Terman recognized that salesmen needed a special vocabulary for selling the new tests to teachers, upon whose cooperation the success of the tests ultimately depended. Shortly after the school year began in 1920, Terman confided to a sales representative for the World Book Company that the importance of mental tests to education should be explained to teachers metaphorically. Tell them, he wrote, that "the intellectual ability of children is, in a sense, the raw material which conditions the effectiveness of all the schools' efforts." He advised the salesman to use a concrete example: "To work without definite knowledge of this raw material is as inexcusable as it would be for a spoke factory not to know what kinds of wood it receives and what the suitability of each is for its particular purpose."[34]

Henry Herbert Goddard, the host at Vineland for the psychologists' brainstorming session on wartime testing, gave up army work to return to his post at the Training School. He explained to a colleague that the army testing had been so reduced to mechanical routine that he doubted the need for highly trained experts.[35] Nevertheless, Goddard enthusiastically adopted the engineering vocabulary so prevalent among the army psychologists and used it both to link his own work with the army program and to promote his favorite political cause, eugenics. In a series of lectures delivered at Princeton University in 1919, Goddard argued that mental tests "enable us to know a very fundamental fact about the human material," its mental "strength." Echoing Cattell and Terman, Goddard explained, "The mechanical engineer could never build bridges or houses if he did not know the strength of his materials, how much of a load each will support. Of how infinitely greater importance it is then when we seek to build up a social structure that we should know the strengths of our materials."[36] Goddard celebrated the contributions of Yerkes's Psychology Committee and Scott's Personnel Committee; the war work had elevated mental testing from an "experiment" of "doubted value" to "an exact science." The army test results, Goddard told his Princeton audience, had important implications for civilian life: "The facts revealed by the Army tests cannot be ignored. Greater efficiency, we are always working for. Can these new facts be used to increase our efficiency? No question! We only await the Human Engineer who will undertake the work."[37]

For the psychologists and for much of their public, the war had proved that psychology was no frivolous entertainment or academic game, but a scientific discipline of practical import; a profession. In a popular article for *Harper's* magazine, Edward Lee Thorndike wrote that "not only philanthropists and philosophers" but "hard-headed" businessmen were looking to psychology for the principles of "human engineering" to guide the "efficient private and public management of man-power or 'personnel.'"[38]

Just as psychologists could turn the medical metaphor against doctors, they could turn the engineering metaphor against engineers. Inasmuch as there was much less direct competition between psychologists and engineers than there was between psychologists and physicians, this semantic turnabout occurred less frequently in the case of engineering than in the case of medicine. But Robert Yerkes pointed out in a 1919 speech that psychologists were strongest where engineers were weakest, in the consideration of human problems. While praising engineers for their dealings with "physical problems of quality, capacity, stress and strain," Yerkes criticized engineers for ignoring the same problems in the realm of human behavior. Engineers, he complained, "have tended to think of problems of human conduct and experience either as unsolved or unsolvable." This ignorance has resulted in the neglect of "human factors" in most "practical situations."[39] Problems of mental engineering, Yerkes proposed, should be given the

117

same (or greater) serious attention that was given the problems of mechanical engineering, and psychologists—human engineers—were the men for the job.

Engineering language, like the medical language that evoked public health, associated psychology with the solution of major social problems. Certain engineering analogies emphasized the dire consequences that would attend society's failure to appreciate the importance of psychology. Comparing the social structure to a bridge (*ad nauseum*), Goddard observed, "It is a maxim in engineering that a bridge is not stronger than its weakest part."[40] Goddard, who worked almost entirely with feeble-minded and delinquent "children," argued that these "weak links" should not be used in the social structure but should be segregated in institutions and gradually reduced in number through eugenical breeding. These positions, and the medical and engineering language in which they were cast, had appeared earlier in Bellamy's utopia: "I should not fail to mention, resumed the doctor, that for those too deficient in mental or bodily strength, we have a separate grade . . . a sort of invalid corps, the numbers of which are provided with a light class of tasks fitted to their strength."[41]

Robert Yerkes applied the same logic in his recommendations for future psychological work in the army. In making assignments to army units, officers should not risk creating "weak links in the army chain" by assigning disproportionate numbers of "inferior men" to single units. Such "random" or "unintelligent" assignments were a much more serious problem, in Yerkes's view, than problems of uneven or inadequate training.[42] The engineering metaphors in which psychologists framed their work thus had specific policy implications, and the psychologists' policy recommendations were lent credence by the metaphors.

In 1922, the National Society for the Study of Education held a major conference on educational testing, the first since the war. The convergence of engineering metaphors in education and in psychology was evident in nearly every paper presented. Columbia University psychologist Edward Lee Thorndike set the tone for the conference in the opening paper. Thorndike argued that the very future of education depended on mental measurement: "Education is one form of human engineering and will profit by measurements of human nature and achievement as mechanical and electrical engineering have profited by using the foot-pound, calorie, volt and ampere."[43] At the same conference, Rudolph Pintner, one of Thorndike's colleagues at Columbia and another veteran of the army testing program, adopted engineering language when he explained that mental tests were in teachers' best professional interests. "A teacher should not be blamed for the poor raw material with which she may have to deal," Pintner sympathized. But, he warned, "we should see to it also that she makes efficient use of the good raw material." Shifting slightly to a conservation metaphor, he spoke of an optimistic future when the "present wastage of good intelligence" would be eliminated, and early "discovery" of mental ability would allow it to be "thoroughly utilized." This would guarantee future educational efforts of "larger educational returns."[44]

Complementary Language

During the war, the use of engineering as a professional model helped psychologists address accusations from military officers that the testing work was an impractical nuisance, an intellectual indulgence, and a self-serving academic research ploy. Before and after the war, engineering language converged with the popular vocabulary of efficiency spoken in educational circles, helping psychologists emphasize the practical importance of their work to education.

Medical and engineering language complemented one another in the professional discourse of psychologists and in the psychologists' presentation of themselves to their public. If suspected of being too academic, intellectually effete, or impractical, psychologists could talk like engineers, who could hardly be more pragmatic and cost-conscious. If accused of being crassly commercial, psychologists could speak as physicians, who (in the metaphor, at least) placed the welfare of others above their own, and explicitly strove to cure the very ills upon which their livelihood depended.

Although the best-remembered attack on mental tests was that launched in 1922 by Walter Lippmann, scattered criticism of the psychologists' new enterprise emerged very early, a decade before the wartime testing program put psychology on the front page.[45] Interestingly, much of this early criticism was aimed squarely at the metaphors that guided both the testing project and the Progressive-Era enthusiasm for educational efficiency. Even as psychologists modeled their work after medicine and engineering, educators and others who were critical of the efficiency movement began their critique by shattering those linguistic models.

Among the professional leaders whom scientifically minded psychologists and educators emulated was the engineer and social reformer Morris Llewellyn Cooke. Cooke, a latecomer to Frederick Taylor's scientific management group, was Taylor's favorite student. Cooke's empiricist slogan, "One Best Way," became a rallying cry for anyone—including school officials—who wanted to show allegiance to scientific method.[46]

Following Cooke's 1911 Carnegie Foundation report on educational and industrial efficiency, Professor R. C. Maclaurin of the Massachusetts Institute of Technology wrote a sharp reply in James McKeen Cattell's journal, *Science*. Maclaurin began by attacking the metaphorical basis of Cooke's influential report. In education, he wrote, "we are not making shoes or bricks or cloth, but are dealing with material of the utmost complexity and variety." He explained, "Uniformity in the product is not only unattainable, it is not even desirable, and factory methods are entirely out of place." Noting that Cooke was hardly alone in promoting "the snap and vigor" of business methods for education, Maclaurin warned that even without such reports, "there are already forces at work to give sufficient prominence to mechanical conceptions and mechanical tests." He wryly concluded, "the value of snap in the domain of education may very easily be overestimated."[47]

In 1912 an editor of the progressive *Nation* magazine wrote a scathing attack on mental measurement, entitled "Measuring the Mind." The entire editorial was a critical appraisal of the analogies on which psychological testing was (and is) based. The author (probably Harold DeWolf Fuller) focused particularly on the work of psychologist Edward Lee Thorndike and educational surveyor Leonard P. Ayres, author of *Laggards in Our Schools*. The editorial is worth quoting at length, for it demonstrates a striking linguistic sensitivity: "Much of the reasoning urged on behalf of this new system is by analogy. To offset the objection that the personal work of education is not in the domain of exact science, we are reminded that 'mothers do not love their babies less who weigh them.' Yet they would love them less if they thought of them purely in terms of pounds and ounces." Turning his sights on Ayres's principles of scientific school management, the journalist continued: "'We have ceased exalting the machinery,' says Mr. Ayres, 'and have commenced to examine the product.' And he proceeds to explain what marvels scientific management has wrought in brick laying. But bricks is bricks! . . . If properly wrenched, it is true, any analogy is useful. There is just enough truth in all this propaganda to create a following. Our youth are indeed to be pitied if the fad of scientific management ever has full sway in the schools."[48] The logical difficulties of analogic reasoning in general, and of technical analogies in particular, were already apparent in 1912.

Even among psychologists, some found the mechanical engineering metaphor inappropriate. Alfred Binet himself warned that his scale of intelligence was not, "in spite of appearances, an automatic method, comparable to a scale which, when one stands upon it, throws out a ticket on which one's weight is printed." Binet feared that it would lead physicians to apply the tests in institutional settings without proper attention to procedure. Concerning the individually administered test, Binet cautioned, "It is not a mechanical method, and we predict to the busy physician who wishes to apply it in hospitals, that he will meet with disappointments."[49]

Another critic of mental tests, New York Supreme Court justice John W. Goff, refused to admit Binet test results as legal evidence, remarking that "standardizing the mind is as futile as standardizing electricity."[50] Unlike other critics, Goff accepted the electrical engineering metaphor, but used it to make an opposing argument. This "co-opting" is a common rhetorical tactic; the editor of the *Nation* used the same tactic in criticizing

Thorndike's "baby" metaphor. When a metaphor takes hold, it orders even the logic of those who would oppose its original implications. Metaphor is so powerful an organizing feature of debate that it seems to demand acknowledgment. This "power" lies not in the words, however, but in the degree to which they attract consensus, a socially and historically specific phenomenon. In other words, the power of a metaphor to shape even opposing points of view depends on its resonance in a particular political, historical context. This meant that the few critics of mental testing often found themselves addressing the psychologists' medical and engineering metaphors before they could address mental testing as a scientific or educational technique.

One such critic argued in 1922 against the material metaphor that was the basis for engineering analogies. Writing in John Dewey's reformist journal *School and Society*, this author, too, aimed his criticism at the psychologists' language: "In all the recent discussions of mental measurement we hear such phrases as the 'amount' of intelligence, and the 'quantity' of intelligence, as if intelligence were a substance like matter which could be weighed, or measured as a length or a surface is measured."[51] The "atomistic" theory of mind, the author argued, sees "a more absolute and ultimate reality in the results of analysis than it does in the whole or synthesis which has been analyzed." It is all too easy, he worried, for psychologists and educators under the sway of this concept to forget the qualitative and human properties of the subjects under study.

The same author warned of a further pitfall in the quantitative study of intelligence, namely, the "surrender of . . . concrete effects to the axiomatic symbolism of mathematics." He cautioned that unless fellow psychologists always remembered the great logical distance separating "abstract number-symbols" from the concrete, qualitative behavioral effects of intelligence, they committed "the fallacy of fancying that when we are studying intelligence quotients we are necessarily studying intelligence."[52] John Dewey, to whom much of the efficiency ethos was anathema, argued that the new "scientific" vocabulary in education merely created the illusion of change. In a 1922 article entitled "Education as Engineering," Dewey wrote that the so-called new education was the same old stuff, "masquerading

122

in the terminology of science." The new vocabulary made little difference, Dewey thought, "except for advertising purposes."[53] Such advertising, however, is a major item in the budget of professionalization.

The medical metaphor also became a focus of criticism. In 1914, an article in *Living Age* parodied the "Soothing Syrup of Psychology."[54] Walter Lippmann in his *New Republic* series on the army tests adopted the medical vocabulary of the psychologists whom he criticized, but called the testers "quacks," not physicians.[55] The medical metaphor was more difficult to criticize than engineering language, however, because it rang so true, having a stronger literal component. Psychologists practicing during this period nearly always did have some training in physiology; among the older generation, many held medical degrees or had studied medicine before entering psychology.

In a 1923 article entitled "The Intelligence Testing Program and Its Objectors—Conscientious and Otherwise," psychologist Guy Montrose Whipple, who had worked with Yerkes and Terman on the army tests, acknowledged that he and his colleagues were not infallible. "It would be too much to claim that the applied psychologist is the only practitioner who never made a mistake," Whipple admitted. "Like the physician, he probably does err at times in diagnosis, prescription and prognosis. But I ask: Are there many of these cases?"[56] Whipple implied that to question the whole psychological enterprise on the basis of a few mistakes would be to undermine an important institution for the sake of an unreasonably perfectionistic standard of professional skill. Whipple's colleague Goddard used a similar analogy to emphasize that the psychologist practiced, by necessity, according to a *higher* standard than that of medicine: "He must not make too many mistakes!" Goddard wrote to a colleague in Chicago, "He cannot bury *his* mistakes; they will run around during a long life to torment him!"[57]

Lewis Terman had even harsher words for his postwar critics. Advocating a three-track educational system in Berkeley, California, Terman declared, "I have no patience with those who condemn this plan as undemocratic." Mixing his metaphors only slightly, he called the traditional one-track system a "straight [*sic*] jacket," and added, "The educational sentimentalists who defend it, who fear mental tests and ignore or deny individual differences, are of a class with those who stake their lives on a coue [*sic*] formula, fear doctors and deny the actuality of disease."[58] Terman equated critics of the tests with superstitious fanatics: Christian Scientists, and followers of Emile Coué, whose system of psychotherapy based on autosuggestion of health led patients to reject conventional medical care. Terman argued that differentiated schooling, according to the "three-track" plan, was no more "undemocratic" than differentiated medical treatment. He agreed heartily with his student Virgil Dickson, who responded to critics' calling the testing plan undemocratic by arguing, "Who could estimate the danger to human life were the physician to prescribe identical treatment for all who came to seek advice? Just as dangerous for the social life of the individual has been our school practice of prescribing the same educational treatment for all." Terman judged this insight to be one of Dickson's most important contributions to the field; it *was* a brilliant turn of the medical metaphor.[59] This medical metaphor resolved an inherent contradiction in the industrial engineering model of education: if followed to its logical conclusion, the industrial model dictated *uniform* education for all children, a policy eminently compatible with democratic theory. Yet the whole point of mental testing was the determination of individual differences in ability; hence the contradiction. By shifting back to the medical model, Terman and his student could justify policy recommendations for differentiated schooling, based on intelligence tests, without seeming to affront democratic theory or to deny the industrial engineering concept of school administration. No one could argue that modern medicine and modern industry were incompatible institutions.

Thus after World War I the engineering and medical models for psychological testing survived side by side, one serving where the other did not suffice to explain and justify the new profession. Each metaphor was the product of complex cultural traditions and historical circumstance, each a sort of *lingua franca* that allowed diverse people to operate as an intellectual community. Their common language united two warring camps of psychologists only superficially, though sufficiently to garner them political power as a professional community. Their common vocabulary, a blend of the older medical language, scientific-management jargon, and the wartime engineering language, made the psychologists appear during the war as one cohesive profession, not only to contemporary observers, but to many historians since. The versatility of this interlocking vocabulary, and its ready appeal to popular contemporary culture and the symbols of technical progress, gave psychologists the social and epistemological cohesion that insulated them from effective criticism until their enterprise had been thoroughly capitalized, by 1925. Thereafter the commercial test industry, and university graduate programs, each employing thousands of experts in measurement psychology, became largely self-justifying.

The *Lingua Franca* of Progressivism

The familiar 'method' of Science, whatever its logical
and epistemological virtue, also has tremendous
rhetorical power. If applied correctly, it has
overwhelming persuasive force.
(J. M. Ziman, *Public Knowledge: An Essay
Concerning the Social Dimension of Science* [1968])

The Americans, who love to do things big, often publish
experiments made on hundreds and even thousands
of persons. They believe that the conclusive
value of a work is proportional to the
number of observations made.
(Alfred Binet,
L'étude experimentale de l'intelligence [1903])

PROFESSIONAL ENGINEERS and physicians during the Progressive Era shared a technical voice that reflected and celebrated their considerable theoretical and practical accomplishments. In addition to adopting the language of medicine and engineering, psychologists adopted this cool, impersonal technical style as their own. Their style implied, syntactically, that the research results and policy recommendations growing out of psychological testing were purely factual, matters of wide consensus, or even facts of nature, and unrelated to the political interests of the researchers. As several historians of progressivism have noted, this language of politically neutral efficiency came out of the ubiquitous scientific laboratory.[1]

A prominent feature of scientific and professional language is its virtual obliteration of personal opinion stated as such. The passive voice prevails: "The contention here supported is that human efficiency is a variable quantity that [varies] according to law."[2] In instances where the statement does require a personal pronoun, *we* is often substituted for *I*, lending a subtle atmosphere of consensus to one author's opinion: "Our efforts have too long been directed by 'trial and error'"; "Greater efficiency, we are always working for."[3] Members of the opposition do not get the same rhetorical company; in professional discourse, third person is usually singular. Thus one psychologist wrote of the army testing program, "Early experience showed that a soldier's own estimate of his own skill could not be trusted, even when he had the best intentions."[4] This subtle shift in number in the expression of general or impersonal statements implies that "we" professional scientists are many; our subject, or potential critic, is alone. In small grammatical and syntactic ways, psychologists allied themselves with an informed and intelligent majority, and upheld the public good against (semantically) isolated critics and doubters.

As the psychologists of the testing movement understood it, science and scientific method, unlike traditional "philosophical" methods, led inevitably to consensus. Scientific method was therefore equally useful in the laboratory and in the political arena. Among the scientists most admired and most often cited by the psychologists was the British statistician Karl Pearson, a student of Francis Galton and his biographer. Pearson is remembered for his statistical invention, "Pearson's r." In 1892 Pearson articulated the scientific approach to social policy in *The Grammar of Science*: "It is because the so-called philosophical method does not . . . lead, like the scientific, to practical unanimity of judgment, that science, rather than philosophy, offers the better training for modern citizenship."[5] Conceiving scientific truth as consensus leads to the question, Whose opinions must be taken into account? The psychologists of the testing movement were not oblivious to this problem, but they answered it with reasoning that was tautological at best. According to Edward Lee Thorndike, "The rule then is that what the expert in the science of education deems scientific has the greatest probability of being so."[6] Thorndike's student Truman Lee Kelley boldly stated that consensus of opinion, in order to be scientific, must be a "weighted consensus" among experts. "Where there is disagreement," concluded Kelley, "the minority is in error."[7]

The publication of the numerical results of psychological tests and surveys contributed to the persuasive force of psychology's scientific method. The author of a school survey taken in

St. Paul, Minnesota, in 1917 explained that the facts, as elicited by mental tests, spoke for themselves: "The results are given in tables of figures and in graphic representations. They are thus rendered objective and tangible. Any reader may interpret them in any manner he finds possible." Publication in and of itself, the author argued, automatically rendered the data objective. This absolved the reporter of responsibility for the test results: "The writer of this report is as little responsible for the facts of the tables and graphs as he would be for the heights of the men in a regiment of soldiers which he had measured with a meter stick. The facts revealed tell their own story which may be read by any who have learned the language of educational measurement."[8]

The psychologists held that the large number of questions in a given test, and of individuals in a given group tested, were sufficient to factor out any taint of personal opinion that, in the view of test advocates, commonly polluted traditional examinations.[9] The larger the sample of individuals tested, and the more questions in each test, the more objective were the results expected.[10] Sheer agglomeration distinguished the new tests from old-fashioned methods. Although the new tests were always standardized against the "known" intelligence of subjects, a knowledge usually based on the opinions of schoolteachers, psychologists claimed on the basis of large numbers of figures that the new tests were superior to "mere" opinion. Thorndike, who spent his career in the company of teachers, attributed the superiority of scientific tests to their plurality. In "Educational Diagnosis" Thorndike explained science in evangelical tones: "Experiments measuring the effects of school subjects and methods seem pedantic and inhuman beside the spontaneous tact and insight of the gifted teacher. But his personal work is confined by time and space to reach only a few; their results join the free common fund of science which increases the more, the more it is used, and lives forever."[11] Numbers, it seemed, guaranteed not only truth but immortality.

Unlike traditional evaluations, psychologists asserted, the new scientific tests were not compromised by personal, ethnic, or political circumstances. In the context of widely perceived conflict concerning school politics, this neutrality was a powerful asset. Educator Paul Hanus and psychologist Edward Lincoln, both of Harvard University, emphasized this asset in reporting on their survey of twelve Massachusetts Cape towns: "These measuring instruments . . . yield results which are not influenced by friendship, family ties, local patriotism, or any form of prejudice. They are not perfect measuring instruments, but have been found to be much more dependable than the subjective judgments of teachers."[12] This stance of political neutrality mimicked that of contemporary physicians and engineers. Physicians argued that their profession let them carry the "flag of truce" in all social conflicts. According to historian Edwin Layton's study of engineering-society presidential addresses, Progressive-Era engineers saw themselves as logical thinkers, free from personal bias and thus suited to the role of arbiter between classes.[13] Sociologists and historians of the professions also have identified this neutrality as a key characteristic of aspiring professional groups.[14] As I have emphasized, there was a direct connection in the logic of progressivism between intelligence, scientific method, and the resolution of conflicting political and economic interests; thus the period is characterized by widespread professionalizing activities.

Professionals seek to achieve political neutrality by exchanging personal opinion for group authority. As Paul Starr observes, "They claim authority not as individuals, but as members of a community that has objectively validated their competence." Starr explains, "The professional offers advice, not as a personal act based on privately revealed or idiosyncratic criteria, but as a representative of a community of shared standards."[15] Psychologists, like the doctors and engineers who were their models, found two kinds of strength in numbers. Psychologists gathered themselves in large numbers into professional associations, and they gathered volumes of statistics on mental characteristics and their correlates. Thus on both the social and the epistemological level, numbers were a significant aspect of professional power. Because psychologists explicitly defined scientific truth in terms of consensus, their ability to augment their membership and create consensus within their professional community through the use of metaphor and the technological voice and their ability to conduct numerous large-scale school surveys with published, quantitative results were key features of their cultural authority and political success. The psychologists worked during an era characterized by a fondness for large numbers; both their language, which made a small profession appear larger, and their numerical research methods, by which hitherto immeasurable phenomena were gauged and counted, contributed to their professional prestige within this cultural context.[16]

School Surveys: Power in Numbers

Beginning in 1904 with the publication of Edward Lee Thorndike's textbook on mental and social measurements in education, school officials became increasingly enthusiastic about the potential for dramatic policy changes that might result from quantitative investigations of the public schools. These surveys, modeled both after the industrial and administrative investigations of efficiency engineers and after public health surveys, were conducted in hundreds of schools in the years between 1909 and 1944. As historian Robert Wiebe has put it, "it seems there was hardly a state or local school system in America that was not surveyed."[17] The surveys generally were commissioned by city or state governments with the primary aim of justifying tax expenditures, but they were welcomed by various reform groups who used the resulting statistics to promote specific educational policies.

The prototypical school survey, of Gary, Indiana, was an exhaustive study of every imaginable aspect of school administration.[18] Students' performance in spelling, arithmetic, and geography was studied, measured, and recorded along with classroom lighting, heating, and sanitation conditions; incidence of contagious and congenital "defects" and diseases was also listed. Often special attention was paid to the nativity and socioeconomic status of schoolchildren and teachers, and children were frequently classified and compared according to race and gender. Researchers attempted to correlate the school system's expenditures on certain kinds of instruction with children's achievement in the same area. Correlations between the results of medical inspections and classroom performance were particularly common, for they often justified medical programs while excusing or explaining poor educational performance.

By 1910, public health reformers had achieved considerable political success by amassing statistics on the efficiency of one or another public health technique.[19] Municipal governments were gathering similar figures about their various operations, to account for the use of tax dollars. Robert Wiebe aptly observes, "It seemed that the age could only be comprehended in bulk," and everything from sinners to telephones was counted.[20] In his introduction to the progressive social policy statement, *The Wisconsin Idea* (1912), Theodore Roosevelt argued that "without means of attainment and measures of result an ideal becomes meaningless." Social progress, Roosevelt argued, depended on measurement: "The real idealist is a pragmatist and an economist. He demands measurable results. . . . Only in this way is social progress possible."[21]

The "Wisconsin Idea," which entailed government utilization of university research, gave a philosophical rationale and institutional structure to the already popular enterprise of counting and measuring.[22] Progressive intellectuals, responding in part to Frederick Jackson Turner's famous frontier thesis, argued that "the test-tube and the microscope, not the axe and rifle," were the necessary tools on the new American frontier of science.[23] An "information fever" pervaded Progressive-Era social reform, inevitably infecting the vulnerable administrators of the public schools, already weakened by intense public criticism.[24]

Many beleaguered school officials welcomed the school surveys, for in the very welcoming gesture they raised their own professional status.[25] One educationist noted, referring to Salt Lake City's impending school survey, "That the city has asked for a plain statement of actual conditions is an indication of a progressive educational spirit."[26] Frank W. Ballou, Boston's superintendent of schools, saw the movement for educational measurement and school surveys as a boon to "educational efficiency." In 1914, he praised the leaders of the measurement movement: "They have realized that the increased prestige of the educational profession depends on the adoption by the profession of the scientific attitude. The profession demands it, the public demands it, and in this direction lies the opportunity of our profession."[27] Another writer concerned with the status of education hoped that "units and scales of measurement" would "do much toward convincing the honest critics of the schools of the real value of the work being done, as well as toward placing teaching more firmly on a professional basis."[28] These writers welcomed almost any measuring device that would help answer critics of the schools' efficiency, and it was in this context that the psychologists introduced their new mental tests into the schools. It was the act of measuring, even more than specific results, that constituted proof of a progressive, professional spirit in education.

Years before psychologists began to speak of "human engineering" and the efficient use of "pupil material," educators themselves were mimicking engineers by adopting the self-consciously "scientific" language of statistics in order to enhance their own professional status. The president of the Boise, Idaho, school board praised the results of a quick school survey done in 1913 by some of Edward Thorndike's students. The president was glad to see that education had "at last reached a stage of development that it is indeed a profession." The Boise survey, he observed, "will certainly compare favorably with expert reports made by engineers etc."[29]

Proponents of the school survey frankly admitted that statistical studies were educators' best defense against critical attack.[30] The first school surveys, done by independent journalists in the late 1890s, relied heavily on traditional tests of school achievement. Most influential among these studies were the investigations of Joseph Mayer Rice, a physician turned muckraker. His national study of public schools, printed first in *The Forum* magazine, then as *The Public School System of the United States* in 1893, was a scathing assault on traditional pedagogy. In his 1913 best-seller *Scientific Management in Education* Rice administered the progressive panacea to the ailing schools and earned himself a name in the measurement movement. His status as a physician likely did him no harm; Rice himself had developed standardized achievement tests for spelling and arithmetic as early as 1900.

This kind of achievement testing became the basis for Leonard P. Ayres's famous exposé *Laggards in Our Schools*, published in 1909. Ayres had already written *Medical Inspection of Schools* in 1908 with the physician and health reformer Luther Halsey Gulick. Medical investigations of the health of schoolchildren, like the mental tests they anticipated, served in part to relieve schools and teachers of the blame for educational failure. This is not to say that proponents of school hygiene harbored only base motives, but that the pervasive defensiveness among educators in the prewar decade encouraged them to welcome any explanation for deteriorating school conditions and rising costs that would not undermine their own shaky profession.[31] By mounting large-scale investigations of the schools, resulting in pages of statistics, educators made their defense in terms that critics could not easily answer—simply because no school board or city government was likely to commission more than one survey, so great was the expense and so tedious were the methods involved.[32]

By 1917 many major cities already had established bureaus of educational research: Boston, Detroit, Dubuque, Kansas City, Louisville, New York, Oakland, Rochester, and St. Paul all boasted these progressive institutions. Psychologists were thus able to use the existing framework of the school survey to promote their new intelligence tests. They argued that achievement tests (the favorite tool of school efficiency engineers) were virtually meaningless unless each pupil's innate capacity for learning was also known. This argument had even greater appeal to teachers than the arguments for achievement testing, for it divided responsibility for success or failure among the pupils, rather than burdening teachers with it.[33] As one surveyor explained, intelligence tests show "the sort of pupil material with which the classroom teacher has to work."[34] Just as, in the school hygiene movement, medical examinations of schoolchildren had succeeded sanitary inspections of the school buildings, intelligence tests succeeded achievement tests. In both cases, the latter development emphasized the innate qualities or chronic condition of the schoolchild rather than the school environment itself.

Authors of school surveys alternated engineering metaphors

with medical terms, such that words like *gauge, diagnose, treatment,* and *material* lost all metaphorical sense and became standard technical vocabulary. When metaphors thus become part of a technical vocabulary, their larger implications become less obvious, less open to question. In a 1913 survey of Portland, Oregon, schools, a Stanford research team studying child hygiene, directed by Ellwood P. Cubberley and including Lewis Terman, advised that children too old for their grades be organized into separate classes, "so that they may receive the treatment that their condition requires."[35] It was Cubberley who brought Lewis Terman to his first academic post at Stanford University; Cubberley's vision of education as a panacea for social ills was extremely influential in teacher training during and after the Progressive Era, and drew the test psychologists to the schools. Cubberley was to teacher education what Cattell was to measurement psychology during this period. In another survey, a Teachers College research group reported having "fairly measured" the "products of the St. Paul schools." Peoria surveyors used the Illinois test "for measuring the quality of pupil material."[36] Boston school superintendent Jeremiah Burke requested a school survey to acquire "a body of statistical information relating to the age, retardation, elimination, persistency and salvage of pupils."[37] In a survey of schools in Buffalo, New York, researchers recommended that a permanent department of measurement be established for "diagnosing problem cases on a scientific basis." Such a "laboratory" or "clinic," the authors recommended, "should not be confined to making routine psychological tests," but should be equipped for "complete mental, physical and social study of the child, for diagnosis of his difficulties, and for recommendation for treatment."[38] As the joint projects of city accountants, school administrators, and psychologists, school survey reports were melting pots for the several vocabularies of their professional authors.

Educators and psychologists were quick to notice that school surveys could accelerate school reform; the surveys themselves, apart from their results, afforded publicity for the problems they investigated. Schoolmen found that the first result of a survey was a welcome increase in the school budget.[39] Specific reforms, too, profited by the surveys. The survey results were brought to bear in reform proposals on everything from special classes for the feebleminded to school dental clinics. In an article for Goddard's *Training School Bulletin*, one author praised the Salt Lake City survey by observing that "school surveys can do much to emphasize the extent and importance of the problem of feeblemindedness."[40]

As early as 1914, education researchers for the National Society for the Study of Education proposed that all school surveys include the new Binet Scale of Intelligence as part of their statistical instrumentation.[41] The 1915 Salt Lake City school survey featured a promotion of Terman's forthcoming manual for the Binet test, *The Measurement of Intelligence* (1916).[42] Ellwood P. Cubberley directed the Salt Lake City survey, assisted by his newly appointed junior colleague at Stanford, Lewis Terman. Cubberley, like George Strayer, who directed many surveys in eastern and midwestern cities, had trained in statistics at Teachers College, under Edward Lee Thorndike.[43] This professional community expanded as school surveys became *de rigeur* for every progressive school system.

In addition to drawing attention to certain educational problems (and away from others, e.g., low pay for teachers), the school surveys were advertisement for the methods they entailed. The director of many surveys done by the Harvard Graduate School of Education, Paul Hanus, frankly admitted that his purpose in using intelligence tests in school surveys was twofold: "(1) to gain information concerning the student body, and (2) to suggest that the perennial use of measurement is an indispensable aid in studying . . . school problems."[44] Such surveys also helped employ the burgeoning numbers of students graduating from the new departments of psychology.

Where school surveyors considered mental testing—and nearly all surveys after 1920 did—they invariably judged existing facilities and programs inadequate and recommended expansion. Most surveys included a recommendation that the school system establish a separate Bureau of Measurement, and strongly implied that schools without such a department labored under pitiable conditions.[45] One psychologist hinted that in the absence of a broad program of mental measurement schools failed to maintain basic American values: "If the junior high school is to be a democratic institution, it will attempt to discover the differences in pupils' special gifts, and train each pupil to be happy and effective in making his particular contribution to human happiness as efficiently as possible."[46] This patriotic appeal, coming on the heels of the Red Scare and the 1919 Palmer raids, anticipated the furor over the tests that arose in 1922 and 1923 through Walter Lippmann's attacks on the army tests in the pages of *The New Republic*. In more restrained tones, and without appeal to democratic principles, Thorndike's protegé George Strayer concluded in his 1928 survey of a small New Jersey school system that although "a large mass of material is now available" to aid in the establishment of mass testing programs, the school under survey "in common with the large mass of other schools, has not as yet organized to take advantage of these materials."[47] This school system was not so much a threat to democracy as it was merely backward.

Though it seemed to Strayer that progress in mental testing was slow, by the mid-1920s about four million children were being tested annually by one or another of the commercial tests. Most popular were Terman's Group Intelligence Test, the Dearborn General Intelligence Test, and the National Intelligence Scale, the last a version of the army Alpha tests.[48] Terman's test alone sold over half a million copies in 1923.[49]

The importance of the school survey in institutionalizing testing practices in the schools should not be underestimated; it was these preexisting links between the research universities and the public schools, as much as the army testing program, that produced the great expansion of mental testing after World War I. In many schools, children were first subject to intelligence and achievement tests not as part of an internal school examination program but as part of a school survey conducted by outside "experts." Although many large cities had established bureaus of educational research, New York City alone seems to have used intelligence tests on a wide scale before 1917.[50] This educational progressivism in New York was consistent with pioneering efforts there in school hygiene and in public health generally; New York had been among the first American cities to institute medical inspection of schools on a large scale.

After World War I, as a result of popular interpretations of the army test results, the momentum increased to include intelligence tests in school surveys. By 1920, schoolchildren in Detroit were all taking group intelligence tests in the first grade as a basis for homogeneous grouping through their first six years of schooling. A similar plan obtained in the industrial city of Jackson, Michigan.[51] The Terman Group Test was introduced to school officials in Atlanta the same year.[52] In the spring of 1921, Boston schools adopted both the individual Stanford-Binet and the Terman group intelligence tests as an aid to promotion and grading in the city schools.[53]

Even tiny rural schools, if they were conveniently located near universities with education departments, underwent testing in the immediate aftermath of the war. Oconee County in the northwest corner of South Carolina had a school population of 5513 in 1920, scattered among fifteen one-room schools and forty-nine schools of "two or more" teachers. In Oconee County, with an average of nine pupils per school, the assessment of children's intelligence was hardly the large-scale "production" problem for which tests had been designed. Nonetheless, in June of 1923 the children were duly tested with the eighteen-minute Pressey Mental Survey, administered by students of the Clemson Agricultural College Division of Education.[54]

By 1926 Springfield, Massachusetts; Peoria, Illinois; Trenton, New Jersey; and Buffalo, New York, were among the many cities that had adopted mass intelligence testing as part of school routine. Springfield students were tested for intelligence upon entering high school. In Peoria, all sixth- and eighth-graders took the Illinois test. Trenton schoolchildren had their "M.A.'s" (mental ages) recorded alongside their "C.A.'s" (chronological ages) on hospital-style charts. In Buffalo, children in grades four through eight took the Illinois Group Intelligence Test in 1926, and kindergarteners were each tested individually every spring thereafter. In Oakland and Berkeley, California, mental testing thrived under the direction of Terman, Cubberley, and their students at Stanford.[55]

Overseas, too, testing spread rapidly after the Great War. In 1921 Terman gave permission for *The Measurement of Intelli-*

gence to be translated into Japanese, and in 1923, Spanish; his earlier book, *The Hygiene of the School Child* (1913) had already been published in Chinese. In 1921 the English psychologist Cyril Burt began work on a British version of the Stanford-Binet. A psychologist from the Psychological Institute in Kristiana, Norway, in 1923 asked Terman's permission to have the army Alpha tests translated for use in the Norwegian navy.[56]

The language of medicine and engineering and the symbolism of mathematics not only structured the logic of intelligence research but ordered the logic of its critique. So pervasive was this interlocking linguistic system of "scientific" metaphor that the whole enterprise of mental measurement could hardly be discussed without reference to it. And although contemporary critics of mental testing were able to recognize the logical fallacies hidden in metaphorical and numerical symbols, they did not suggest an alternative metaphorical system that matched the considerable persuasive power of medical and engineering language in the context of Progressive-Era society. Critics of mental testing, until they launched their own quantitative studies of intelligence in the 1940s, had no basis for their criticism except the rhetoric of democratic theory. Since that vocabulary was also employed with some ingenuity by the advocates and practitioners of mental testing, critics were in a weak position to turn it against the tests. Their critiques of medical and engineering metaphors, and of metaphor in general, went only halfway toward upsetting the measurement industry. For by 1922 mental testing was no longer an experimental technique but a commercial enterprise in which many individuals and institutions had a stake. Most criticisms of the tests, and of the analogical reasoning that supported them, came too late in the profession's development to have great effect. Moreover, critics were unable to muster competing metaphors that would have made alternatives to testing plausible. Such competing metaphors would have had to refute the very importance of quantitative research, in which some critics had as large a stake as the testers.

Psychology's newly institutionalized authority, having a commercial basis that linked textbook companies such as Houghton Mifflin with the school administration and schoolteaching professions, was for the time being impervious to the political-philosophical critiques of testing launched by democratic social critics John Dewey, Walter Lippman, and others. Once such institutional links had been established, and a new generation of psychologists and educators had been schooled in the medical-engineering lexicon of the testing enterprise, the project became self-sustaining. The psychologists' work justified itself, and the quantitative and metaphorical languages by which the first generation defined their professional authority became the received wisdom of the next.[57]

✦ *Notes* ✦

INTRODUCTION

1. James McKeen Cattell, "The Conceptions and Methods of Psychology," *Popular Science Monthly* (December 1904), 176–86.

2. In focusing on "control," Cattell echoed John Dewey and sociologist Edward A. Ross. See Dewey, "Psychology and Social Practice," in *John Dewey, The Middle Works, 1899–1924*, ed. JoAnn Boydston (Carbondale: Southern Illinois University Press, 1976), 1:149–50; Ross, *Social Control* (New York: Macmillan, 1901), as cited in Dorothy Ross, "American Social Science and the Idea of Progress," in *The Authority of Experts: Studies in History and Theory*, ed. Thomas L. Haskell (Bloomington: Indiana University Press, 1984), pp. 157–75, esp. pp. 161–64; see also Morris Janowitz, "Sociological Theory and Social Control," *American Journal of Sociology* 81 (1975): 82–108.

3. I do not endorse the psychologists' chiliastic view by noting, as a historian, that they believed in the social good of their program. I have come to the ethical view that the testing enterprise is not a marked improvement over less bureaucratic forms of evaluation, but my primary historical interest is in discovering how psychologists created a persuasive rationale for their enterprise, enabling them to implement mental tests on a massive scale within a very short period of time.

4. On education in democratic theory, and democratic theory in educational policy, see Rush Welter, *Popular Education and Democratic Thought in America* (New York: Columbia University Press, 1969); Carl F. Kaestle, *Pillars of the Republic: Common Schools and American Society, 1780–1860* (New York: Hill and Wang, 1984).

5. See Paul Davis Chapman, *Schools as Sorters: Lewis M. Terman, Applied Psychology, and the Intelligence Testing Movement, 1890–1930* (New York: New York University Press, 1988), pp. 1, 146–70; James McKeen Cattell, "Mental Tests and Measurements," *Mind* 15 (1890): 373–80; Gertrude A. Hildreth, *A Bibliography of Mental Tests and Rating Scales* (New York: Psychological Corporation, 1933); W. S. Deffenbaugh, "Uses of Intelligence and Achievement Tests in 215 Cities," City School Leaflet 20 (Washington, D.C.: Government Printing Office, 1925). As Chapman points out, tests of mental capacity for the purposes of school classification were a small part of the entire testing enterprise, but popular sources did not make this distinction, and "IQ" testing came to represent the entire phenomenon. See J. K.

Hart, "Who's Intelligent Now?" *Survey* 52 (1924); "Intelligence, Limited," *Saturday Evening Post* 196 (1923): 19; Raymond Dodge, "Mental Engineering After the War," *Review of Reviews* 59 (1919): 606–10; H. B. English, "Is America Feeble-Minded?" *Survey* 49 (1922): 79–81; Arthur S. Otis, "Some Queer Misconceptions Regarding Intelligence Tests," *American School Board Journal* 75 (1927): 42, 134; Charles G. Reigner, "The Measurement Movement—and the Man in the Street," *Education* 44 (1924): 571–75. Otis was an editor at World Book Company.

6. On the "false start" of anthropometric testing in the 1890s, see Michael Sokal, "James McKeen Cattell and Mental Anthropometry: Nineteenth-Century Science and Reform and the Origins of Psychological Testing," in *Psychological Testing and American Society*, ed. Michael Sokal (New Brunswick, N.J.: Rutgers University Press, 1987), pp. 21–45. On nineteenth-century antecedents, see Milos Bondy, "Psychiatric Antecedents of Psychological Testing Before Binet," *Journal of the History of the Behavioral Sciences* 10 (1974): 180–94; Stephen Jay Gould, *The Mismeasure of Man* (New York: Norton, 1981); Richard Hofstadter, *Social Darwinism in American Thought* (Philadelphia: University of Pennsylvania Press, 1944); Merle Curti, *The Social Ideas of American Educators* (Totowa, N.J.: Littlefield, Adams, 1935); John Higham, *Strangers in the Land: Patterns of American Nativism, 1860–1925* (1963; New York: Atheneum, 1970); Daniel Calhoun, *The Intelligence of a People* (Princeton: Princeton University Press, 1973).

7. See Lawrence Cremin, *The Transformation of the School: Progressivism in American Education, 1876–1957* (New York: Knopf, 1961); David B. Tyack, *The One Best System: A History of American Urban Education* (Cambridge, Mass.: Harvard University Press, 1974); Joel H. Spring, *Education and the Rise of the Corporate Order* (Boston: Beacon Press, 1972); Raymond E. Callahan, *Education and the Cult of Efficiency: A Study of the Social Forces That Have Shaped the Administration of the Public Schools* (Chicago: University of Chicago Press, 1962).

8. See Daniel Rodgers' essay "In Search of Progressivism," *Reviews in American History* 10 (1982): 113–32, on the three "languages of progressivism": antimonopoly, social bonds, and efficiency. I would argue that in the context of urban educational reform, these are not independent languages; rather, the critique of monopoly was cast in the ameliorative language of social harmony or social control, and that resolution was sought in practical techniques, such as standardized testing, referred to as "efficiency." The successful implementers of mass testing—psychologists and administrators—often managed to use the "antimonopoly," democratic terms of their critics against those critics by explaining hierarchy as efficiency and comparing

equality of treatment to "lockstep" standardization. This tighter relation among the languages of educational progressivism makes sense
in light of the centrality of educational policy to democratic theory
during this period. See James McKeen Cattell, "The American Association for the Advancement of Science: Science, Education, and Democracy," *Science* 39 (1914): 154–64, 22; Tyack, *The One Best System*.

9. Others have written such accounts. The best is Thomas Pogue
Weinland's unpublished doctoral thesis, "The History of the I.Q. in
America, 1890–1941" (Columbia University, 1970); see also Raymond
E. Fancher, *The Intelligence Men: Makers of the IQ Controversy* (New
York: Norton, 1985); Sokal, ed., *Psychological Testing and American
Society*.

10. This work has suggested to me that metaphorical discourse is
at the heart of every concerted effort to form social groups, whether
for commercial, institutional, professional, religious, or political purposes. Some of these implications are addressed in my current work
on hygiene as political metaphor.

11. Eric Hobsbawm and Terence Ranger, eds., *The Invention of
Tradition* (New York: Cambridge University Press, 1983); J.G.A.
Pocock, "Time, Institutions and Action: An Essay on Traditions and
Their Understanding," in *Politics and Experience: Essays Presented to Mi-
chael Oakeshott on the Occasion of His Retirement*, ed. Preston B. King and
B. C. Parekh (Cambridge: Cambridge University Press, 1968).

12. The most insightful analyses of profession are to be found in
Andrew Abbott, *The System of Professions: An Essay on the Division of
Expert Labor* (Chicago: University of Chicago Press, 1988), a brilliant
book that I regret I came to well after most of my work on this book
was completed, and Magali Sarfatti Larson, *The Rise of Professionalism:
A Sociological Analysis* (Berkeley: University of California Press, 1977).
On the centrality of testing to the professionalization of psychology
see Thomas M. Camfield, "The Professionalization of American Psychology, 1870–1917," *Journal of the History of the Behavioral Sciences* 9
(1973): 66–75; Franz Samelson, "Putting Psychology on the Map: Ideology and Intelligence Testing," in *Psychology in Social Context*, ed.
Allan Buss (New York: Irvington Press, 1979), pp. 103–68; Lee J.
Cronbach, "Five Decades of Controversy Over Mental Testing," *American Psychologist* 30 (1975): 1–14.

13. Lee Cronbach, *Essentials of Psychological Testing* (New York:
Harper Brothers, 1960), p. 157. On the extent of testing in the
schools, see Deffenbaugh, "Uses of Intelligence" and "Cities Reporting the Use of Homogeneous Grouping and of the Winnetka Technique and the Dalton Plan," City School Leaflet 22, (Washington,
D.C.: Government Printing Office, 1926).

14. See, for instance, the difference between Robert Yerkes's supportive letters to colleague Lewis Terman and his express criticism of the testing enterprise, and of Terman, in letters to Walter Lippmann. Robert Mearns Yerkes Papers, Sterling Memorial Library, Yale University.

15. Most professions make similar chiliastic claims; see, for example, the contemporaneous claims of dentists, as outlined in Steven L. Schlossman, JoAnne Brown, and Michael Sedlak, *Preventive Dentistry and American Public Education* (Santa Monica, Calif.: The Rand Corporation, 1985). On the "good" and the "practical" as modes of legitimation, and hence bases of authority, see Peter L. Berger and Thomas Luckman, *The Social Construction of Reality: A Treatise in the Sociology of Knowledge* (Garden City, N.Y.: Doubleday, 1966), esp. pp. 92–126. Clearly, not all psychologists were interested in, or invested in, mental testing. However, testing remains the single most salient and coherent practical technology offered for social consumption by professional psychology. Other powerful psychological systems, including psychoanalysis and behaviorism, have had profound cultural and social impact without presenting this technological coherence. A similar study could be made of these systems, or of any concerted effort, professional or political, toward social change; such a study may force the revision of these relative claims of importance for testing. Such revisions, besides being inevitable, are to be welcomed.

16. On the primacy of knowledge as the basis of profession, see A. M. Carr-Saunders and P. A. Wilson, *The Professions* (Oxford: Clarendon Press, 1933); for a powerful revision of this premise, see Abbott, *The System of Professions*, esp. pp. 52–57, 206, 286, 298. See also E. B. Huey to James McKeen Cattell, March 18, 1902, James McKeen Cattell Papers, Manuscripts Division, Library of Congress.

17. I have not addressed a fourth category: the experimental subject, who in the case of the social sciences and social professions is often different from the client. See Michel Foucault, "The Subject and Power," *Critical Inquiry* 8 (1982): 777–95. A very fine start is made in Kurt Danziger, *Constructing the Subject: Historical Origins of Psychological Research* (Cambridge: Cambridge University Press, 1990). On laboratories as social settings, see Jill G. Morawski, ed., *The Rise of Experimentation in American Psychology* (New Haven: Yale University Press, 1988); Bruno Latour, *Laboratory Life: The Social Construction of Scientific Facts* (Beverly Hills: Sage Publications, 1979); Harry M. Marks, "Local Knowledge: Experimental Communities and Experimental Practices, 1918–1950" (Paper presented at the Conference on Twentieth Century Health Sciences, University of California, San Francisco, May 23–24, 1988).

18. The expert knowledge of nurses, computer engineers, and automobile mechanics has not guaranteed their being understood as professionals. Conversely, the maintenance of a clientele without a monopoly over expert knowledge usually is called quackery. Peter Novick asserts, "De jure or de facto monopoly is the aspiration of every professionalizing group, and historians are no exception." Novick follows with a discussion on popularization, which he does not frame as the opposite of monopoly, but as part of the process of monopolization (in the case of interwar historians, a failure). Peter Novick, *That Noble Dream: The "Objectivity Question" and the American Historical Profession* (New York: Cambridge University Press, 1988), pp. 185, 192–94.

19. Again, I suspect this does not make the psychologists unique or less sincere in what they were doing; the observation merely challenges conventional wisdom on the order of things.

20. By "primed to accept" I mean that medical and engineering achievements were very widely celebrated in the popular cultural sources of the period. For similar usage among professionalizing historians, see William E. Dodd to Albert B. Hart, December 22, 1926, as cited by Novick, *That Noble Dream*, p. 194, where historical practice is held up to legal and medical authority in a discussion about licensing historians.

21. As I explain later, the metaphorical references to medicine and engineering that permeated psychologists' public declarations about their project were nearly absent in their private correspondence with one another. This is one of the observations that leads me to refer to their metaphorical discourse as "advertisement."

22. Henry Herbert Goddard of the Vineland (New Jersey) Training School led the movement based in schools to study the feeble-minded. Lewis Madison Terman of Stanford University led the movement to study the gifted. See, respectively, Leila Zenderland, "The Debate over Diagnosis: Henry Herbert Goddard and the Medical Acceptance of Intelligence Testing," in *Psychological Testing and American Society*, ed. Sokal, pp. 46–74; Chapman, *Schools as Sorters*; Henry L. Minton, *Lewis M. Terman: Pioneer in Psychological Testing* (New York: New York University Press, 1988).

23. On the historical congruence between eugenics and other "progressive" reform programs, see Donald K. Pickens, *Eugenics and the Progressives* (Nashville: Vanderbilt University Press, 1968). Throughout, I use the term *progressive* to describe the self-understanding and contemporaneous usage of social critics and reformers who worked under this broad banner. The "Progressives" were a vast and varied group whose primary coherence stemmed from their be-

lief in the possibility of social progress, as they variously described it, through the thoroughgoing diffusion of scientific knowledge and its application to social problems. In my own political view, their many accomplishments were of mixed political and moral value, indisputably long-lived, but their faith was inherently conservative insofar as it marginalized politics in favor of technology, presuming ends as predetermined in order to focus on means. I believe this to be the key to their many successes in implementing programs of social reform in education, public health, and law. The most articulate contemporaneous social critic to make this point about ends and means was William Chandler Bagley. See his *Determinism in Education* (Baltimore: Warwick and York, 1925).

24. I use the term *technological progressivism* to emphasize the focus on means. On the historiography of progressivism, see Rodgers, "In Search of Progressivism."

25. One element in both the labor movement and the conservation movement was a typically "progressive" emphasis on the intelligent and efficient management of land and labor—by both workers and owners—rather than on land or labor itself. Thus labor leader Samuel Gompers came to accept some of Frederick Winslow Taylor's principles of scientific management; teachers came to accept the incursions of psychologists. In my study of the field of psychological testing I found surprisingly little express resistance to the testing enterprise on the part of parents or teachers. Another study could be written that made response and resistance to these professional efforts the central focus; such a study would require the use of socialist, labor union, African-American, and foreign-language sources, among others, and might cause me to revise my strong opinion that the "success" of the testing enterprise rested on the ability of the psychologists to marginalize opposition to testing by defining the enterprise in technical, and therefore (by their definition) apolitical, terms. Technology is not inherently apolitical—to call technology neutral is as much a political gesture as is calling it political—but in the terms of Progressive-Era discourse about social reform and the uses of human ingenuity, technology was seen as a replacement for politics. On the technological fix for labor strife, see Milton J. Nadworny, *Scientific Management and the Unions, 1900–1932: A Historical Analysis* (Cambridge, Mass.: Harvard University Press, 1955); David F. Noble, *America by Design: Science, Technology and the Rise of Corporate Capitalism* (New York: Knopf, 1977); on conservation see Samuel P. Hays, *Conservation and the Gospel of Efficiency: The Progressive Conservation Movement, 1890–1920* (Cambridge, Mass.: Harvard University Press, 1959).

26. See Noble, *America by Design*; Tyack, *The One Best System*; Ray-

mond E. Callahan, *Education and the Cult of Efficiency: A Study of the Social Forces That Have Shaped the Administration of the Public Schools* (Chicago: University of Chicago Press, 1964); Charles McCarthy, *The Wisconsin Idea* (New York: Macmillan, 1912); Samuel P. Hays, "The Politics of Reform in Municipal Government in the Progressive Era," *Pacific Northwest Quarterly* 55 (1964): 157–69; Frederick Winslow Taylor, *The Principles of Scientific Management* (New York and London: Harper Brothers, 1911); Samuel Haber, *Efficiency and Uplift: Scientific Management in the Progressive Era* (Chicago: University of Chicago Press, 1964). These different groups all called themselves "progressive" and shared this essential confidence in the power of intellectual resources mobilized in social technologies. I am of course not arguing that this is the only important aspect of their shared political views.

27. This understanding of progressivism as a cultural movement is based on my own reading of the primary and secondary literature on social reform movements of the period between 1880 and 1930. See the bibliographic essay for a complete list of sources. Many of these principles are given dramatic life in Edward Bellamy's utopian novel *Looking Backward 2000–1887* (1888; New York: World Publishing Company, 1945), a best-seller since its publication in 1888.

28. David O. Edge, "Technological Metaphor and Social Control," *New Literary History* 6 (1974–1975): 135–47; Murray Edelman, *Political Language: Words That Succeed and Policies That Fail* (New York: Academic Press, 1977). See also Jürgen Habermas, *Toward a Rational Society* (Boston: Beacon Press, 1970), chap. 6.

29. See, for instance, Walter Lippman's series of articles in *The New Republic*: "The Mental Age of Americans," 32 (1922): 213–15; "The Mystery of the 'A' Men," 32 (1922): 246–48; "The Reliability of Intelligence Tests," 32 (1922): 275–77; "Tests of Hereditary Intelligence," 32 (1922): 328–30; "A Future for the Tests," 33 (1922): 9–11. See also Lewis Terman's reply, "The Great Conspiracy, or the Impulse Imperious of Intelligence Testers Psychoanalyzed and Exposed by Mr. Lippmann," 33 (1922): 1–15. Note Terman's use against Lippmann of then-suspect (post-Palmer) allegiances to the leftist critique of empire and to psychoanalysis, which Terman likened to spiritualism. The internal psychological critique came primarily from William Chandler Bagley in "Professor Terman's Determinism," *Journal of Educational Research* 6 (1922): 376–85, and *Determinism in Education*; see Terman's reply, "The Psychological Determinist, or Democracy and the IQ," *Journal of Educational Research* 6 (1922): 57–62. For a contemporaneous overview of the controversy and defense of the tests, see Guy M. Whipple, "Educational Determinism: A Discussion of Professor Bagley's Address at Chicago," *School and Society* 15 (1922):

599–602, and "The Intelligence Testing Program and Its Objectors—Conscientious and Otherwise," *School and Society* 17 (1923): 561–68; note the implications of subversion and treachery linked to the wartime language of "self-determination" and "conscientious objectors." On the cultural politics of the home front, and justifications for war during World War I, see David Kennedy, *Over Here: The First World War and American Society* (New York: Oxford University Press, 1977).

30. It was not until the 1940s that social-scientific evidence was produced to challenge the hereditarian assumptions of the mental testing movement; see also Chapman, *Schools as Sorters*, pp. 159–71; Henry L. Minton, "The Iowa Child Welfare Research Station and the 1940 Debate on Intelligence: Carrying on the Legacy of a Concerned Mother," *Journal of the History of the Behavioral Sciences* 20 (1984): 160–76.

31. On the force of numbers in several respects, see JoAnne Brown, "Mental Measurements and the Rhetorical Force of Numbers," in *The Estate of Social Knowledge*, ed. JoAnne Brown and David van Keuren (Baltimore: Johns Hopkins University Press, 1991), pp. 134–52; Patricia Cline Cohen, *A Calculating People: The Spread of Numeracy in Early America* (Chicago: University of Chicago Press, 1982); James H. Cassedy, *American Medicine and Statistical Thinking, 1800–1860* (Cambridge, Mass.: Harvard University Press, 1984).

32. Hannah Arendt, "Totalitarian Imperialism," *Journal of Politics* 20 (1958): 25.

33. Karl Marx and Friedrich Engels, *The German Ideology* (New York: International Publishers, 1969), p. 19.

34. Actual relations between the abstract categories of "language" and "social structure," "language" and "event," and "language" and "thought" are circular, intimate, and multiple. Trying to separate these concepts in a useful historiographic way presents us with complex political and epistemological dilemmas.

35. See Jill G. Morawski and Gail A. Hornstein, "The Quandary of the Quacks: The Struggle for Expert Knowledge in American Psychology, 1890–1940," in *The Estate of Social Knowledge*, ed. Brown and van Keuren, pp. 106–33; Brown, "Mental Measurements," pp. 134–52.

36. See the insightful discussion of "local knowledge" in Marks, "Local Knowledge."

37. Works addressing historically the subject of professional expertise and authoritative language are David Hollinger, "Historians and the Discourse of Intellectuals," in *New Directions in American Intellectual History*, ed. John Higham and Paul Conkin (Baltimore: Johns Hopkins University Press, 1979), pp. 42–43; Gerald L. Geison, ed.,

Professions and Professional Ideologies in America (Chapel Hill: University of North Carolina Press, 1983), p. 9; Kenneth Hudson, *The Jargon of the Professions* (London: Macmillan, 1978); Edelman, *Political Language*; Stanley Fish, "Anti-Professionalism," in his *Doing What Comes Naturally: Change, Rhetoric, and the Practice of Theory in Literary and Legal Studies* (Durham, N.C.: Duke University Press, 1989). While Andrew Abbott gives almost no direct attention to the language issue in *The System of Professions*, it seems to me that my theoretical assertions fit very well into Abbott's much larger conceptual scheme of professionalism, and may be generalized further into the realm of politics and cultural authority (from whence they came, via Edelman and Pocock).

38. This effort is consistent with, and beholden to, the following ongoing conversations about language, cultural authority, and scientific knowledge: the social psychology of "symbolic interactionism," after George Herbert Mead; the sociology of knowledge, after Karl Mannheim; philosophy of language, after Susanne K. Langer, Ernst Cassirer, and Ludwig Wittgenstein; linguistics, after Lev Vygotsky, Benjamin Lee Whorf, and Edward Sapir; political philosophy, after Hannah Arendt; political theory, after Antonio Gramsci and Jürgen Habermas; cultural anthropology, after Clifford Geertz; sociolinguistics, after William Labov and Basil Bernstein; philosophy and history of science, after Thomas Kuhn, Donald Schön, and Mary Hesse; and certain aspects of critical theory, after Sigmund Freud's concept of "overdetermination" and Michel Foucault's idea of "the subject." As eclectic as this list is, it is only a sketch to orient the reader. These ongoing conversations that have begun to redefine the boundaries of the disciplines in some American universities are by no means identical or even always compatible, but they are predicated upon similar questions about the historical, cultural, social, and symbolic constitution of what people understand to be "reality," in the sense of "something that exists independently of ideas concerning it." The authors cited here share a conviction that I find compelling, namely, that although what we call "reality" is socially, historically, and linguistically constructed, this premise does not make the concept of knowledge meaningless. Theirs, if I understand them, and mine, is an agnostic position, rather than an atheistic or nihilistic one.

39. The best exposition of language-as-metaphor is George Lakoff and Mark Johnson, *Metaphors We Live By* (Chicago: University of Chicago Press, 1980).

40. This is a completely circular process; but circles are no less "true" than straight lines. Additionally, metaphors about language abound. I reject as simplistic and unpersuasive the "weapon," "tool,"

and "mirror" models, but "storehouse" is useful primarily to make the historical and social points above, and not others. Richard Rorty's observation that we can no more get outside language than we can get outside our skins is helpful, for this situation does not preclude our understanding skin as separate from self. Clearly, this is the subject for another study on the historical metaphors for language itself. On personal experience and persuasive metaphor, see Chapter 4.

41. This profound distrust of rhetoric as a form of deception is not a view that I find persuasive, although the possibility of deception is contained in the possibilities of communication and representation; deception is one of many uses for language, and is not confined to certain sorts of language like political "speechifying" or professional advertisement. By denying that language is primarily a form of deception I am not denying the capability of language to deceive. On the problem of thought as distinguished from language, see Lev Semenovich Vygotsky, *Thought and Language* (Cambridge, Mass.: MIT Press, 1962); Anthony Wootton, *Dilemmas of Discourse: Controversies about the Sociological Interpretation of Language* (London: Allen and Unwin, 1975), pp. 20–21; and the essays of J.G.A. Pocock in *Politics, Language and Time: Essays on Political Thought and History* (New York: Atheneum, 1971).

42. For a summary of this development, see John E. Toews, "Intellectual History After the Linguistic Turn: The Autonomy of Meaning and the Irreducibility of Experience," *American Historical Review* 92 (1987): 879–907. See also the introduction to Michael J. Shapiro, ed., *Language and Politics* (New York: New York University Press, 1984) for a broader view of the several disciplines; Terry Eagleton, *Literary Theory: An Introduction* (Minneapolis: University of Minnesota Press, 1983).

43. Kuhn's term *paradigm* could be introduced here in place of *analogy*, insofar as it can be argued that the linguistic turn has been a revolution. See Thomas S. Kuhn, "Reflections on My Critics," in *Criticism and the Growth of Knowledge*, ed. Imre Lakatos and Alan Musgrave (Cambridge: Cambridge University Press, 1970), and "Second Thoughts on Paradigms," in *The Structure of Scientific Revolutions*, ed. F. Suppe (Urbana: University of Illinois Press, 1974), where Kuhn asserts that paradigms *are* languages.

44. On other kinds of educational reform aimed at addressing the increasing diversity and size of the school population, see Tyack, *The One Best System*; Cremin, *The Transformation of the School*.

45. H. L. Wilensky, "The Professionalization of Everyone?" *American Journal of Sociology* 70 (1964): 137–58; Hudson, *The Jargon of the Professions*.

46. The brilliant, entertaining, and exasperating essays of Stanley Fish are especially pertinent to understanding these internecine conflicts. See his *Doing What Comes Naturally*, esp. p. 570 n. 43, on Stephen Toulmin's *Human Understanding*, and *Is There a Text in This Class? The Authority of Interpretive Communities* (Cambridge, Mass.: Harvard University Press, 1980).

47. An important series of questions allowed by this method are those pertaining to language and violence. On this subject see Claus Mueller, with the assistance of Carol Coe Conway, *The Politics of Communication: A Study in the Political Sociology of Language, Socialization, and Legitimation* (New York: Oxford University Press, 1973); Elaine Scarry, *The Body in Pain: The Making and Unmaking of the World* (New York: Oxford University Press, 1985), on torture and the obliteration of speech in totalitarian regimes.

48. Talcott Parsons, ed., *Essays in Sociological Theory, Pure and Applied* (New York: The Free Press, 1949).

49. That is, the philosophical effort across the disciplines and in critical legal studies to reconceptualize language as a social activity constituting social reality. Here again, by stressing the need for a "connection" between "language" and "reality" I unwillingly sustain the conventional false dichotomy between these two "things." A new vocabulary is needed.

50. That is, the work of Hughes, Freidson, Larson, and Abbott.

51. See n. 17 above.

52. See Novick, *That Noble Dream*, p. 194, for an interesting discussion of popularization efforts and worries among historians before World War II. Novick cites Louis Gottschalk, who wrote to the MGM Studios in 1935 about the film *The Scarlet Pimpernel*, "If cinema art is going to draw its subjects so generously from history, it owes it to its patrons and its own higher ideals to achieve a greater accuracy. No picture of a historical nature ought to be offered to the public until a reputable historian has had a chance to criticize and revise it." Novick does not counterpose monopolization and popularization, but his evidence suggests the contradiction; see also George Bancroft, "What's the Matter with History?" *Saturday Review of Literature* 19 (1939): 3–4, 16, as cited in Novick, *That Noble Dream*, pp. 195–96.

53. I have not explored the distinctions between spoken and written texts in this book. For our purposes, it is important to remember that only the surviving written texts, and not hallway gossip, professional conversation, and lost ephemera, were available to me as evidence. I use the term *listener* here because *reader* has more than one sense, which may be confusing here.

54. See Bruce Fraser, "The Interpretation of Novel Metaphors," in *Metaphor and Thought*, ed. Andrew Ortony (New York: Cambridge University Press, 1979), pp. 172–85; George Herbert Mead, *Mind, Self and Society: From the Standpoint of a Social Behaviorist* (1934; Chicago: University of Chicago Press, 1962), p. 55.

55. Karl Mannheim speaks to this point, known as "Mannheim's paradox," in *Ideology and Utopia* (New York: Harcourt, Brace and World, 1936).

56. Lakoff and Johnson, *Metaphors We Live By*; Mark Johnson, *The Body in the Mind* (Chicago: University of Chicago Press, 1987).

57. See the bibliography in Ortony, ed., *Metaphor and Thought*, for references to discussions of these problems.

58. Again, another vocabulary for emphasizing the intimate relations between language and reality would be useful here.

59. On the practical claims of professionals and their consequences for garnering outside resources, see Magali Sarfatti Larson, "The Production of Expertise and the Constitution of Expert Power," in *The Authority of Experts*, ed. Haskell, p. 71 n. 18.

60. See Thomas L. Haskell, *The Emergence of Professional Social Science: The American Social Science Association and the Nineteenth Century Crisis of Authority* (Urbana: University of Illinois Press, 1977), on interdependence, with regard to this point.

61. On brand names and mass marketing, see Susan Strasser, *Satisfaction Guaranteed: The Making of the American Mass Market* (New York: Pantheon, 1989).

CHAPTER ONE
THE SEMANTICS OF PROFESSION: A THEORY

1. Introduction to Paul S. Boyer and Stephen Nissenbaum, eds., *Salem-Village Witchcraft: A Documentary Record of Local Conflict in Colonial New England* (Belmont, Calif.: Wadsworth Publishing, 1972).

2. Sidney E. Ahlstrom, *A Religious History of the American People* (New Haven: Yale University Press, 1972), pp. 472–87; 1019–29; Joseph F. Kett, *The Formation of the American Medical Profession: The Role of Institutions, 1780–1860* (New Haven: Yale University Press, 1968); Carr-Saunders and Wilson, *The Professions*, pp. 68–70, 290–94; Larson, *The Rise of Professionalism*, p. 22; John S. Haller and Robin M. Haller, *The Physician and Sexuality in Victorian America* (New York: Norton, 1974) p. x.

3. Wilensky, "The Professionalization of Everyone?"

4. Everett C. Hughes, "Professions," in *The Professions in America*, ed. Kenneth S. Lynn (Boston: Houghton Mifflin, 1965), p. 2; Bernard

Barber, "Some Problems in the Sociology of the Professions," in ibid.; Donald Scott, "The Profession That Vanished: Public Lecturing in Mid–Nineteenth Century America," in *Professions and Professional Ideologies*, ed. Geison, p. 14; Eliot Freidson, "Are Professions Necessary?" in *The Authority of Experts*, ed. Haskell, p. 10; Paul Starr, *The Social Transformation of American Medicine* (New York: Basic Books, 1982), p. 15; Abbott, *The System of Professions*, introduction and p. 318.

5. Freidson, "Are Professions Necessary?"

6. The Hans Christian Andersen story "The Emperor's New Clothes" can be read as a parody of "professionalizing" craft-work, and speaks to this distinction.

7. Starr, *The Social Transformation of American Medicine*, p. 140.

8. Charles E. Rosenberg, "The Therapeutic Revolution," in *The Therapeutic Revolution: Essays in the Social History of American Medicine*, ed. Morris Vogel and Charles E. Rosenberg (Philadelphia: University of Pennsylvania Press, 1979).

9. Starr, *The Social Transformation of American Medicine*, p. 86, citing Erving Goffman, *The Presentation of Self in Everyday Life* (Garden City, N.Y.: Doubleday, 1959), p. 33.

10. For an extended discussion of this view, see Edelman, *Political Language*. As Stanley Fish has argued, this point does not necessarily damn professions as empty deceptions; such a judgment depends on one's attitude toward the importance and value of language as a form of action. See Fish, *Doing What Comes Naturally*, pp. 215–46.

11. Wilensky, "The Professionalization of Everyone?"

12. I do not mean to argue that acquiescence is passive, complete, consistent, or peaceable. There is a need for historical study of anti-professionalism and other forms of resistance among targeted clientele.

13. Wilensky, "The Professionalization of Everyone?" p. 148.

14. This loose, historically variable definition is, I think, compatible with Abbott's views in *The System of Professions*; see pp. 315–26.

15. Magali Sarfatti Larson observes that professional work produces "fictitious commodities" that cannot be detached from the rest of life, stored, or mobilized. See *The Rise of Professionalism*, p. 14.

16. Starr, *The Social Transformation of American Medicine*, p. 12.

17. I am using *metaphor* here in its everyday, nontechnical sense. Under the term *metaphor* I include simile, trope, and analogy. I use *analogy* and *metaphor* interchangeably. As Philip Wheelwright observes, distinctions of grammar are not to the point; what is important is the nature of the semantic transformation. Further, some would argue that much of my evidence concerns "models" rather than metaphors. I hold that it is the exceptional case where the object of emula-

tion is directly perceived; it is far more usual for language to convey the object of emulation, generalize it, and serve as the immediate inspiration for professional activity. It is not a question of insistence on models *versus* metaphors, or metaphors *versus* models, but on the interaction between the two and the advantages—in terms of portability, among other things—of the linguistic forms of action, including the creation and use of metaphor.

18. Hudson, *The Jargon of the Professions*, p. 1.

19. Ibid.

20. Susan Sontag, *Illness as Metaphor* (New York: Farrar, Straus and Giroux, 1978); Rosenberg, "The Therapeutic Revolution." See also Sontag, *AIDS and Its Metaphors* (New York: Farrar, Straus and Giroux, 1989); David A. Hollinger, "Inquiry and Uplift: Late Nineteenth-Century American Academics and the Moral Efficacy of Scientific Practice," in *The Authority of Experts*, ed. Haskell, pp. 142–56.

21. George S. Morison, Address before the American Society of Civil Engineers, 1895, cited in Edwin T. Layton, Jr., *The Revolt of the Engineers* (Cleveland: The Press of Case Western Reserve University, 1971), pp. 58–59; see also Dugald C. Jackson, *Present Status and Trends in Engineering Education* (New York: Engineers' Council for Professional Development, 1939), p. 97; Frederick Newell, "Awakening of the Engineer," *Engineering News* 74 (1915): 568; Frederick Newell, "A Practical Plan of Engineering Education," *Journal of the Cleveland Engineering Society* 9 (1917): 311.

22. I doubt that there is any such thing as a "mere" metaphor: in this instance, Cotton Mather referred both to common practice and to the metaphorical implications of medicine and theology as models for one another. I wish to undermine what I see as a false distinction between *metaphor* and *reality*.

23. John C. Burnham, "Change in the Popularization of Health in the United States," *Bulletin of the History of Medicine* 58 (1984): 184. Burnham emphasizes a shift from religious to secular contexts in the popularization of health principles. On theological metaphors in the health professions, see also Annie M. Brainard, *The Evolution of Public Health Nursing* (Philadelphia: W. B. Saunders, 1922), p. 420; Starr, *The Social Transformation of American Medicine*, p. 39; Peter Dobkin Hall, "The Social Foundations of Professional Credibility: Linking the Medical Profession to Higher Education in Connecticut and Massachusetts, 1700–1830," in *The Authority of Experts*, ed. Haskell; Charles E. Rosenberg, "Piety and Social Action: Some Origins of the American Public Health Movement," in *No Other Gods: On Science and American Social Thought*, ed. Charles E. Rosenberg (1961; Baltimore: Johns Hopkins University Press, 1976), pp. 109–22.

24. This is a subject of further research in my forthcoming book on hygienic practice and hygiene as political metaphor.

25. Dr. Albert C. Reed, "Immigration and the Public Health," *Popular Science Monthly* 83 (1913): 317. *Taint* was a word then in common usage with regard to the purity of food and milk, and with reference to venereal disease. See Allan M. Brandt, *No Magic Bullet: A Social History of Venereal Disease in the United States since 1800* (New York: Oxford University Press, 1985).

26. JoAnne Brown, "Tuberculosis: A Romance" (Paper presented to a seminar in Science, Technology, and Society, Massachusetts Institute of Technology, Cambridge, Mass., April 1991). The "lesser" professions are no less willing to borrow authority from the classical professions: in a recent letter to the editor of *Glamour* magazine, a hairdresser objected to a do-it-yourself feature entitled "Got a Friend? Get a Great Haircut!" "What next?" raged the cosmetician, "'Got a Friend? Get a Great Appendectomy!'?"

27. On metaphor and social policy see Donald A. Schön, "Generative Metaphor: A Perspective on Problem-Setting in Social Policy," in *Metaphor and Thought*, ed. Ortony, pp. 254–83.

28. For a thoughtful firsthand account of this case, see Sontag, *Illness as Metaphor*. Sontag mistakenly insists that by practitioners' abolishing metaphorical constructs of disease, they can better serve the patient with a purer scientific medicine.

29. Lakoff and Johnson, *Metaphors We Live By*.

30. Hollinger, "Historians and the Discourse of Intellectuals," pp. 42–43; Gerald L. Geison, editor's introduction to *Professions and Professional Ideologies*, p. 9; Hudson, *The Jargon of the Professions*, p. 1; Stephen Botein, "What We Shall Meet Afterwards in Heaven: Judgeship as a Symbol for Modern American Lawyers," in *Professions and Professional Ideologies*, ed. Geison; Starr, *The Social Transformation of American Medicine*, p. 11; Berger and Luckman, *The Social Construction of Reality*, pp. 92–126.

31. Edward Spicer, "Persistent Identity System," *Science* 4011 (1971): 799; Mead, *Mind, Self and Society*; Leonard Bloomfield, *Language* (New York: Holt, 1933); Charles F. Hockett, "Implications of Bloomfield's Algonquin Studies," in *Language in Culture and Society*, ed. Dell Hymes (New York: Harper and Row, 1964); Dell Hymes, *Foundations in Sociolinguistics: An Ethnographic Approach* (Philadelphia: University of Pennsylvania Press, 1974). See also William Labov, "The Logic of Nonstandard English," *Georgetown Monograph Series in Language and Linguistics* 22 (1969): 1–44; Joshua Fishman, "Childhood Indoctrination for Minority Group Membership," *Daedalus* 90 (1961): 329–49.

32. Mead, *Mind, Self and Society*, pp. 189–90.

33. On analogies and creativity, see Mary Brenda Hesse, *Models and Analogies in Science* (London and New York: Sheed and Ward, 1963), pp. 2–3; Norman Robert Campbell, *Physics, the Elements* (Cambridge: Cambridge University Press, 1920), p. 129. On the metaphorical basis of all language, see Lakoff and Johnson, *Metaphors We Live By*.

34. See Schön, "Generative Metaphor"; Karl W. Deutsch, "Mechanism, Organism and Society: Some Models in Natural and Social Science," *Philosophy of Science* 18 (1951): 230–52; Richard H. Brown, "Metaphore et methode: de la logique et la decouverte en sociologie," *Cahiers internationeaux de sociologie* (1977): 61–73; Robert Oppenheimer, "Analogy in Science," *The American Psychologist* 11 (1956): 127–35; Michael A. Overington, "The Scientific Community as Audience: Toward a Rhetorical Analysis of Science," *Philosophy and Rhetoric* 10 (1977): 143–63.

35. Recently several historical studies have appeared that treat the language of disciplines and professions: Donald McCloskey, *The Rhetoric of Economics* (Madison: University of Wisconsin Press, 1985); Fish, *Doing What Comes Naturally*; John S. Nelson, Allan Megill, and Donald N. McCloskey, eds., *The Rhetoric of the Human Sciences: Language and Argument in Scholarship and Public Affairs* (Madison: University of Wisconsin Press, 1987).

36. Barbara Melosh, *The Physician's Hand: Work Culture and Conflict in American Nursing* (Philadelphia: Temple University Press, 1982), p. 21.

37. Larson, *The Rise of Professionalism*, p. xvii (emphasis mine).

38. Starr, *The Social Transformation of American Medicine*, pp. 9–11.

39. Charles Rosenberg's work demonstrates a keen sensitivity to language and metaphor without a lot of explicit theorizing.

40. J. L. Austin, *How to Do Things with Words* (Oxford: Clarendon Press, 1975), pp. 151–62, 5. J.G.A. Pocock brought Austin's work to historians' attention.

41. Ibid., p. 5; see also C. S. Lewis, *Studies in Words* (Cambridge: Cambridge University Press, 1960), p. 6; Ludwig Wittgenstein, *Philosophical Investigations* (Oxford: Basil Blackwell, 1968), secs. 546, 23. Law is the preeminent exemplar of language as political action, with inexorable material consequences, often of a life-or-death nature. The critical legal studies movement takes this as a central premise. See Peter Novick's summary in *That Noble Dream*, pp. 555–57; Mark Tushnet, "Legal Scholarship: Its Cause and Cure," *Yale Law Journal* 90 (1981): 1205–23. Stanley Fish points out how quickly this challenge to positivism in legal theory can devolve into radical nihilism: see "Anti-Professionalism," in *Doing What Comes Naturally*, pp. 226–27.

42. See William J. Goode, "Encroachment, Charlatanism and the Emerging Profession: Psychology, Sociology and Medicine," *American Sociological Review* 25 (1960): 902–14.

43. Edelman, *Political Language*, p. 61.

44. On the important differences between written and oral language, see Jack R. Goody and Ian Watt, "The Consequences of Literacy," in *Literacy in Traditional Societies*, ed. Jack R. Goody (Cambridge: Cambridge University Press, 1968), pp. 28–68; David D. Hall, "The World of Print and Collective Mentality," in *New Directions in American Intellectual History*, ed. Higham and Conkin, pp. 166–80; John T. Taylor, *Early Opposition to the English Novel* (New York: King's Crown Press, 1943).

45. Lakoff and Johnson, *Metaphors We Live By*, p. 4.

46. Alison Lurie gives a fictional account of one such academic assault by an unmet critic on an English professor at "Corinth College" (Cornell University) in her Pulitzer Prize–winning novel *Foreign Affairs* (New York: Random House, 1984), pp. 5–8. Another way to view this is to note that unless *community* is defined broadly, and in part by communication (after Dewey and Mead), then *professional community*, in the sense of neighborhood or village, is metaphorical.

47. Other kinds of symbols, e.g., visual symbols, such as the psychiatrist's couch or the cosmetologist's white lab coat, are subsumed under the concepts of hegemony and ideology; these kinds of nonlinguistic symbols deserve further attention, but for the purposes of this discussion they are considered analogous to language.

48. Berger and Luckman, *The Social Construction of Reality*, pp. 39–46. On the "time-binding" function of language, that is, its historical function, see A. Korzybski, *Science and Sanity* (Lancaster, Pa.: Science Press, 1933), cited in Alden Wessman and Bernard Gorman, "Emergence of Human Awareness and Concepts of Time," in their *Personal Experience of Time* (New York: Plenum Press, 1977) p. 19.

49. Berger and Luckman, *The Social Construction of Reality*, p. 39.

50. Ibid., p. 68.

51. Antonio Gramsci, *Prison Notebooks* (New York: International Publishers, 1971).

52. Antonio Gramsci, *I materialismo storico e la filosophiia di Benedetto Croce*, vol. 2 of *Collected Works* (1948), p. 11, cited in Joseph Femia, "Hegemony and Consciousness in the Thought of Antonio Gramsci," *Political Studies* 23: 33.

53. Pocock, *Politics, Language and Time*, p. 36, *The Machiavellian Moment: Florentine Political Thought and the Atlantic Republican Tradition* (Princeton: Princeton University Press, 1975), and *Virtue, Commerce,*

and History: Essays on Political Thought in History, Chiefly in the Eighteenth Century (New York: Cambridge University Press, 1985).

54. Historians David Hollinger and Thomas Bender have also preferred to study language rather than ideas. See Hollinger, "Historians and the Discourse of Intellectuals"; Bender, "The Cultures of Intellectual Life."

55. Edelman, *Political Language*, p. 59.

56. Ibid., p. 144.

57. Ibid., p. 23.

58. Murray Edelman, *The Symbolic Uses of Politics* (Urbana: University of Illinois Press, 1964), p. 131.

59. Murray Edelman, *Politics as Symbolic Action: Mass Arousal and Quiescence* (New York: Academic Press, 1971), p. 72.

60. In arguing that such usage was systematic while not necessarily conscious I mean to say that the historian, in retrospect, may perceive patterns of which the historical actors themselves may not have been aware. These social patterns may nonetheless have influenced the past situation.

CHAPTER TWO
PSYCHOLOGY AS A SCIENCE

1. *Oxford English Dictionary*, vol. 12, s.v. "psychology."

2. This phrase is from John Stuart Mill, *A System of Logic, Ratiocinative and Inductive: Being a Connected View of the Principles of Evidence and the Methods of Scientific Investigation* (London: Longmans, Green, 1900), bk. 6, chap. 3, sec. 1.

3. David Hothersall, *History of Psychology* (Philadelphia: Temple University Press, 1984), p. 319.

4. On the pragmatic philosophy of scientific progress, see David Hollinger, "The Problem of Pragmatism in American History," *Journal of American History* 67 (1980): 88–107; James T. Kloppenberg, *Uncertain Victory: Social Democracy and Progressivism in European and American Thought 1870–1920* (New York: Oxford University Press, 1986).

5. Ross, "American Social Science," pp. 157, 162. For a definitive history of the social sciences see idem, *The Origins of American Social Science* (New York: Cambridge University Press, 1991). See also Brown and van Keuren, eds., *The Estate of Social Knowledge*; Haskell, *The Emergence of Professional Social Science*; Mary O. Furner, *Advocacy and Objectivity: A Crisis in the Professionalization of American Social Science, 1865–1905* (Lexington: University of Kentucky Press, 1975).

6. Daniel N. Robinson, *Toward a Science of Human Nature: Essays on*

the Psychologies of Mill, Hegel, Wundt and James (New York: Columbia University Press, 1982), p. 127.

7. Ernest R. Hilgard, *Psychology in America: A Historical Survey* (New York: Harcourt Brace Jovanovich, 1987), pp. 29–33.

8. Robinson, *Toward a Science of Human Nature*, p. 172. It can also be argued that German science heavily influenced American medicine and engineering and so these were similarly dependent on the same general American admiration for the Germans prior to 1914.

9. Karl Pearson, *The Life, Letters, and Labours of Francis Galton* (Cambridge: Cambridge University Press, 1914–1930), 3A: 56–57, cited in Daniel J. Kevles, *In the Name of Eugenics: Genetics and the Uses of Human Heredity* (Berkeley: University of California Press, 1985), p. 17. See also Chapter 8 of this book, on quantification.

10. This emphasis on social control through social science, analogous to perceived control of nature through natural science, was best articulated by John Dewey, whose subtle and complex discussions of "social control" helped provoke, half a century later, the revisionist historiography known as the "social control" thesis. For Dewey's articulation, see his "Psychology and Social Practice," pp. 149–50, as cited in Ross, "American Social Science," p. 162. For an example of the "social control" historiography, see David Rothman, *The Discovery of the Asylum: Social Order and Disorder in the New Republic* (Boston: Little, Brown, 1971).

11. Hamilton Cravens, *The Triumph of Evolution: American Scientists and the Heredity-Environment Controversy 1900–1941* (Philadelphia: University of Pennsylvania Press, 1978), pp. 64, 65, 71.

12. G. Stanley Hall, "Research, the Vital Spirit of Teaching," *The Forum* 17 (1894): 558–70; and Robert S. Woodworth, "The Adolescence of Psychology," *Psychological Review* 50 (1943): 10–32. The definitive biography of G. Stanley Hall is Dorothy Ross's *G. Stanley Hall: The Psychologist as Prophet* (Chicago: University of Chicago Press, 1972).

13. The Hopkins laboratory was the first in the United States with a continuous history: see Cravens, *The Triumph of Evolution*, p. 64; Hilgard, *Psychology in America*, p. 32.

14. Lewis Terman to Joseph Peterson, author of *Early Conceptions and Tests of Intelligence*, January 14, 1925, Lewis Madison Terman Papers, Box 1, Stanford University; see also G. Stanley Hall, *Life and Confessions of a Psychologist* (New York: D. Appleton, 1924), p. 14.

15. Daniel J. Kevles gives a succinct account of Galton's and Binet's importance to eugenics through their work in statistics and mental testing in *In the Name of Eugenics*, pp. 76–77. See also Weinland, "A History of the I.Q. in America, 1890–1941."

16. Hothersall, *History of Psychology*, p. 304.

17. Mannheim, *Ideology and Utopia*, pp. 70–71ff. On the personal equation, see Edwin G. Boring, *A History of Experimental Psychology*, 2d ed. (New York: Appleton-Century-Crofts, 1957), pp. 134–53; the term enters psychology via astronomy and physiology.

18. Hothersall, *History of Psychology*, p. 330.

19. Cohen, *A Calculating People*; Kevles, *In the Name of Eugenics*, chap. 2.

20. For the full-blown version of progressive science as a secular religion, see Albert Wiggam, *The New Decalogue of Science* (Indianapolis: Bobbs-Merrill, 1923). Wiggam was an active correspondent with Lewis Terman, author of the Stanford-Binet revision.

21. Historian Frederick Jackson Turner's speech before the 1893 meeting of the American Historical Association in Chicago gave historical weight to the 1890 census director's observation that "there can hardly be said to be a frontier" as of 1890.

22. Edward Bellamy's utopian novel *Looking Backward 2000–1887* articulated late-nineteenth-century bourgeois sympathies toward the underclass.

23. The most insightful and succinct treatment of progressivism to date is Rodgers' article "In Search of Progressivism." On conservation and efficiency, see Hays, *Conservation and the Gospel of Efficiency*; Haber, *Efficiency and Uplift*. Lewis Terman often referred to "the Conservation" of talent and health. See Terman, "The Conservation of Talent," *School and Society* 19 (1924): 359–64.

24. See Laurence R. Veysey, *The Emergence of the American University* (Chicago: University of Chicago Press, 1965), pp. 133–79; Hollinger, "Inquiry and Uplift."

25. On science and progress see Dewey, "Psychology and Social Practice"; Charles R. Mann, "Science in Civilization and in Education," *School Review* 14 (1906): 664–70; Edward Lee Thorndike, "Quantitative Study of Education," *The Forum* 36 (1905): 443–48.

26. See Herbert Spencer, *The Principles of Psychology* (New York: Appleton-Century, 1896). Psychology's link with Darwinism was in part hereditary: Sir Francis Galton, the British scholar who founded eugenics and inspired the search for heritable mental capacities, was a cousin and follower of Charles Darwin. See Daniel N. Robinson, *An Intellectual History of Psychology* (New York: Macmillan, 1976), pp. 320–24; Ross, "American Social Science"; Gould, *The Mismeasure of Man*.

27. See Stanley Joel Reiser, *Medicine and the Reign of Technology* (New York: Cambridge University Press, 1978); John Harley Warner, *The Therapeutic Perspective: Medical Practice, Knowledge and Identity in America 1820–1885* (Cambridge, Mass.: Harvard University Press,

1986), pp. 86, 91; on a similar analytical point regarding clinical trials, see Harry M. Marks, "Notes from the Underground: The Social Organization of Therapeutic Research," in *Grand Rounds*, ed. Russell C. Maulitz and Diana E. Long (Philadelphia: University of Pennsylvania Press, 1988), pp. 297–336.

28. See Noble, *America by Design*; Nelson Kellog, "Gauging the Nation: Samuel Wesley Stratton and the Invention of the National Bureau of Standards" (Ph.D. diss., Johns Hopkins University, 1991).

29. See David McCullough, *The Path Between the Seas: The Creation of the Panama Canal 1870–1914* (New York: Simon and Schuster, 1977).

30. Morton White, *Social Thought in America: The Revolt Against Formalism* (New York: Viking Press, 1949); Ross, "American Social Science."

31. On the relationship between intelligence, happiness, and labor unrest see Henry Herbert Goddard, *Human Efficiency and Levels of Intelligence* (Princeton: Princeton University Press, 1920), p. 60; Goddard's thinking is imbued with the ideas of Edward Bellamy's nationalism. Compare Goddard to Bellamy, *Looking Backward 2000–1887*, pp. 129, 135. On democracy and education see John Dewey, *Democracy and Education* (New York: Macmillan, 1916); Welter, *Popular Education*.

32. The best account of these associations remains John Higham, *Strangers in the Land: Patterns of American Nativism 1860–1925*, 2d ed. (New Brunswick, N.J.: Rutgers University Press, 1988).

33. "Negative" eugenics consisted primarily of sterilization or incarceration; "positive" eugenics emphasized education in sexual hygiene and marital choice. See Mark H. Haller, *Eugenics: Hereditarian Attitudes in Social Thought* (New Brunswick, N.J.: Rutgers University Press, 1963); Pickens, *Eugenics and the Progressives*; Kevles, *In the Name of Eugenics*.

CHAPTER THREE
EDUCATION AS A PROFESSION

1. John C. Burnham, "The Struggle Between Physicians and Paramedical Personnel in American Psychiatry, 1917–1941," *Journal of the History of Medicine* 29 (1974): 101. Testing developed in four distinct arenas: public schools, schools for the feebleminded, industrial corporations, and the criminal court system. In this study I deal primarily with the first. See also Chapman, *Schools as Sorters*.

2. Still the best discussion of education in this period is Cremin, *The Transformation of the School*. On urban education in the same pe-

riod, see Tyack, *The One Best System*. See also Callahan, *Education and the Cult of Efficiency* (1964); David B. Tyack and Elizabeth Hansot, *Managers of Virtue: Public School Leadership in America, 1820–1980* (New York: Basic Books, 1982).

3. See the *National Education Association Proceedings* for these years; Tyack and Hansot, *Managers of Virtue*, pp. 136–40, 180–85.

4. Joseph Mayer Rice, *The Public School System of the United States* (1893; New York: Arno Press, 1969); "New York City Superintendent Report Shows Increasing Lack of Room in City Schools," *New York Times*, November 23, 1905, p. 18; cartoon, *New York Times*, September 18, 1910, p. 16; United States Senate, *Reports of the Immigration Commission 29: The Children of Immigrants in Schools* (Washington, D.C.: Government Printing Office, 1911), 1:15, 97; Tyack, *The One Best System*, p. 230; Cremin, *The Transformation of the School*; Paul S. Boyer, *Urban Masses and Moral Order* (Cambridge, Mass.: Harvard University Press, 1978), pp. 123–27. On teachers there are few secondary works: see Barbara Joan Finklestein, "Governing the Young: Teacher Behavior in American Primary Schools, 1820–1880" (Ph.D. diss., Teachers College, Columbia University, 1970).

5. On the "new" versus the "old" immigration see Thomas J. Archdeacon, *Becoming American: An Ethnic History* (New York: Free Press, 1983), p. 113 and chaps. 4 and 5.

6. Callahan, *Education and the Cult of Efficiency* (1962), p. 53.

7. Tyack, *The One Best System*, p. 230, citing United States Senate, *The Children of Immigrants in Schools*, 1:14–15.

8. United States Senate, *The Children of Immigrants in Schools* 1:15, 97, 165.

9. Ibid., p. 151. To complicate matters, the pupils and teachers often were not of similar immigrant background.

10. Ibid., pp. 136, 139, 140.

11. Tyack and Hansot, *Managers of Virtue*, pp. 180–201.

12. Jürgen Herbst, "Professionalization in Public Education, 1890–1920: The American High School Teacher" (mimeographed, 1984), p. 46. See also Edward Lee Thorndike, "The Feminization of American Education," ca. 1909, Edward Lee Thorndike Papers, Box 2, Library of Congress.

13. United States Bureau of the Census, *Historical Abstracts of the United States, Colonial Times to the Present* (Washington, D.C.: Government Printing Office, 1975); United States Senate, *The Children of Immigrants in Schools* 1:584–85, 724–26. On the feminization of teaching see Keith Melder, "Woman's High Calling: The Teaching Profession in America, 1830–1860," *American Studies* 13 (Fall 1972); Willard S. Elsbree, *The American Teacher: Evolution of a Profession in a*

Democracy (New York: American Book Company, 1939), pp. 199–208; Tyack, *The One Best System*, chap. 2; Kaestle, *Pillars of the Republic*, pp. 126ff.; Herbst, "Professionalization in Public Education, 1890–1920." Paul Mattingly's *The Classless Profession: American Schoolmen in the Nineteenth Century* (New York: New York University Press, 1975) deals little with the majority of teachers, who were women. See also James McKeen Cattell's harsh indictment of "spinsters" as teachers, "The School and the Family," *Popular Science Monthly* 74 (1909): 92–93; Ann Douglas, *The Feminization of American Culture* (New York: Knopf, 1977).

14. In South Omaha, Nebraska, 35 percent of teachers had fewer than five years' experience; in New Orleans, 32.2 percent; in Duluth, 31.1 percent; in Shenandoah, Pennsylvania, 26.1 percent. See United States Senate, *The Children of Immigrants in Schools* 1:584–85, 724–26.

15. Tyack, *The One Best System*, pp. 61–63.

16. On interdependence as an emergent perception among intellectuals of this period, see Haskell, *The Emergence of Professional Social Science*. On conflict and consensus in the Progressive Era, see Robert H. Wiebe, *Search for Order, 1877–1920* (New York: Hill and Wang, 1967). On women in the professions and sciences, see esp. Margaret W. Rossiter, *Women Scientists in America: Struggles and Strategies to 1940* (Baltimore: Johns Hopkins University Press, 1982); Daniel Walkowitz, "The Making of a Feminine Professional Identity: Social Workers in the 1920s," *American Historical Review* 95 (1990): 1051–75; Joan Jacobs Brumberg and Nancy Tomes, "Women in the Professions: A Research Agenda for American Historians," *Reviews in American History* 10 (1982): 275–96.

17. Interestingly, *scientific management*, the term used by Frederick Winslow Taylor to describe his industrial system, was earlier coined by medical sectarians in the nineteenth century to describe negatively the intrusive methods of allopathic man-midwives. See Susan Cayliff, *Wash and Be Healed* (Philadelphia: Temple University Press, 1987).

18. It is certainly true that medicine and engineering were both conspicuous examples of applied science in the Progressive Era, but they were no more conspicuously "scientific" than chemistry or physics, and no more fully professionalized than law or the clergy. *Science* is so universal an approbation during this period that, like *eugenical* or *progressive*, it loses explanatory power. My focus on medical and engineering language is an effort to recapture the very particular definition of *science* that psychologists embraced.

19. Ellwood P. Cubberley, director, *Report of the Survey of the Public School System of School District No. 1, Multnomah County, Oregon*, November 1, 1913.

20. See Michael Sedlak, *A History of Social Services Delivered to Youth, 1880–1977*, Final Report to the National Institute of Education, Contract 400–79–0017, 1982; Roy Lubove, *The Professional Altruist: The Emergence of Social Work as a Career* (Cambridge, Mass.: Harvard University Press, 1965); Schlossman, Brown, and Sedlak, *Preventive Dentistry*.

21. Lewis Terman and John Almack, *The Hygiene of the School Child* (New York: Houghton Mifflin, 1929); S. Josephine Baker, *Child Hygiene* (New York: Harper and Brothers, 1925); Lillian Wald, "Medical Inspection of Public Schools," *Annals of the American Academy of Political and Social Sciences* 25 (1905): 297–98. The 1913 Buffalo, New York, Congress on School Hygiene brought together public health, mental asylum, and public-school officials, who adopted a shared "hygienic" vocabulary. See Thomas A. Storey, ed., with the assistance of Frederic A. Woll and Julian Park, *Transactions of the Fourth International Congress on School Hygiene* (Buffalo, N.Y.: Courier, 1914).

22. James H. Cassedy, *American Medicine and Statistical Thinking 1800–1860* (Cambridge, Mass.: Harvard University Press, 1984); Cohen, *A Calculating People*; Gail A. Hornstein, "Quantifying Psychological Phenomena: Debates, Dilemmas, and Implications," in *The Rise of Experimentation*, ed. Morawski, pp. 1–34.

23. Irving Fisher, *Report on National Vitality: Its Wastes and Conservation*, Committee of One Hundred on National Health, Bulletin 30 (Washington, D.C.: Government Printing Office, 1909). This report inspired Lewis Terman to speak of education as "conservation." Fisher, a Yale economist, was a leader in the American eugenics movement. On the scale of scientific research and the public's ability to scrutinize it, see Marks, "Notes from the Underground"; Brown, "Mental Measurements."

24. See Starr, *The Social Transformation of American Medicine*, chap. 5.

25. Ibid.; Larson, *The Rise of Professionalism*, pp. 57–63.

26. "Discussion," *Minnesota Medicine* 6 (1923): 445, cited in Starr, *The Social Transformation of American Medicine*, p. 141.

27. J. A. Larrabee, "The Schoolroom as a Factor in the Production of Disease," *Journal of the American Medical Association* 11 (1888): 613–14, cited in John Duffy, "School Buildings and the Health of American School Children in the Nineteenth Century," in *Healing and History*, ed. Charles E. Rosenberg (New York: Science History Press, 1979).

28. Luther Halsey Gulick, M.D., and Leonard P. Ayres, *Medical Inspection of Schools* (New York: Charities Publication Committee, 1908), pp. 25–27; J. E. Wallace Wallin, *The Mental Health of the School Child: The Psycho-Educational Clinic in Relation to Child Welfare: Contributions to*

a New Science of Orthophrenics and Orthosemantics (New Haven: Yale University Press, 1914), pp. 1–12; Baker, *Child Hygiene*.

29. Gulick and Ayres, *Medical Inspection of Schools*, pp. 25–27.

30. Louis Dufestel, "La nouvelle organization de l'inspection medicale des écoles de la ville de Paris," in *Transactions of the Fourth International Congress on School Hygiene*, pp. 135–44. See also Gulick and Ayres, *Medical Inspection of Schools*, pp. 18–28.

31. Gulick and Ayres, *Medical Inspection of Schools*, p. 36.

32. Ibid., pp. 49, 48.

33. Starr, *The Social Transformation of American Medicine*, pp. 180–89; Jacob Sobel, "Prejudices and Superstitions Met With in the Medical Inspection of Schoolchildren," in *Transactions of the Fourth International Congress on School Hygiene*, pp. 78–88.

34. Starr, *The Social Transformation of American Medicine*, p. 189.

35. Susan Lederer, "Noguchi Hideo's Luetin Experiment and the Anti-Vivisectionists," *Isis* 76 (1985): 31–48.

36. "Lower East Side Parents Storm Schools After Being Told Their Children Were Being Killed," *New York Times*, June 28, 1906, sec. 4, p. 3; "Throat-Cutting Rumors Lead Frantic Italians to Mob Three NYC Buildings," *New York Times*, June 29, 1906, sec. 9, p. 1. According to contemporary medical theory, "mouth breathing" that resulted from swollen adenoids was a sign that insufficient oxygen was reaching the brain, resulting in symptoms of feeblemindedness. Adenoidectomies were credited with improving children's school performance, and were performed in great numbers. The operation results in temporary heavy bleeding, which no doubt fostered the rumors of murder.

37. Sobel, "Prejudices and Superstitions," pp. 78–88.

38. J. E. Wallace Wallin, "Experimental Oral Euthenics: An Attempt Objectively to Measure the Relation Between Community Mouth Hygiene and the Intellectual Efficiency and Educational Progress of Elementary School Children," *Dental Cosmos* 54 (1912): 404–13; 545–66.

39. Leonard P. Ayres, *Laggards in Our Schools* (New York: Russell Sage Foundation, 1909).

40. William B. Ebersole, *Report of the Scientific Experiments Conducted in the Cleveland Schools for the Purpose of Ascertaining the Value of Healthy Conditions of the Mouth* (Cleveland: National Mouth Hygiene Association, 1912); Alfred Fones, "Report of Five Years of Mouth Hygiene in the Public Schools of Bridgeport, Connecticut," *Dental Cosmos* 61 (July 1919).

41. See Cordelia O'Neill, "Mouth Hygiene: What It Has Done for Us—What It Can Do for You," in *Transactions of the Fourth Interna-*

tional Congress on School Hygiene, pp. 206–13; and "Oral Hygiene as It Appeals to Educators," in *A Brief History of Mouth Hygiene in Cleveland*, ed. Harris Wilson (Cleveland: S. P. Maunt Printing, 1929), pp. 69–117; W. B. Ebersole, "History of the Oral Hygiene Campaign as Inaugurated by the Oral Hygiene Committee of the National Dental Association," *Dental Cosmos* 53 (1911): 1386–93; Ebersole, *Report of the Scientific Experiments*.

42. O'Neill, "Oral Hygiene," p. 19; Ebersole, *Report of the Scientific Experiments*, pp. 24–25.

43. Schlossman, Brown, and Sedlak, *Preventive Dentistry*. My discussion of dentistry is based on this collaborative research.

44. Ibid.

45. Ibid.

46. Ibid.; Larson, *The Rise of Professionalism*, pp. 56–63; Charles E. Rosenberg, *The Care of Strangers: The Rise of America's Hospital System* (New York: Basic Books, 1987).

47. Hugo Münsterberg, *Psychology and Industrial Efficiency* (New York: Houghton Mifflin, 1913); on physicians' animosity toward psychologists and psychiatrists, see Leila Zenderland, "Psychologists, Physicians, and Mental Measurements" (Paper presented at May 1984 meeting of the American Association for the Advancement of Science, revised and published in *Psychological Testing and American Society*, ed. Sokal; John C. Burnham, "Psychology, Psychiatry, and the Progressive Movement," *American Quarterly* 12 (1960): 457–65.

48. Wald, "Medical Inspection of Public Schools."

49. Lewis Terman, *The Hygiene of the School Child* (New York: Houghton Mifflin, 1914), p. 1. On the Progressive-Era conservation ideal, see Hays, *Conservation and the Gospel of Efficiency*.

50. Gail Hamilton [Mary Abigail Dodge], *Our Common School System* (Boston: Estes and Lauriat, 1880), p. 91, cited in Tyack, *The One Best System*, p. 82.

51. Starr, *The Social Transformation of American Medicine*, p. 117. I am indebted to Barbara Melosh for pointing out the correspondence between gender-defined social roles and the plausibility of the medical metaphor in education versus psychology.

52. On the prevalence of the factory model, see Tyack, *The One Best System*; Callahan, *Education and the Cult of Efficiency* (1962); Carl F. Kaestle, *Joseph Lancaster and the Monitorial School Movement: A Documentary History* (New York: Teachers College Press, 1973); Herbert M. Kliebard, "Bureaucracy and Curriculum Theory," in *Freedom, Bureaucracy and Schooling, 1971 Yearbook of the Association for Supervision and Curriculum Development*, ed. Vernon Haubrich (Washington, D.C.: Association for Supervision and Curriculum Development, 1971).

53. David O. Edge writes, "As the metaphor begins to 'bite' cognitively, it brings with it attitudes appropriate to its literal referent." But metaphors are created all the time, yet only some take hold: "we might profitably inquire as to the social forces which may determine the use of metaphor, predisposing us to assimilate it into our imagination, and to 'take it seriously.'" Edge, "Technological Metaphor and Social Control," pp. 141, 137. See the Introduction and Chapter 4 on metaphor.

Chapter Four
The Biographical Referents of Metaphor

1. On the history of intelligence testing see Weinland, "The History of the I.Q. in America, 1890–1941"; Gould, *The Mismeasure of Man*. Also helpful are Camfield, "The Professionalization of American Psychology"; Camfield, "Psychologists at War: The History of American Psychology and the First World War" (Ph.D. diss., University of Texas at Austin, 1969); Daniel Kevles, "Testing the Army's Intelligence: Psychologists and the Military in World War I," *Journal of American History* 55 (1968): 565–81; Cravens, *The Triumph of Evolution*; Florence Goodenough, *Mental Testing: Its History, Principles and Applications* (New York: n.p., 1949); Franz Samelson, "World War I Intelligence Testing and the Development of Psychology," *Journal of the History of the Behavioral Sciences* 13 (1977): 274–82.

2. On personal experience as the "storehouse of potential metaphors," see Donald A. Schön, *Invention and the Evolution of Ideas* (London: Tavistock, 1967), p. 67.

3. Contrary to contemporaneous and historical assumptions, Binet did not complete his medical studies: see Theta H. Wolf, *Alfred Binet* (Chicago: University of Chicago Press, 1973). I am grateful to Michael Sokal for pointing out this fact.

4. On G. Stanley Hall, see Ross, *G. Stanley Hall: The Psychologist as Prophet*; on Münsterberg, see Matthew Hale, Jr., *Human Science and Social Order: Hugo Münsterberg and the Origins of Applied Psychology* (Philadelphia: Temple University Press, 1980); on Cattell, see Michael Sokal, "The Educational and Psychological Career of James McKeen Cattell" (Ph.D. diss., Case Western Reserve University, 1972).

5. James McKeen Cattell, "Mental Tests and Measurements," *Mind* 15 (1890): 373–80.

6. James McKeen Cattell to his parents, December 25, 1890, Cattell Papers, Box 55, file "September–December 1890."

7. See Sokal, "The Educational and Psychological Career of James McKeen Cattell."

8. Stephen S. Colvin, "Principles Underlying the Construction and Use of Mental Tests," in *Intelligence Tests and Their Uses, 21st Yearbook of the National Society for the Study of Education*, ed. Guy Montrose Whipple (Bloomington, Ill.: Public School Publishing, 1922), p. 25.

9. On the sharply rising opportunity costs of medical education, see Starr, *The Social Transformation of American Medicine*, pp. 116–24.

10. Joseph Ben-David and Randall Collins, "Social Factors in the Origins of a New Science: The Case of Psychology," *American Sociological Review* 31 (1966): 451–65, esp. pp. 462–63. The authors view American psychology as having stalled, relative to European examples. They reach this conclusion because their research stops at 1910, before experimental psychology "took off" in the United States. On the experimentalists, see also Morawski, ed., *The Rise of Experimentation*.

11. Hale, *Human Science and Social Order*.

12. Hugo Münsterberg to James McKeen Cattell, February 25, 1898, Hugo Münsterberg Papers, Boston Public Library.

13. Hale, *Human Science and Social Order*; death notices, file 2499b.774, Münsterberg Papers.

14. Robert S. Woodworth to James McKeen Cattell, August 4, 1904, Cattell Papers, Box 46.

15. George Haines and Frederick Jackson, "A Neglected Landmark in the History of Ideas," *Mississippi Valley Historical Review* 34 (1947): 201–20; A. W. Coates, "American Scholarship Comes of Age: The Louisiana Purchase Exposition of 1904," *Journal of the History of Ideas* 22 (1961): 404–17; Hale, *Human Science and Social Order*.

16. On instrumentation see Merriley Borrell, "Instruments and an Independent Physiology: The Harvard Physiological Laboratory, 1871–1906," in *Physiology in the American Context, 1850–1940*, ed. Gerald L. Geison (Bethesda, Md.: American Physiological Society, 1987), pp. 293–322.

17. Raymond E. Fancher to JoAnne Brown, personal communication, July 1985. See also Fancher, *The Intelligence Men*.

18. Michael M. Sokal, "James McKeen Cattell and the Failure of Anthropometric Testing, 1890–1901," in *The Problematic Science: Psychology in Nineteenth-Century Thought*, ed. William R. Woodward and Mitchell G. Ash (New York: Praeger, 1982).

19. Adolph Meyer to Henry Herbert Goddard, February 8, 1906, Henry Herbert Goddard Papers, Archives of the History of Psychology, University of Akron, Ohio.

20. Henry Herbert Goddard, diary entries of April 4, 1907, and April 25, 1907, Box M43; E. C. Sanford to Henry Herbert Goddard, December 3, 1906, Box M33; George Morris Philips, Principal, Penn-

sylvania State Normal School, to Henry Herbert Goddard, May 3, 1904, Box M35.2, Goddard Papers; Clara Harrison Town, "The Binet-Simon Scale and the Psychologist," *The Psychological Clinic* 5 (1912): 239–44; "List of Apparatus Necessary for a Complete Course in Experimental Psychology," undated, Cattell Papers, Box 85. See also Borrell, "Instruments and an Independent Physiology."

21. Hale, *Human Science and Social Order*, pp. 5ff.

22. Starr, *The Social Transformation of American Medicine*, pp. 118–20.

23. Yerkes received his first A.B. from Ursinus College in 1897. Robert Mearns Yerkes, diary entries of June 8 and 24, September 10, 18, and 29, and October 3 and 27, 1898, Yerkes Papers, Box 169; Robert M. Yerkes, "Early Days of Comparative Psychology," *Psychological Review* 50 (1943): 74–76; Robert M. Yerkes, "Psychobiologist," *A History of Psychology in Autobiography*, ed. Carl Murchison (Worcester, Mass.: n.p., 1930–1952), 2:383–84.

24. Robert Mearns Yerkes, diary entries of October 3 and 27, 1898, Yerkes Papers, Box 169.

25. Robert Mearns Yerkes, diary entry of December 31, 1898, Yerkes Papers, Box 169.

26. Ibid.

27. Yerkes, "Psychobiologist," pp. 383–84.

28. Lewis Madison Terman, "Trails to Psychology," in *A History of Psychology in Autobiography*, ed. Murchison, 2:299–300.

29. Ibid., p. 318.

30. Historian Paul Davis Chapman has called the years 1905–1910 Terman's "fallow period," minimizing the connection between school hygiene and mental testing; I argue that this public health interest was integral to Terman's career in psychology. See Chapman, *Schools as Sorters*, p. 24.

31. Lewis Terman, transcript of interview with A. E. Wiggam, December 14 and 15, 1925, p. 4, Terman Papers, Box 8, file 2.

32. Lewis Terman, "Medical Inspection in Schools of California," *The Psychological Clinic* 5 (1911): 58; idem, "Social Hygiene: The Real Conservation Problem," *North American Review* 198 (1913): 404–12; idem, "School Clinics for Free Medical and Dental Treatment," *The Psychological Clinic* 5 (1912): 271–78.

33. Terman, "Trails to Psychology," p. 324. Terman's son, an engineer, later suffered from the same disease.

34. See the bibliography of Terman's works, Terman Papers. His books on school hygiene include *The Teacher's Health: A Study in the Hygiene of an Occupation* (Boston: n.p., 1914), *The Hygiene of the School Child*, and *Health Work in the Schools*, authored with E. B. Hoag (Bos-

ton: Houghton Mifflin, 1914). On Terman, see also Chapman, *Schools as Sorters*, and Minton, *Lewis M. Terman*.

35. Terman, "Medical Inspection in Schools of California," p. 58.

36. Terman, "Trails to Psychology," p. 324.

37. Ibid., p. 311n.

38. See, for example, Goddard's description of the married couples research, *Program: Twenty-fifth Anniversary of Vineland Laboratory, 1906–1931* (Vineland, N.J.: Smith Printing House, 1932), pp. 67–68.

39. See Leila Zenderland's essay "The Debate over Diagnosis," pp. 46–74.

40. Henry Herbert Goddard, notes, undated, Goddard Papers, Box M33, file AA3.

41. Henry Herbert Goddard, diary entry of May 6, 1907, Goddard Papers, Box M43; ticket to Congrès International de la Hygiène Scolaire, Paris, 1910, Goddard Papers.

42. Peter Tyor, transcript of interview with Lillian Edwards Brown Capell, Goddard's assistant, Goddard Papers, p. 4.

43. Goddard, *Human Efficiency and Levels of Intelligence*, p. 75.

44. Rosenberg, *The Care of Strangers*.

45. Robert S. Woodworth to James McKeen Cattell, July 19, 1901, Cattell Papers, Box 46, Woodworth files, 1899–1903. "Lusk" is Graham Lusk, physiologist. I am grateful to Harry M. Marks for this information.

46. Robert S. Woodworth to James McKeen Cattell, June 2, 1903, Cattell Papers, Box 46, Woodworth files, 1899–1903.

47. Joseph Ben-David and Randall Collins, "Social Factors in the Origin of a New Science: The Case of Psychology," *American Sociological Review* 31 (1966): 461–63.

48. Geraldine M. Jonçich, *The Sane Positivist: A Biography of Edward Lee Thorndike* (Middletown, Conn.: Wesleyan University Press, 1968), pp. 96–98; 121–22.

49. Edward Lee Thorndike, "Autobiography," in *A History of Psychology in Autobiography*, ed. Murchison, vol. 3; Thorndike, "Measurement in Education," in *Twenty-first Yearbook of the National Society for the Study of Education*, ed. Whipple, pt. 1, pp. 1–9.

50. Thorndike, "Autobiography."

51. Edward Lee Thorndike, *An Introduction to the Theory of Mental and Social Measurements* (New York: Teachers College Press, 1904); George D. Strayer, *City School Expenditures* (New York: Teachers College Press, 1905); Ayres, *Laggards in Our Schools*; see also the following city and county school surveys directed by Cubberley: Multnomah County, Oregon (1913); Salt Lake City, Utah (1915); Palo Alto, California (1931)—and by Strayer—St. Paul, Minnesota (1917); Stamford,

Connecticut (1922–1923); Springfield, Massachusetts (1923–1924); Lynn, Massachusetts (1927); Closter, New Jersey (1928); Watertown, Massachusetts (1931); Hartford, Connecticut (1937); Boston, Massachusetts (1944). On the school survey movement see Chapter 3.

52. On women in psychology and related pursuits, see Rossiter, *Women Scientists*; Elizabeth Scarborough and Laurel Furumoto, *Untold Lives: The First Generation of Women Psychologists* (New York: Columbia University Press, 1987); Barbara F. Reskin, "Sex Differentiation and the Social Organization of Science," *Social Inquiry* 48 (1978): 6–37; Laurel Furumoto, "Shared Knowledge: The Experimentalists, 1904–1929," in *The Rise of Experimentation*, ed. Morawski.

53. Ross, *G. Stanley Hall: The Psychologist as Prophet*. See also E. L. Thorndike to James Cattell, July 6, 1904, Cattell Papers; Jonçich, *The Sane Positivist*, pp. 35, 62–63, 96; Carl Murchison, ed., *A History of Psychology in Autobiography*; M. D. Boring and E. G. Boring, "Masters and Pupils among American Psychologists," *American Journal of Psychology* 61 (1948): 527–34. See Charles E. Rosenberg, "Piety and Social Action: Some Origins of the American Public Health Movement," in his *No Other Gods: On Science and American Social Thought* (Baltimore: Johns Hopkins University Press, 1961), pp. 109–22; Charles E. Rosenberg, *The Cholera Years: The United States, 1832, 1849, and 1866* (Chicago: University of Chicago Press, 1962), p. 132; Brown, "Tuberculosis: A Romance"; Elizabeth B. Keeney, *The Botanizers* (Chapel Hill: University of North Carolina Press, 1992), on the religious aspects of scientific research in the nineteenth century; Haller and Haller, *The Physician and Sexuality in Victorian America*. Note the current usage of salvation language and crusade rhetoric in medicine.

54. Rosenberg, *The Care of Strangers*; Terman, "School Clinics"; Terman, "The Significance of Intelligence Testing for Mental Hygiene," *Journal of Psycho-Asthenics* 18 (1914): 119–27. The term *clinical psychology* was used more loosely during this period than it is today, I believe, and was at times synonymous with *the new psychology*, at times specific to clinical settings.

CHAPTER FIVE
HISTORICAL MEANINGS OF MEDICAL LANGUAGE

1. Reiser, *Medicine and the Reign of Technology*, pp. 110–21; Daniel M. Musher, Edward A. Dominguez, and Ariel Bar-Sela, "Edouard Seguin and the Social Power of the Thermometer," *New England Journal of Medicine* 316 (1987): 115; J. Worth Estes, "Quantitative Observations of Fever and Its Treatment before the Advent of Short Clinical Thermometers," *Medical History* 35 (1991): 214; Warner, *The*

Therapeutic Perspective, pp. 154–55. I am grateful to my colleague Harry M. Marks for several of these citations.

2. Henry Herbert Goddard, "The Binet Tests and the Inexperienced Teacher," *The Training School Bulletin* 10 (1913): 9. Goddard liked this metaphor, and repeated it verbatim in "The Binet Measuring Scale of Intelligence: What It Is and How It Is To Be Used," *The Training School Bulletin* 11 (1916): 88. Edward A. Dominguez, Ariel Bar-Sela, and Daniel M. Musher, "Adoption of Thermometry into Clinical Practice in the United States," *Reviews of Infectious Diseases* 9 (1987): 1198; I. Kraft, "Edouard Seguin and the Moral Treatment of Idiots," *Bulletin of the History of Medicine* 35 (1961): 393–418. Other psychologists adopted the thermometer metaphor: see also Walter Dill Scott, *Aids in the Selection of Salesmen* (Pittsburgh: Carnegie Institute of Technology, 1916), p. 36; Robert Yerkes, ed., *The New World of Science: Its Development During the War* (New York: The Century Company, 1920), p. 385, comparing the calibration of thermometers to the "calibration" of trade tests.

3. C. S. Lewis, *Studies in Words*, p. 3.

4. Pocock, *Politics, Language and Time*, p. 36; see also Quentin Skinner, "Meaning and Understanding in the History of Ideas," *History and Theory* 8 (1969): 3–53, and "Some Problems in the Analysis of Thought and Action," *Political Theory* 2 (1974): 277–303. The "thermometer" analogy is a metonym for the larger system that I call "medical metaphor."

5. Cattell, "The Conceptions and Methods of Psychology." See also idem, "Our Psychological Association and Research," *Science* 45 (1917): 275–84.

6. Lewis Terman, "Genius and Stupidity: A Study of Seven 'Bright' and Seven 'Stupid' Boys," *Pedagogical Seminary* 13 (1906): 312.

7. Daniel Nelson, *Managers and Workers: Origins of the New Factory System in the United States, 1880–1920* (Madison: University of Wisconsin Press, 1975), p. 12.

8. F. G. Cobbe, *Fortune Review*, 1888, as cited in the *Oxford English Dictionary*.

9. Thorndike, *An Introduction to the Theory of Mental and Social Measurements*, as cited in the *Oxford English Dictionary*. [The *Oxford English Dictionary* gives 1905 as publication date, presumably relying on a British edition.]

10. Starr, *The Social Transformation of American Medicine*, p. 15; see also Murray Edelman, "The Political Language of the Helping Professions," in his *Political Language*, p. 60. Starr does not remark, however, on the linguistic character of the borrowed authority.

11. Sontag, *Illness as Metaphor*. Sontag does not pair her historical linguistics on the metaphor of disease with a history of medicine. Her

focus is on the hidden morality of literal medical language: illness as metaphor for moral life. On the essentially metaphorical character of everyday speech, see Lakoff and Johnson, *Metaphors We Live By.*

12. On the more recent uses of medical language in the "helping professions," see Edelman, *Political Language*, pp. 57–75.

13. See Johnson, *The Body in the Mind.*

14. George E. Dawson, "A Youthful Study of Degeneracy," *Pedagogical Seminary*, December 1896, p. 258. In another example, Wisconsin's eugenical marriage laws were likened to the abolition of the common drinking cup: filler article, *Journal of Education*, August 14, 1913.

15. The *Oxford English Dictionary* gives *sterilize* as a medical term as the metaphorical extension of *sterile*, meaning "barren" or "infertile." Metaphors, however, have a way of reciprocating changes in meaning; thus *sterilize* became popular in eugenics over the term *desexualize* because it carried, by the early twentieth century, the medical meaning of "germ-free" or "clean."

16. Goddard, *Human Efficiency and Levels of Intelligence*, p. 92. Goddard also used physician-patient language when discussing feeble-mindedness and crime; this he may have adopted from Samuel Butler's inversion of the crime-disease equation, in Butler, *Erewhon or Over the Range*, ed. Hans-Peter Breuer and Daniel F. Howard (1872; Newark: University of Delaware Press, 1981), pp. 113–17.

17. Haller, *Eugenics*; Pickens, *Eugenics and the Progressives.*

18. Walter E. Fernald, "Care of the Feeble-minded," *Proceedings, National Conference of Charities and Corrections*, 1904, p. 383.

19. See John W. Dower's discussion of race hatred in his *War Without Mercy: Race and Power in the Pacific War* (New York: Pantheon, 1986), introduction; Robert N. Proctor, "Eugenics Among the Social Sciences," in *The Estate of Social Knowledge*, ed. Brown and van Keuren, pp. 175–208.

20. Edelman, *Political Language*, p. 59. Edelman observes, "Political metaphors can vividly, potently and persuasively evoke changed worlds in which the remedies for anxieties are clearly perceived and self-serving courses of action are sanctified." Edelman, *Politics as Symbolic Action*, p. 71.

21. Alfred Binet, *Les Idées modernes sur les enfants* (Paris: E. Flammarion, 1909).

22. Reiser, *Medicine and the Reign of Technology*, p. 141.

23. Ibid.

24. Starr, *The Social Transformation of American Medicine*, pp. 10, 12. On the professional ideal of objectivity as the relinquishing of personal opinion, see Joseph Mayer Rice, *Scientific Management in Education* (New York and Philadelphia: Hinds, Noble and Eldredge, 1913), pp. xv, xvii; Marion R. Trabue and Frank Parker Stockbridge, *Mea-*

sure Your Mind: The Mentimeter and How to Use It (New York: Doubleday, Page, 1922) pp. 13–14; Edward A. Lincoln, *Beginnings in Educational Measurement* (Philadelphia: Lippincott, 1924), pp. 57, 60; Ralph W. Tyler, "The Specific Techniques of Investigation: Examining and Testing Acquired Knowledge, Skill and Ability," in *Thirty-seventh Yearbook of the National Society for the Study of Education*, 1938, 2:341–55; Edward Lee Thorndike, "What Is 'Scientific' Method in the Study of Education?" in *Twenty-first Yearbook of the National Society for the Study of Education*, ed. Whipple, pp. 81–82; Joseph Peterson, *Early Conceptions and Tests of Intelligence* (Yonkers-on-Hudson, N.Y.: World Book Company, 1925), pp. 157, 213; David Snedden, "Increasing the Efficiency of Education," *Journal of Education* 78 (1913): 62–63; Karl Pearson, *The Grammar of Science* (1892; London: Adam and Charles Black, 1900), p. 19; Edward Lee Thorndike, "Educational Diagnosis," *Science* 37 (1913): 138–39; Yerkes, ed., *The New World of Science*, p. 358.

25. A. C. Rogers, M.D., to Henry Herbert Goddard, February 24, 1911, Goddard Papers, Box 615, file "Correspondence P-R-Q."

26. Henry Herbert Goddard to A. C. Rogers, M.D., March 3, 1911, Goddard Papers, Box 615, file "Correspondence P-R-Q."

27. J. E. Wallace Wallin, *Experimental Studies of Mental Defectives* (Baltimore: Warwick and York, 1912), p. 1.

28. Ibid.

29. J. E. Wallace Wallin, *Odyssey of a Psychologist: Pioneering Experiences in Special Education, Clinical Psychology and Mental Hygiene with a Comprehensive Bibliography of the Author's Publications* (Wilmington, Del.: author, 1955), p. 44.

30. J. E. Wallace Wallin, "The Distinctive Contribution of the Psycho-Educational Clinic to the School Hygiene Movement," in *Transactions of the Fourth International Congress on School Hygiene* 3:428.

31. J. E. Wallace Wallin, *The Function of the Psychological Clinic* (1914).

32. Edgar A. Doll, review of Wallin's *The Function of the Psychological Clinic*, *The Training School Bulletin* 11 (1914): 10–12. See also Chapter 3 on the relation between school hygiene and mental testing.

33. Lewis Terman, *The Measurement of Intelligence*, ed. Ellwood P. Cubberley (Boston: Houghton Mifflin, 1916), p. 22.

34. On these epidemic diseases as perceived threats, see James E. McCulloch, ed., *The New Chivalry—Health* (Nashville: Southern Sociological Congress, 1915), p. 33.

35. On the immense social "capital" of medicine, see Larson, *The Rise of Professionalism*, pp. 38–39.

36. John Duffy, "American Perceptions of the Medical, Legal and Theological Professions," *Bulletin of the History of Medicine* 58 (1984): 1–15.

37. Starr, *The Social Transformation of American Medicine*, pp. 39–40, and Carr-Saunders and Wilson, *The Professions*, pp. 68–70, on the early conjunction of medicine and theology. On the religious roots of medical practice, see Hall, "The Social Foundations of Professional Credibility." Interesting examples of theological metaphor used to popularize health reform are found in Burnham, "Change in the Popularization of Health," and Rosenberg, *No Other Gods*.

38. Dr. A. C. Rogers to Henry Herbert Goddard, November 25, 1910; Goddard to Rogers, November 29, 1910; Rogers to Goddard, February 24, 1911; Goddard to Rogers, March 3, 1911; Century Company Publishers to Goddard, October 8, 1914; Goddard to Century Company Publishers, October 14, 1914, Goddard Papers, Box M615. See also H. L. Mencken to Henry Herbert Goddard, February 12 and 23, 1935; Honorable Mr. Justice Middleton to Goddard, January 20, 1931, Goddard Papers, Box M32; H. L. Mencken, *The American Language: An Inquiry into the Development of the English Language in the United States*, 4th ed. rev. (New York: Knopf, 1943), p. 175.

39. As Murray Edelman observes, after Sapir, 'A word or phrase which has become established as connoting threat of reassurance for a group thus can become a cue for releases of energy 'out of all proportion to the apparent triviality of meaning suggested by its mere form.' " See Edelman, *The Symbolic Uses of Politics*, p. 116, citing Edward Sapir, "Symbolism," in *Encyclopedia of the Social Sciences* (New York, 1934), pp. 492–95.

40. See also Thomas Dawes Eliot, "A Limbo for Cruel Words," *Survey*, June 15, 1922, pp. 389–91.

41. Elizabeth Irwin, "Tests and Methods of Testing," *The Training School Bulletin*, September 1916, pp. 120–23; see also Honorable George S. Addams, "Defectives in the Juvenile Court," *The Training School Bulletin* 11 (1914): 51, and *The Training School Bulletin* 10 (1913): entire volume. On the Wasserman test, developed in 1906, see Starr, *The Social Transformation of American Medicine*, p. 137. On the euphemistic "social hygiene" movement to prevent venereal disease, see Brandt, *No Magic Bullet*.

42. On metaphor and contradiction, see Edelman, *Political Language*, chap. 1. On logical category shift, see Colin Turbayne, *The Myth of Metaphor* (New Haven: Yale University Press, 1962), p. 17, and Norwood Russell Hanson, *Patterns of Discovery: An Inquiry into the Conceptual Foundations of Science* (Cambridge: Cambridge University Press, 1958).

43. Pocock, *Politics, Language and Time*, p. 18.

44. See Brandt, *No Magic Bullet*, for an excellent discussion of the history of venereal disease.

45. On parental resistance to school examinations, including medical exams and mental tests, see William J. Reese, *Power and the Promise of School Reform: Grassroots Movements during the Progressive Era* (Boston: Routledge and Kegan Paul, 1986), esp. chap. 8; on Terman and the public schools, see Chapman, *Schools as Sorters*.

46. Personal communication with Elizabeth Lunbeck, November 1990, Baltimore, Md. The Irwin quote is the only such reference I found among psychologists.

47. See C. A. Ulrich to Lewis Terman, May 19, 1952, Terman Papers, Box 20, file 14.

48. Ellwood P. Cubberley, editor's introduction to Terman, *The Measurement of Intelligence*. On blood counting techniques during this period, see A. Wright, "On Some New Procedures for the Examination of the Blood and Bacterial Cultures," *Lancet* 2 (1902): 11; M. L. Verso, "The Evolution of Blood-Counting Techniques," *Medical History* 8 (1964): 149–58; Richard C. Cabot, *A Guide to the Clinical Examination of the Blood for Diagnostic Purposes*, 3d ed. rev. (New York: William Wood, 1898), chap. 2, "Counting the Corpuscles," pp. 11–25; John C. DaCosta, Jr., *Clinical Hematology*, 2d ed. rev. (Philadelphia: P. Blakiston's Son, 1907), pp. 55–74.

49. Julia Richman, in 1884 the first female principal of a New York City public school, was named district superintendent of schools in 1903, a post she held until 1912.

50. Edward Lee Thorndike, report to Julia Richman, Principal, Public School #77, 1904, Thorndike Papers. By the time Thorndike had finished his investigation, Richman had been named district superintendent of schools.

51. Thorndike, "Educational Diagnosis," pp. 138–39. Compare this article to Edouard Seguin's discussions of home thermometry in *Family Thermometry: A Manual of Thermometry, for Mothers, Nurses, Hospitals, etc., and All Who Have Charge of the Sick and the Young* (New York: G. P. Putnam, 1873).

52. Reiser, *Medicine and the Reign of Technology*, pp. 43–44.

53. Ibid., p. 109.

54. Lincoln, *Beginnings in Educational Measurement*, p. 57.

55. A. R. Gilliland and R. H. Jordan, *Educational Measurement and the Classroom Teacher* (New York: The Century Company, 1924), p. 47.

56. Thorndike, "Educational Diagnosis," pp. 138–39.

57. Charles B. Barnes, "Feeble-mindedness as a Cause for Homelessness," *The Training School Bulletin*, March 1916, p. 10.

58. On the objectivity of mental tests as against personal opinion, see Yerkes, *The New World of Science*, p. 358; Lincoln, *Beginnings in Educational Measurement*, p. 57; Rice, *Scientific Management in Education*, p. xv.

59. Goddard, "The Binet Tests and the Inexperienced Teacher," p. 9.

CHAPTER SIX
HUMAN ENGINEERING

1. Layton, *The Revolt of the Engineers*, pp. 4, 55; Louis Galambos, with the assistance of Barbara Barrow Spence, *The Public Image of Big Business in America, 1880–1940: A Quantitative Study in Social Change* (Baltimore: Johns Hopkins University Press, 1975), p. 8.

2. Numerous scholars have commented on the "natural" life cycle of metaphors. See the index to Warren Shibles' encyclopedic *Metaphor* (Whitewater, Wis.: n.p., 1971).

3. Carl F. Kaestle, *Education and Social Change in Nineteenth-Century Massachusetts* (New York: Cambridge University Press, 1980); Tyack, *The One Best System*, p. 41. On the romance of technology, see Leo Marx, *The Machine in the Garden: Technology and the Pastoral Ideal in America* (New York: Oxford University Press, 1964).

4. Haber, *Efficiency and Uplift*, p. xii.

5. This notion was compatible with the nineteenth-century thermodynamic model of brain physiology in relation to intellect. See Charles Rosenberg, "Science and American Social Thought," in *Science and Society in the United States*, ed. David D. Van Tassel and M. G. Hall (Homewood, Ill.: Dorsey Press, 1966).

6. Marx, *The Machine in the Garden*, esp. chap. 4.

7. Hays, *Conservation and the Gospel of Efficiency*, esp. chaps. 1 and 13; Rodgers, "In Search of Progressivism"; Callahan, *Education and the Cult of Efficiency* (1962); Haber, *Efficiency and Uplift*; Noble, *America by Design*.

8. H. L. Mencken, *The American Language* (New York: Knopf, 1943), pp. 286–91, citing the *Engineering News-Record*, April 19, 1923, and January 15, 1925.

9. *National Education Association Proceedings*, 1915, p. 319, cited in Callahan, *Education and the Cult of Efficiency* (1962), p. 151.

10. Henry Suzzalo, "The Effective American University System," *Educational Record* 4, cited in Noble, *America by Design*, p. 224.

11. Larson, *The Rise of Professionalism*, p. 27; Layton, *The Revolt of the Engineers*, chap. 3; Noble, *America by Design*, chap. 3; Monte A. Calvert, *The Mechanical Engineer in America, 1830–1910* (Baltimore:

Johns Hopkins University Press, 1967), chap. 7; Thorstein Veblen, *The Engineers and the Price System* (New York: B. W. Heubsch, 1921).

12. By his own report, Cattell also wrote of eugenics in 1895 as a way of "altering the quantities of gold and iron in the world," but this classical allusion is not an obvious engineering metaphor. See Cattell, "Our Psychological Association and Research," p. 284. See also Robert Routledge, *Discoveries and Inventions of the Nineteenth Century* (London and New York: George Routledge and Sons, 1891), p. 2.

13. James McKeen Cattell, "Examinations, Grades and Credits," *Popular Science Monthly* 66 (1904–1905): 367.

14. Thorndike, *Mental and Social Measurements*, pp. 5–6. Note the thermometer analogy; see my Chapter 5 on thermometry.

15. Rice, *The Public School System of the United States*; idem, *Scientific Management in Education*; idem, "Why Our Improved Educational Machinery Fails to Yield a Better Product," *The Forum*, July–September 1904, pp. 96–114.

16. Rice, *Scientific Management in Education*, p. 248.

17. See Chapter 3 on education as a profession.

18. Cecelia Tichi, *Shifting Gears: Technology, Literature, Culture in Modernist America* (Chapel Hill: University of North Carolina Press, 1987).

19. Bellamy's work was so popular after 1888 that the absence of direct references to him is not surprising.

20. Bellamy, *Looking Backward 2000–1887*, p. 45.

21. Ibid., p. 98n. The passage continues: "The vast majority of my contemporaries, though nominally free to do so, never really chose their occupations at all, but were forced by circumstances into work for which they were relatively inefficient, because not naturally fitted for it."

22. Goddard, *Human Efficiency and Levels of Intelligence*, p. 60.

23. Trabue and Stockbridge, *Measure Your Mind*.

24. "Intellectual gospel" is David Hollinger's term; see also suggestions to this effect in Christopher Lasch, *The New Radicalism in America, 1889–1963: The Intellectual as a Social Type* (1965; New York: Norton, 1986), chap. 1.

25. See also Trabue and Stockbridge, *Measure Your Mind*, p. 6.

26. For example, John Palmer Garber, *Current Activities and Influences in Education* (Philadelphia: Lippincott, 1913), p. 144, includes "scientific management," "efficiency," and "conservation of the young" in the same paragraph.

27. See J. M. Greenwood, superintendent of Kansas City, Missouri, schools, "Scientific Management in Education," *Journal of Education* 77 (1913): 174–75, on teachers as workmen. See also Hamilton, *Our Com-*

mon School System, p. 91, rejecting the factory model in favor of a hospital model.

28. Martin made his speech six years before Frederick Taylor published *The Principles of Scientific Management* in 1911.

29. George H. Martin, "Comparison of Modern Business Methods with Educational Methods," *National Education Association Proceedings*, 1905, pp. 320–25; George D. Strayer and Edward Lee Thorndike, "Means of Measuring Educational Products," in *Educational Administration*, ed. George D. Strayer (New York: Macmillan, 1913); Frances E. Spaulding, "Application of the Principles of Scientific Management to School Systems," *National Education Association Proceedings*, 1913, pp. 259–79.

30. On the political dimensions of technique there is a vast literature. With specific reference to education, see Callahan, *Education and the Cult of Efficiency*; Steven Selden, "Curricular Metaphors: From Science to Symbolism," *Educational Theory* 25 (1975): 243–62, and "Conservative Ideology and Curriculum," *Educational Theory* 27 (1977): 205–22; Michael Apple, *Ideology and Curriculum* (Boston: Routledge and Kegan Paul, 1979).

31. Such lax usage may also reflect the relatively broader diffusion of the language of efficiency. See Ludwik Fleck, *Genesis and Development of a Scientific Fact* (1935; Chicago: University of Chicago Press, 1979), pp. 112, 115. *"Every communication and, indeed, all nomenclature tends to make any item of knowledge more exoteric and popular"* (p. 114; emphasis in original).

32. Franklin Bobbitt, "The Elimination of Waste in Education," *The Elementary School Teacher* 12 (1912): 260. On Bobbitt see Kliebard, "Bureaucracy and Curriculum Theory"; Herbert M. Kliebard, "The Drive for Curriculum Change in the United States" (pts. 1 and 2), *Journal of Curriculum Studies* 11 (1979): 191–202, 273–86; Callahan, *Education and the Cult of Efficiency*.

33. Garber, *Current Activities*, pp. 261, 144. See also Terman, "The Conservation of Talent"; Hays, *Conservation and the Gospel of Efficiency*.

34. Taylor, *The Principles of Scientific Management*, pp. 120, 123, 124, 126; see also Cattell, "Examinations, Grades and Credits."

35. Frank Gilbreth and Lillian Moller Gilbreth, *Applied Motion Study* (New York: Macmillan, 1919), pp. 23, 167–68.

36. This reciprocal use of metaphor among engineers and educators exemplifies in the social realm a phenomenon that Max Black has noted at a different level, namely, that to call a man a wolf is to make the wolf more human. See Max Black, *Models and Metaphors* (Ithaca: Cornell University Press, 1962), p. 40; see also Edelman, "The Political Language of the Helping Professions," and Robert

Mearns Yerkes, *Introduction to Psychology* (New York: Henry Holt, 1911), p. 51.

37. Yerkes, *Introduction to Psychology*, p. 53. On the fascination with electricity, see Carolyn Marvin, "Dazzling the Multitude: Imagining the Electric Light as a Communications Medium," in *Imagining Tomorrow: Technology and the American Future*, ed. Joseph J. Corn (Cambridge, Mass.: MIT Press, 1986).

38. Terman, *The Measurement of Intelligence*, p. 4.

39. Terman advocated testing the intelligence of schoolchildren, not the effectiveness of teaching materials, in contrast to Greenwood, "Scientific Management in Education," p. 174, where "material" refers to schoolbooks.

40. Routledge, *Discoveries and Inventions of the Nineteenth Century*, p. 213.

41. Terman, *The Measurement of Intelligence*, p. 44.

42. See Marvin, "Dazzling the Multitude," p. 204.

43. As cited by Layton, *The Revolt of the Engineers*, p. 69; see Lewis Terman's correspondence with Caspar Hodgson, his publisher at the World Book Company, Terman Papers.

44. Noble, *America by Design*, p. 38.

45. The medical analogy did not as easily allow for commercialization, as the medical profession expressly disavowed mercenary interests.

CHAPTER SEVEN
THE GREAT WAR

1. Goddard soon resigned to return to Vineland. Lewis Terman was a member both of Yerkes's wartime Committee on the Psychological Examination of Recruits and of Scott's Committee on Classification of Personnel. See Minton, *Lewis M. Terman*, p. 64n.

2. Clarence S. Yoakum and Robert M. Yerkes, *Army Mental Tests* (New York: Henry Holt, 1920), p. 199.

3. Estimates vary by tenfold. Michael Schudson, "Organizing the 'Meritocracy': A History of the College Entrance Examination Board," *Harvard Educational Review* 42 (1972): 34, estimates thirty to forty million tests as of 1929, but Weinland, "The History of the I.Q. in America, 1890–1941," estimates only three to four million. Schudson's figures include achievement tests.

4. Minton's is the best account to date of the wartime committee efforts. See also Richard T. von Mayrhauser, "Walking Out at the Walton" (Paper presented at the Cheiron Society annual meeting, Philadelphia, June 12–15, 1985, subsequently revised and published

as "The Manager, the Medic and the Mediator: The Clash of Professional Styles and the Wartime Origins of Group Mental Testing"), in *Psychological Testing and American Society*, ed. Sokal, pp. 128–57. Portions of my doctoral thesis, "The Semantics of Profession," were presented as the invited lecture at this Cheiron Society meeting. See also Samelson, "World War I Intelligence Testing."

5. Noble, *America by Design*, pp. 275–76; Milton J. Nadworny, *Scientific Management and the Unions, 1900–1932* (Cambridge, Mass.: Harvard University Press, 1952), p. 111. See Lillian Moller Gilbreth, *The Psychology of Management: The Function of the Mind in Determining, Teaching and Installing Methods of Least Waste* (New York: Sturgis and Walton, 1914).

6. See Noble, *America by Design*; Callahan, *Education and the Cult of Efficiency*; Schudson, "Organizing the 'Meritocracy.'"

7. For example, the journal *Industrial Psychology*, subtitled *The Journal of Human Engineering*, founded in 1926.

8. See Samelson, "World War I Intelligence Testing"; Weinland, "The History of the I.Q. in America, 1890–1941"; Gould, *The Mismeasure of Man*; Camfield, "The Professionalization of American Psychology"; Camfield, "Psychologists at War"; Kevles, "Testing the Army's Intelligence"; Robert Yerkes, "Psychology in Relation to the War," *Psychological Review* 25 (1918): 85–115.

9. Yerkes, "Psychology in Relation to the War," p. 95.

10. Robert Mearns Yerkes, ed., *Psychological Examining in the United States Army*, vol. 15 of the *Memoirs of the National Academy of Sciences* (Washington, D.C.: Government Printing Office, 1921), p. 98; Samelson, "World War I Intelligence Testing," p. 276. Yerkes apparently did not view the Sanitary Corps as the prestigious medical division that he considered the Medical Reserve Corps, although both comprised medical officers.

11. Robert Yerkes, war diary, July 15, 1918, Yerkes Papers, Box 171, file 22663.

12. On the history of behaviorism during this early period, see Kerry Wayne Buckley, "Behaviorism and the Professionalization of Psychology: A Study of John Broadus Watson, 1878–1958" (Ph.D. diss., University of Massachusetts, Amherst, 1982) (subsequently published as *Mechanical Man: John Broaches Watson and the Beginnings of Behaviorism* [New York: Guilford Press, 1989]); Laurence D. Smith, *Behaviorism and Logical Positivism: A Reassessment of the Alliance* (Stanford: Stanford University Press, 1986). Buckley characterizes behaviorism as a form of radical environmentalism; as such, I would argue, it is antithetical to the hereditarian faith of the mental test psychologists. Also see John M. O'Donnell, *The Origins of Behaviorism in*

American Psychology 1870–1920 (New York: New York University Press, 1985).

13. Noble, *America by Design*, pp. 297, 230; Loren Baritz, *Servants of Power: A History of the Use of Social Science in American Industry* (Westport, Conn.: Greenwood Press, 1974), pp. 35–36; Fred H. Rindge, Jr., "Solving the Problem of 'Human Engineering,'" *Engineering News* 70 (1913): 962–63.

14. Noble, *America by Design*, p. 208.

15. See Noble, *America by Design*, for exhaustive detail on the activities of engineers and corporate managers during World War I; on industrial psychology see Leonard W. Ferguson's comprehensive series *The Heritage of Industrial Psychology* (n.p., 1964), Archives of the History of American Psychology, University of Akron, Ohio.

16. See Lewis Terman, "Suggestions for Revising, Extending and Supplementing the Binet Intelligence Tests," and William H. Pyle, "The Value to Be Derived from Giving Mental Tests to All School Children," in *Transactions of the Fourth International Congress on School Hygiene*, vol. 5.

17. Lewis Terman to Henry Herbert Goddard, March 29, 1917, Goddard Papers, Box 615.

18. Lewis Terman to Robert Yerkes, May 2, 1917, Yerkes Papers, Box 46, file 907.

19. So effective were psychologists at preserving the illusion of wartime unity that historians only recently have recognized how deeply divided they were. See von Mayrhauser, "The Manager, the Medic and the Mediator," pp. 128–58.

20. Robert Yerkes, war diary, January 23, 1918, and January 11, 1919, Yerkes Papers, Box 171, file 2663; see also Winthrop D. Lane to Henry Herbert Goddard, October 31, 1917, and Goddard's reply, November 10, 1917, Goddard Papers, Box 615. Lane was editor of *The Survey* magazine.

21. "Proceedings of the American Psychological Association," *School and Society*, February 12, 1916, cited in *The Training School Bulletin*, September 1916, p. 114.

22. See the correspondence between Lewis Terman and the Houghton Mifflin Company, 1919–1927, on permissions to reprint test material, Terman Papers, Box 20, file 11; and the lengthy correspondence between Terman and the popular science writer Albert E. Wiggam, Terman Papers, Box 16, file 12.

23. Robert Yerkes, war diary, March 17, 1918, Yerkes Papers, Box 171, file 2663.

24. "March of the Psychos," *Camplife Chickamauga*, clipping, Yerkes Papers, Box 94, file 1782.

25. Robert Yerkes, war diary, June 20 and 25, 1918, Yerkes Papers, Box 171, file 2663.

26. "Examiner's Guide for Psychological Examining in the Army," 2d ed., July 1918, in Yoakum and Yerkes, *Army Mental Tests*, pp. 58 ff.

27. Robert Yerkes, war diary, September 22, 1918, Yerkes Papers, Box 171, file 2663, p. 142.

28. Robert Yerkes, war diary, March 16, 1919, Yerkes Papers, Box 172, file 2664.

29. Illinois senator Lawrence Sherman, *Congressional Record*, 65th Congress, 2d Session, p. 9877 (September 3, 1918), cited in Jonçich, *The Sane Positivist*, p. 435.

30. Robert M. Yerkes, "Report of the Psychology Committee of the National Research Council," *Psychological Review* 26 (1919): 149; Raymond Dodge, "Mental Engineering During the War," *Review of Reviews* 59 (1919): 504–8, and "Mental Engineering After the War."

31. On the split between Yerkes's National Research Council Committee and Walter Dill Scott's Committee on Classification of Personnel, see von Mayrhauser, "The Manager, the Medic and the Mediator." On cooperation, see Yoakum and Yerkes, *Army Mental Tests*, p. 204; Edward L. Thorndike, "Intelligence and Its Uses," *Harper's*, January 1920, pp. 227–35; Dodge, "Mental Engineering During the War"; Walter V. Bingham, "Cooperative Business Research," *Annals of the American Academy of Political and Social Sciences* 110 (1923): 179–89; Goddard, *Human Efficiency and Levels of Intelligence*, p. 46.

32. Taylor, *The Principles of Scientific Management*, p. 140.

33. "The National Reachers Council," unsigned manuscript, not attributed, Cattell Papers, Box 85.

34. Lewis Terman to Mr. E. R. Parker, sales representative in Atlanta for the World Book Company, September 25, 1920, Terman Papers, Box 20, file 18.

35. Henry H. Goddard to Dr. H. W. Chase, November 28, 1917, Goddard Papers, Box M614.

36. Goddard, *Human Efficiency and Levels of Intelligence*, p. 28. See also pp. vii, 8, 10, 34, 46, 116. See Cattell, "Examinations, Grades and Credits," p. 367; Terman, *The Measurement of Intelligence*, p. 4.

37. Goddard, *Human Efficiency and Levels of Intelligence*, p. vii.

38. Thorndike, "Intelligence and Its Uses"; see also Robert Yerkes, war diary, March 16, 1919, Yerkes Papers, Box 172, file 2664.

39. Yoakum and Yerkes, *Army Mental Tests*, p. vii, citing a January 25, 1919, speech. This recalls Goddard's disputes with psychiatrists and physicians. See Zenderland, "The Debate over Diagnosis," pp. 46–74.

40. Goddard, *Human Efficiency and Levels of Intelligence*, p. 34.

41. Bellamy, *Looking Backward 2000–1887*, p. 129.

42. Yoakum and Yerkes, *Army Mental Tests*, pp. 25, 34, 35.

43. Thorndike, "Measurement in Education," p. 1.

44. Rudolph Pintner, "The Significance of Intelligence Testing in the Elementary School," in *Twenty-first Yearbook of the National Society for the Study of Education*, ed. Whipple, pp. 163, 167.

45. See Walter Lippmann's articles in *The New Republic*: "The Mental Age of Americans"; "The Mystery of the 'A' Men"; "The Abuse of the Tests," 32 (1922): 297–98; "A Future for the Tests"; reply from Lewis Terman, "The Great Conspiracy, or the Impulse Imperious of Intelligence Testers Exposed by Mr. Lippmann," 33 (1922): 116–20; discussion, 33 (1922): 145–46, 33 (1923): 201–2, 33 (1923); Lippmann's rejoinder, "Judgment of the Tests," 34 (1923): 322–23. See also the correspondence between Robert Yerkes and Walter Lippmann, Yerkes Papers, and the correspondence between Terman and his publishers about the debate, Terman Papers.

46. Layton, *The Revolt of the Engineers*, pp. 154–78; Tyack, *The One Best System*.

47. R. C. Maclaurin, "Educational and Industrial Efficiency," *Science* 33 (1911): 101–3.

48. "Measuring the Mind," *Nation* 94 (1912): 486.

49. Alfred Binet, cited by Clara Harrison Town, "The Binet-Simon Scale and the Psychologist," *The Psychological Clinic* 5 (1912): 239–44. It is interesting to note that the weight scale, like the thermometer, is both an engineering and a medical tool.

50. "No Psychology in Law," *Literary Digest* 53 (1916): 405, cited in Kevles, "Testing the Army's Intelligence."

51. Thomas J. McCormack, "A Critique of Mental Measurements," *School and Society* 15 (1922): 689.

52. Ibid., p. 688.

53. John Dewey, "Education as Engineering," *The New Republic* 22 (1922): 90.

54. "Soothing Syrup of Psychology," *Living Age* 283 (1914): 573–75.

55. Lippmann, "The Mental Age of Americans" and "A Future for the Tests."

56. Whipple, "The Intelligence Testing Program and Its Objectors—Conscientious and Otherwise," pp. 561–68, 600. Note how the title capitalizes linguistically on the military's prestige.

57. Henry Herbert Goddard to Andrew W. Brown, chairman, Clinical Section of the American Psychological Association, February 15, 1933, Goddard Papers, Box M32, file "Brown Correspondence." See also Edward Lee Thorndike, *The Measurement of Intelligence*

(New York: Teachers College, Columbia University, 1927), p. 79: sample test item, "There was a painter who became a physician, whereupon a citizen said to him: 'You have done well; for before the faults of your work were seen but now they are unseen.'—Francis Bacon."

58. Terman, "The Conservation of Talent," pp. 359–64. "Coué formula" refers to the popular teachings of French psychotherapist Emile Coué, whose system of healing through autosuggestion caused him to promulgate the phrase, "Every day in every way I am getting better and better."

59. Lewis Terman, editor's introduction to Virgil Dickson, *Mental Tests and the Classroom Teacher* (Yonkers-on-Hudson, N.Y.: World Book Company, 1926), p. xiv; Dickson, *Mental Tests*, p. 224; Terman, editor's introduction to Dickson, *Mental Tests*, p. xiv.

Chapter Eight
The *Lingua Franca* of Progressivism

1. See Rodgers, "In Search of Progressivism," p. 126; Neil Harris, "The Lamp of Learning: Popular Lights and Shadows," in *The Organization of Knowledge in Modern America, 1860–1920*, ed. Alexandra Oleson and John Voss (Baltimore: Johns Hopkins University Press, 1979).

2. J. M. Ziman, *Public Knowledge: An Essay Concerning the Social Dimension of Science* (London: Cambridge University Press, 1968), p. 34; Walter Dill Scott, *Increasing Human Efficiency in Business: A Contribution to the Psychology of Business* (New York: Macmillan, 1911), p. 7.

3. Terman, *The Measurement of Intelligence*, p. 4; Goddard, *Human Efficiency and Levels of Intelligence*, p. vii.

4. Dodge, "Mental Engineering During the War," p. 506.

5. Pearson, *The Grammar of Science*, p. 19.

6. Guy Whipple, *Thirty-seventh Yearbook of the National Society for the Study of Education*, 1938, 2:260, citing Edward Thorndike, *Fifth Yearbook of the National Society for the Study of Education*, 1906, 1:81–82.

7. Truman Lee Kelley, *Scientific Method: Its Function in Research and in Education* (Columbus: Ohio State University Press, 1929), pp. 41, 40.

8. George Strayer, director, *Report of a Survey of the School System of Saint Paul*, Minnesota (St. Paul: City Council, 1917), p. 262.

9. Joseph Peterson, *Early Conceptions and Tests of Intelligence* (Yonkers-on-Hudson, N.Y.: World Book Company, 1925), p. 157.

10. Trabue and Stockbridge, *Measure Your Mind*, pp. 13–14.

11. Thorndike, "Educational Diagnosis," p. 142.

12. *Education in Twelve Cape Towns: A Study for the Cape Cod Chamber of Congress by Members of the Staff of the Graduate School of Education, Harvard University* (Norwood, Mass.: Ambrose Press, 1927), pp. 7–8.

13. Layton, *The Revolt of the Engineers*, p. 57.

14. See Geison, ed., *Professions and Professional Ideologies*, p. 3; Lubove, *The Professional Altruist*, p. 121; Talcott Parsons, "The Professions and Social Structure," in *Essays in Sociological Theory*, ed. Parsons; Starr, *The Social Transformation of American Medicine*, p. 191; Haskell, *The Emergence of Professional Social Science*; Abbott, *The System of Professions*.

15. Starr, *The Social Transformation of American Medicine*, p. 12.

16. Callahan, *Education and the Cult of Efficiency* (1962), p. 112; on the national census and the social power of quantification, see Cohen, *A Calculating People*. On the school survey movement, see Tyack, *The One Best System*, and Chapman, *Schools as Sorters*, pp. 39–64.

17. Wiebe, *Search for Order, 1877–1920*, pp. 40–41. On the growth of professional associations, see Cattell, "Our Psychological Association and Research" and "The Psychological Corporation," *Annals of the American Academy of Political and Social Science* 110 (1923): 165–71; Samuel W. Fernberger, "The American Psychological Association, a Historical Summary, 1892–1930," *Psychological Bulletin* 29 (1932): 1–89.

18. George Strayer, *The Gary Public Schools* (New York: General Education Board, 1918).

19. Cassedy, *American Medicine and Statistical Thinking 1800–1860*.

20. Wiebe, *Search for Order, 1877–1920*, pp. 40–41.

21. Theodore Roosevelt, introduction to McCarthy, *The Wisconsin Idea*, p. viii.

22. McCarthy, *The Wisconsin Idea*; Cohen, *A Calculating People*.

23. McCarthy, *The Wisconsin Idea*, pp. 124–25, citing Frederick Jackson Turner.

24. See Boyer, *Urban Masses and Moral Order*, on the "quantification of vice" in the white slavery investigations during this period. Clearly, my own figures of speech ("information fever") and alternating voices are subject to the same critique that I am directing at the psychologists.

25. For an extended analysis of this kind of empiricism among twentieth-century intellectuals, see Robert Booth Fowler, *Believing Skeptics: American Political Intellectuals, 1945–1964* (Westport, Conn.: Greenwood Press, 1978). Fowler examines the roots of liberal skepticism in Progressive-Era political thought.

26. J. Harold Williams, "Backward and Feeble-minded Children in Salt Lake City," *The Training School Bulletin*, September 1915, p. 123.

27. Frank W. Ballou, "The Significance of Educational Measurements," *Journal of Education*, July 16, 1914, pp. 74–76.

28. Garber, *Current Activities*, p. 152.

29. Charles S. Meek, "Report to the National Council," *National Education Association Proceedings*, 1913, pp. 376–80, cited in Callahan, *Education and the Cult of Efficiency* (1962), p. 113.

30. Callahan, *Education and the Cult of Efficiency* (1962), pp. 112–20.

31. In Portland, Oregon, between 1902 and 1912, average daily school attendance doubled, while the school budget increased sixfold. See Cubberley, *Report of the Survey of the Public School System of School District No.1, Multnomah County, Oregon*, p. xv.

32. Jeremiah E. Burke, superintendent, Boston Public Schools, *Annual Report of the Superintendent, October 1925* (Boston: Printing Department, 1925), p. 96.

33. See George Strayer, director, *Report of the Survey of the Schools of Holyoke, Massachusetts* (Holyoke, Mass.: Unity Press, 1930), pp. 240–41.

34. Paul H. Hanus, director, *Report on a Survey of Certain Aspects of the Lancaster, Pennsylvania City School District* (Cambridge, Mass.: Graduate School of Education, Harvard University, 1924–1925), p. 39.

35. Cubberley, *Report of the Survey of the Public School System of School District No. 1, Multnomah County, Oregon*, p. 146. See Lawrence W. Cremin, *The Wonderful World of Ellwood Patterson Cubberley: An Essay on the Historiography of American Public Education* (New York: Bureau of Publications, Teachers College, Columbia University, 1965), p. 4; see also Ellwood P. Cubberley, *Public Education in the United States* (Boston: Houghton Mifflin, 1919).

36. Charles E. Chadsey, director, *Survey of the Peoria Public Schools* (Peoria, Ill.: Schwab Print, 1924), p. 91; see also the Lancaster survey, p. 39.

37. Burke, *Annual Report of the Superintendent, October 1925*, p. 96.

38. Buffalo Municipal Research Bureau, Inc., *Report of the Buffalo School Survey*, 1931, pp. 87–88, 129.

39. Callahan, *Education and the Cult of Efficiency* (1962), p. 115.

40. Williams, "Backward and Feeble-minded Children," p. 129. On the particularly successful efforts in school dentistry, see Schlossman, Brown, and Sedlak, *Preventive Dentistry and American Public Education*.

41. H. L. Smith and Charles H. Judd, eds., *Plans for Organizing School Surveys, Thirteenth Yearbook of the National Society for the Study of Education* (Chicago: University of Chicago Press, 1914), pt. 2, p. 31.

42. Ellwood P. Cubberley, director, *Report of the Survey of the Public School System of Salt Lake City, Utah*, June 30, 1915, p. 212.

43. Geraldine Jonçich, ed., *Psychology and the Science of Education* (New York: Teachers College Press, 1962), p. 15.

44. Hanus, *Report on a Survey of Certain Aspects of the Lancaster, Pennsylvania City School District*, pt. 2, p. 38; pt. 3, p. 57.

45. See, for example, Cubberley, *Report of the Survey of the Public School System of School District No. 1, Multnomah County, Oregon*; idem, *Report of the Survey of the Public School System of Salt Lake City, Utah*, pp. 212–14; Strayer, *Report of a Survey of the School System of Saint Paul, Minnesota*; Hanus, *Report on a Survey of Certain Aspects of the Lancaster, Pennsylvania City School District*, pp. 78, 80; George Strayer, director, *Report of a Survey of the Schools of Lynn, Massachusetts* (New York: Teachers College, Columbia University, 1927), p. 199; Buffalo Municipal Research Bureau, Inc., *Report of the Buffalo School Survey*, pp. 87–88, 98, 129; Strayer, *Report of the Survey of the Schools of Holyoke, Massachusetts*, p. 298.

46. Marion R. Trabue, "The Uses of Intelligence Tests in Junior High Schools," in *Twenty-first Yearbook of the National Society for the Study of Education*, pt. 2, pp. 178–79.

47. George Strayer, director, *Report of the Survey of the Schools of Closter, New Jersey* (New York: Institute of Educational Research, Division of Field Studies, Teachers College, Columbia University, February 1928), p. 103.

48. United States Bureau of Education, *Cities Reporting the Use of Homogeneous Grouping and of the Winnetka Technique and the Dalton Plan*, School Leaflet 22 (Washington, D.C.: Government Printing Office, 1926), pp. 1–11; Lewis Terman to Caspar Hodgson, World Book Company, October 15, 1923, Terman Papers, Box 20, file 19; James McKeen Cattell, copy of address to the Pacific Division of the American Association for the Advancement of Science, Cattell Papers, Box 85, file "Miscellany," p. 1. Michael Schudson cites a figure ten times higher, based on a 1947 estimate by Douglas Scates, but this figure includes achievement tests, which were administered more than once to each child. See Schudson, "Organizing the 'Meritocracy,'" p. 49; Douglas E. Scates, "Fifty Years of Objective Measurement and Research in Education," *Journal of Educational Research* 41 (1947): 249.

49. Terman to Hodgson, October 15, 1923.

50. Barnes, "Feeble-mindedness as a Cause for Homelessness," pp. 10–11. Rudimentary, nonstandardized achievement tests, and anthropometric tests taken in tandem with medical inspections, had been in place since the 1890s.

51. Warren K. Layton, "The Group Intelligence Testing Program of the Detroit Public Schools," in *Twenty-first Yearbook of the National Society for the Study of Education*.

52. Lewis Terman to Mr. E. R. Parker, September 25, 1920, Terman Papers, Box 20, file 18.

53. Boston Public Schools, *Report on Age and Progress of Pupils in the Boston Public Schools: School Document #12–1925* (Boston: Printing Department, 1925), p. 53.

54. Division of Education, Clemson Agricultural College, *Public School Survey of Oconee County, South Carolina* (Clemson, S.C.: author, June 1923).

55. George Strayer, director, *Report of the Survey of Certain Aspects of the Public School System of Springfield, Massachusetts, School Year 1923–4*, p. 160; Chadsey, *Survey of the Peoria Public Schools*, pp. 91–92; memorandum, Trenton Public Schools, Department of Educational Research and Efficiency, September 9, 1925, Vineland Research Laboratory Papers, Box M935, Archives of the History of American Psychology; Buffalo Municipal Research Bureau, Inc., *Report of the Buffalo School Survey*, p. 75; Chapman, *Schools as Sorters*. On hospital charts, see S. Weir Mitchell, "The Early History of Instrumental Precision in Medicine," *Transactions of the Congress of American Physicians and Surgeons* 2 (1891): 159–98; Warner, *The Therapeutic Perspective*, pp. 154–55.

56. See correspondence, Terman Papers, Box 12.

57. See the continued usage of both engineering and medical terms in the standard textbook used in teacher-education graduate schools, N. L. Gage and David C. Berliner, *Educational Psychology* (New York: Rand McNally College Publishing, 1975), introduction. Gage and Berliner also introduce an ecological metaphor throughout to reconcile controversial positions on "nature" versus "nurture."

✤ Bibliographic Essay ✤

The linguistic turn in American historiography is not new. As Peter Novick has shown in his brilliant study of the "objectivity question" in historical scholarship, the historiography of the interwar years (1918–1945) absorbed and reformulated relativist and pragmatic philosophies that included early work on the "fictive nature of abstractions" and "ambiguities of meanings," with implications for both semantics and historiography (Peter Novick, *That Noble Dream: The "Objectivity Question" and the American Historical Profession* [New York: Cambridge University Press, 1988], pp. 161–62). Novick discusses here Walter Lippmann's challenge, ca. 1922, to the journalistic ideal of objectivity, a challenge of a piece with Lippmann's attack on mental testing the same year. See Walter Lippmann, *Public Opinion* (1922), as discussed in Michael Schudson, *Discovering the News: A Social History of American Newspapers* (New York: Basic Books, 1978), pp. 135–58. A fuller discussion of the linguistic turn necessarily would explore in greater depth this period of relativist challenge to the scientific model of objective historical scholarship. An intelligent consideration of relativist social-scientific concepts of "culture" is John Shanklin Gilkeson's essay "The Domestication of 'Culture' in Interwar America, 1919–1941," in *The Estate of Social Knowledge*, ed. JoAnne Brown and David van Keuren (Baltimore: Johns Hopkins University Press, 1991). See also H. Blumer, *Symbolic Interactionism: Perspective and Method* (Englewood Cliffs, N.J.: Prentice-Hall, 1969); Warren Susman, "The Culture of the Thirties," in his *Culture as History: The Transformation of American Society in the Twentieth Century* (New York: Pantheon, 1984); Morton White, *Social Thought in America: The Revolt Against Formalism* (New York: Viking Press, 1949); Novick, *That Noble Dream*, chap. 6. On postwar empiricism, see Robert Booth Fowler, *Believing Skeptics: American Political Intellectuals, 1945–1964* (Westport, Conn.: Greenwood Press, 1978). Other authors have undertaken the historiographic chronicle, notably John Toews in a 1987 review article entitled "Intellectual History After the Linguistic Turn: The Autonomy of Meaning and the Irreducibility of Experience" (*American Historical Review* 92 [1987]: 879–907).

Not all of the currents in the linguistic turn have been relativistic. In 1969 Robert Berkhofer, Jr., called for a new approach to the practice of history, an approach informed by behavioral theory and the methods of social science (Robert F. Berkhofer, Jr., *A Behavioral Approach to Historical Analysis* [New York: The Free Press, 1969], pp.

147–51). Among his suggestions was a call for a new method, "historical semantics," that would have historians consider critically the nature of the linguistic evidence in which they trade. Berkhofer argued that traditional, unscientific practices, and a commonsensical approach to the written word as evidence, were hampering historical analysis by perpetuating sloppy, unsystematic thought about the intellectual and social importance of language. Berkhofer suggested (albeit sketchily) that historians delve into linguistic philosophy, semiotics, and literary criticism to glean useful historiographic rules about the interpretation of written artifacts in relation to past social structures as well as to the history of ideas. Berkhofer's eclectic approach suggested that most of the disciplines, and not literature and linguistics alone, offer insight into language that might be useful to historians. Most historians interested in these problems, however, have since chosen either a literary or an anthropological basis for their methods. See in this vein Roger Chartier, "Texts, Printings, Readings," on book production, in *The New Cultural History: Essays by Aletta Biersack et al.*, ed. Lynn Hunt (Berkeley: University of California Press, 1989); see also Cathy Davidson, *Revolution and the Word: The Rise of the Novel in America* (New York: Oxford University Press, 1986).

Since the early 1960s, in the field of political history, J.G.A. Pocock has argued powerfully for a more complex approach to the related concepts of political language, thought, and action. See especially Pocock, *Politics, Language and Time: Essays on Political Thought and History* (New York: Atheneum, 1971). Pocock and his British colleague Quentin Skinner have urged that past language replace past thought as the subject of intellectual historians' inquiry. Such a focal shift would help place the history of ideas in the context of past social life and, they argue, possibly rescue it from its elitist, ephemeral, and esoteric tendencies. See Hannah Arendt, *On Revolution* (Cambridge, Mass.: Harvard University Press, 1963); Pocock, *Politics, Language and Time*, and his *The Machiavellian Moment: Florentine Political Thought and the Atlantic Republican Tradition* (Princeton: Princeton University Press, 1975); Quentin Skinner, "Meaning and Understanding in the History of Ideas," *History and Theory* 8 (1969): 3–53; Skinner, "Some Problems in the Analysis of Thought and Action," *Political Theory* 2 (1974): 277–303; Jean-Christophe Agnew, *Worlds Apart: The Market and Theater in Anglo-American Thought, 1550–1750* (New York: Cambridge University Press, 1986). Bernard Bailyn's important *Ideological Origins of the American Revolution* (Cambridge, Mass.: Harvard University Press, 1967) and Perry Miller's discussions of "calling," "profession," "errand," and "covenant" in *Errand into the Wilderness* (New York: Harper and Row, 1956) are compatible with, if not derived from, this movement toward a socialized, language-based definition of intellectual history. See also more recently Dorothy Ross, *The Origins of American Social Science* (New York: Cambridge University Press, 1991). In the same Anglo-American tradition, David Hollinger's 1977 Wingspread essay, "Historians and the Discourse of Intellectuals" (in *New Directions in American Intellectual History*, ed. John Higham and Paul Conkin [Baltimore: Johns Hopkins University Press, 1979]), lays out the far-reaching implications of semantic analysis for intellectual historians. Hollinger brings to his colleagues' attention the crucial insight that linguists and philosophers have long taken for granted: "Discourse is a social as well as intellectual activity; it entails interaction between minds, and it revolves around something possessed in common" (see again Hollinger, "Historians and the Discourse of Intellectuals," pp. 42–43). Stefan Collini argues similarly for the importance of social context to the historical study of intellectual discourse in his study of L. T. Hobhouse, *Liberalism and Sociology: L. T. Hobhouse and Political Argument in England, 1880–1914* (Cambridge: Cambridge University Press, 1979). Collini's work is a fine early example of linguistic theory applied to the history of the social sciences. Collini argues that one of the vital imperatives of a socially grounded intellectual history is the uncovering of the "context of refutation" in which past intellectuals worked. (Collini further notes that "while we constantly need to be reminded that the past is another country where they speak . . . a foreign language, the impassability of the divide can be exaggerated. . . . [Foreign languages] are among the things that historians, like other children, can learn." Stefan Collini, *Liberalism and Sociology*, pp. 1–11.) Intellectuals live in social worlds and respond not only to the legacy of ideas that undergird their intellectual work, but to the social, cultural, economic, and political spectacle that they daily observe as participants. In the case of the psychologists who invented and advertised the measurement of intelligence, the context of refutation included the late-nineteenth-century emergence of psychology from philosophy and religion; the labor unrest and extreme concentration of wealth characteristic of the postbellum years; the strains of anti-intellectualism found in populist and socialist ideologies; and the visible demographic changes brought on by massive immigration and internal migration in the United States between 1890 and 1926. Like other progressive reforms, intelligence testing was offered up by its proponents as a refutation both of the excesses of laissez-faire capitalism and of the excesses of socialism.

The literature on progressivism is massive, but several works stand out: Daniel Rodgers' essay "In Search of Progressivism" (*Reviews in American History* 10 [1982]: 113–32) reviews and improves the historiography. Other very useful studies, apart from the histories of progressive education, include Richard Hofstadter, *The Age of Reform* (New York: Knopf, 1955); Samuel P. Hays, *Conservation and the Gospel of Efficiency: The Progressive Conservation Movement, 1890–1920* (Cambridge, Mass.: Harvard University Press, 1959); Samuel Haber, *Efficiency and Uplift: Scientific Management in the Progressive Era* (Chicago: University of Chicago Press, 1964); Robert Wiebe, *Search for Order, 1877–1920* (New York: Hill and Wang, 1967); Charles Forcey, *The Crossroads of Liberalism: Croly, Weyl, Lippmann, and the Progressive Era, 1900–1925* (New York: Oxford University Press, 1967); David J. Rothman, *Conscience and Convenience: The Asylum and Its Alternatives in Progressive America* (Boston: Little, Brown, 1980); Robert M. Crunden, *Ministers of Reform: The Progressive Achievement in American Civilization* (New York: Basic Books, 1982).

One important institutional context for the psychologists' professionalizing activities was the increasingly formalized articulation between research universities and the newly consolidated public schools. (Corporations, the military, courts of law, and universities are the other major settings in which administrators used mental tests to reorganize and "rationalize" existing selection processes.) Yet, this formal articulation by which the mental capacities of students—future workers—were determined, described, and allocated into the corporate system was not merely a response to a preexisting system of capitalist production, but also a thoroughgoing transformation of that system. On the role of personnel (aptitude) testing and intelligence testing in late-nineteenth- and early-twentieth-century corporate capitalism, see David F. Noble, *America by Design: Science, Technology and the Rise of Corporate Capitalism* (New York: Knopf, 1977). It is not my purpose in this book to prove that IQ testing was both cause and effect of the corporate consolidations of the late twentieth century, but rather to describe the logical system that encouraged psychologists and their clientele in the public schools to invest the testing enterprise with such a transformative potential. I am not sure how one would "prove" such a phenomenon, unless to construct a comparative study of the United States and the Soviet Union, an intriguing possibility. I therefore assert that there was no linear cause-and-effect relation between testing and capitalism, but a circular reinforcement of one by the other. The abundant literature on the history of education during this period attests to this circular condition of reform and social propaganda, and forms a link between intellectual and social histories. The most important of these secondary works are Lawrence Cremin's comprehensive *The Transformation of the School: Progressivism in American Education, 1876–1957* (New York: Knopf, 1961); Raymond E. Callahan, *Education and the Cult of Efficiency: A Study of the Social Forces That Have Shaped the Administration of the Public Schools* (Chicago: University of Chicago Press, 1962), on curricular reform and school practice; David B. Tyack, *The One Best System: A History of American Urban Education* (Cambridge, Mass.: Harvard University Press, 1974), on urban schools; Merle Curti, *The Social Ideas of American Educators* (Totowa, N.J.: Littlefield, Adams, 1935, 1959), on ideologies of pedagogical reform; Berenice Fisher, *Industrial Education* (1967); and Noble, *America by Design*, on education and corporate social policy. On the eighteenth and nineteenth centuries, see Rush Welter, *Popular Education and Democratic Thought in America* (New York: Columbia University Press, 1969); Lawrence Cremin, *American Education: The National Experience, 1783–1876* (New York: Harper and Row, 1980); and Carl F. Kaestle, *Pillars of the Republic: Common Schools and American Society, 1780–1860* (New York: Hill and Wang, 1984). I would argue that one reason for the plethora of work on education in the Progressive Era is the very centrality of education to the progressive ethos.

Like intellectual historians, social historians in the United States have begun to think about language. (This discussion focuses primarily on historians who work in and on the United States. The European story is different.) Interestingly, social historians of education have paid little attention to language in spite of there being a large critical literature on metaphor, curriculum, and educational policy. See, for example, the policy work of Steven Selden, including "Curricular Metaphors: From Science to Symbolism," *Educational Theory* 25 (1975): 243–62; Israel Scheffler, *The Language of Education* (Springfield, Ill.: Charles C. Thomas, 1960); Herbert M. Kliebard, "Bureaucracy and Curriculum Theory," in *Freedom, Bureaucracy and Schooling, 1971 Yearbook of the Association for Supervision and Curriculum Development*, ed. Vernon Haubrich (Washington, D.C.: Association for Supervision and Curriculum Development, 1971); Francis Schrag, "Teaching/Healing: The Medical Analogy," *Teachers College Record* 72 (1971): 594–604.

The relationships between social structures and ideas have been approached in a different manner by those social historians who have incorporated linguistic theories into their work. In his superb book *The Work Ethic in Industrial America, 1850–1920* (Chicago: University of Chicago Press, 1974), Daniel T. Rodgers has documented "work rhetoric" as a vital activity in the development of modern work-culture. In his well-known review essay "In Search of Progressivism" Rodgers furthers these insights by describing the amalgam known as progressivism as a series of languages, which then allows him to link these vocabularies both to one another and to the social factors they entail. Rodgers' more recent *Contested Truths: Keywords in American Politicals Since Independence* (New York: Basic Books, 1987), based in part on Raymond Williams' work *Keywords: A Vocabulary of Culture and Society*, rev. ed. (New York: Oxford University Press, 1985), is less satisfying as social history because language is treated as isolated words rather than as a web of metaphorical relations referring to social conditions and lived experiences. In a study of African-American folk culture, Lawrence Levine adopts the sociolinguistics of William Labov, and borrows methods from critical theory, to analyze "texts" that include work songs, religious music, games, and rituals (Lawrence W. Levine, *Black Culture and Black Consciousness* [New York: Oxford University Press, 1977], esp. pp. 138–54, "The Language of Freedom"). John Mack Farragher uses linguistic theory even more explicitly in decoding diaries from the nineteenth century, in *Women and Men on the Overland Trail* (New Haven: Yale University Press, 1979), applying Basil Bernstein's "restricted" and "elaborated" categories of language to his analysis of gender-specific experience during the westward migration. Drew Gilpin Faust's recent work on Confederate women and the narratives of war is among the best-realized U.S. social histories in this genre (Drew Gilpin Faust, "Altars of Sacrifice: Confederate Women and the Narratives of War," *Journal of American History* 76 [1990]: 1200–1228).

Historians of science, influenced by the sociology of knowledge and philosophy of language, have tended to conflate language with other symbolic representations in ways that are quite useful to the case for considering language as a basic form of social action. Those historians of science steeped in the philosophy of science tend to see language as a broad and complex intellectual and social activity, somewhat more so than do historians in other fields. Thomas Kuhn's influential work *The Structure of Scientific Revolutions*, which hinges on the concepts entailed in the "paradigm," can also be read as a contemplation on the social and epistemological roles of analogical language in science, and indeed Kuhn himself has reread the work in this way. See Thomas S. Kuhn, "Reflections on My Critics," in *Criticism and the Growth of Knowledge*, ed. Imre Lakatos and Alan Musgrave (Cambridge: Cambridge University Press, 1970), p. 277. See also Thomas S. Kuhn, "Metaphor in Science," in *Metaphor and Thought*, ed. Andrew Ortony (New York: Cambridge University Press, 1979); Mary Brenda Hesse, *Models and Analogies in Science* (1963; Notre Dame, Ind.: University of Notre Dame Press, 1966); Kenneth Burke, *Permanence and Change: An Anatomy of Purpose* (Indianapolis: Bobbs-Merrill, 1954), chap. 4; Susanne Langer, *Philosophy in a New Key: A Study of the Symbolism of Reason, Rite and Art* (1942; New York: New American Library, 1951); Donald A.

Schön, *Displacement of Concepts* (London: Tavistock, 1963), pp. 191–99; Schön, "Generative Metaphor: A Perspective on Problem-Setting in Social Policy," in *Metaphor and Thought*, ed. Ortony; the entire Ortony volume is useful. On Kuhn's sweeping influence among historians, in the context of antipositivism, see Arthur Danto, *Narration and Knowledge* (1985); see also Novick, *That Noble Dream*, chap. 15, 'The Center Does Not Hold."

The history and philosophy of science have also produced strong scholarship on the epistemological history of particular scientific terms and models. In her book *Models and Analogies in Science* (New York and London: Sheed and Ward, 1963), pp. 2–5, citing M. R. Campbell, *Physics, The Elements* (1920), p. 129, Mary Brenda Hesse argues that analogies, including metaphors, are not mere aids to scientific thinking; they are the essence of theory. Without analogies, she argues, "theories would be completely valueless and unworthy of the name." In this stance, Hesse challenged received wisdom on the status of metaphor, as articulated by Pierre Duhem. According to Duhem, analogies, models, and metaphors were mere stimuli to imagination, with no permanent significance to the theories they helped generate.

The social policy dimensions of metaphor are discussed by Donald Schön, David O. Edge, and Murray Edelman, all of whom have emphasized the stultifying effects of metaphor in the framing of policy questions, where the semantics of question-framing create heuristic limitations in advance. Langer also considers aspects of this problem in *Philosophy in a New Key*.

Symbols other than language are also pertinent to these conversations. Kuhn's term "paradigm" was apparently borrowed from Gombrich's work. Norwood Russell Hansen's *Patterns of Discovery* (Cambridge: Cambridge University Press, 1958) and Rudolf Arnheim's *Visual Thinking* (Berkeley: University of California Press, 1969) explore the cognitive dimensions of visual representation. Victor W. Turner's *Dramas, Fields, and Metaphors: Symbolic Action in Human Society* (Ithaca, N.Y.: Cornell University Press, 1974) represents salient anthropological work in this realm, as does the honorary historian Clifford Geertz's *Interpretation of Cultures: Selected Essays* (New York: Basic Books, 1973). See Donald Schön, *Displacement of Concepts* (New York: Humanities Press, 1963); David O. Edge, "Technological Metaphor and Social Control," *New Literary History* 6 (1974–1975): 135–47; Murray Edelman, *Political Language: Words That Succeed and Policies That Fail* (New York: Academic Press, 1977), esp. chap. 4 on medical language in social welfare policy; R. H. Brown, "Social Theory as Metaphor," *Theory and Society* 3 (1976): 169–98. On discovery, invention, and question-framing see Langer, *Philosophy in a New Key*. See also

Ernst Cassirer, *Language and Myth* (New York: Dover, 1946); Max Black, *Models and Metaphors* (Ithaca, N.Y.: Cornell University Press, 1962); Andrew Ortony, "Why Metaphors Are Necessary and Not Just Nice," *Educational Theory* 25 (1975): 45–53. See also Novick, *That Noble Dream*, chap. 15.

Historians of the professions have also taken up the problems of language, influenced in part by the critical legal studies movement. Stephen Botein's study of religious symbolism among lawyers, Sanford Levinson's work on law as literature, Sybil Lipschultz's essay on social feminism and legal discourse, and Stanley Fish's essays on law, rhetoric, and the professions all take language seriously as historically significant social action. See Stephen Botein, "What We Shall Meet Afterwards in Heaven: Judgeship as a Symbol for Modern American Lawyers," in *Professions and Professional Ideologies in America*, ed. Gerald L. Geison (Chapel Hill: University of North Carolina Press, 1983); Sanford Levinson, "Law as Literature," in *The Authority of Experts: Studies in History and Theory*, ed. Thomas L. Haskell (Bloomington: Indiana University Press, 1984); Sybil Lipschultz, "Social Feminism and Legal Discourse, 1908–1923," *Law and Feminism* 2 (1989): 131–60. For more explicit discussions of language and profession, see Stanley Fish, *Doing What Comes Naturally: Change, Rhetoric, and the Practice of Theory in Literary and Legal Studies* (Durham, N.C.: Duke University Press, 1989); Kenneth Hudson, *The Jargon of the Professions* (London: Macmillan, 1978); Richard K. Fenn, *Liturgies and Trials: The Secularization of Religious Language* (Oxford: Basil Blackwell, 1982). These works are part of a broad revival of historical interest in the professions and the disciplines, signaled by the publication in the last fifteen years of several new theoretical works on professions, and several historical essays on the "division of expert labor" (Andrew Abbott, *The System of Professions: An Essay on the Division of Expert Labor* [Chicago: University of Chicago Press, 1988]).

Magali Sarfatti Larson, in *The Rise of Professionalism: A Sociological Analysis* (Berkeley: University of California Press, 1977), has met historians halfway by rooting her sociological analysis in the historical examples of medicine and engineering. Larson, a student of Everett Hughes and Eliot Freidson, has influenced two major collections of historical essays on the professions: Gerald Geison's edited volume *Professions and Professional Ideologies in America* and Thomas Haskell's *The Authority of Experts*. See also Burton Bledstein, *The Culture of Professionalism* (New York: Norton, 1976). Also indebted to Larson are Andrew Abbott, whose brilliant work *The System of Professions* takes in a broader spectrum of professional histories, and Paul Starr, another historical sociologist, whose work *The Social Transformation of American*

Medicine (New York: Basic Books, 1982) has synthesized most previous scholarship on the subject. Larson, Abbott, and Starr draw insight from thinkers as disparate as Marx and Parsons, continually gauging theory against historical record. They—particularly Abbott—distinguish themselves among scholars of professionalization not only by skillfully fusing two disciplines, but in steadfastly refusing to walk the beaten ideological paths of liberalism or its radical critiques. See Talcott Parsons, "The Professions and Social Structure" (1939), in his *Essays in Sociological Theory, Pure and Applied* (New York: The Free Press, 1954), pp. 34–49; Everett C. Hughes, *Men and Their Work* (New York: The Free Press, 1958); Hughes, "Professions," *Daedalus* 92: 655–68; Eliot Freidson, "The Theory of Professions," in *The Sociology of the Professions*, ed. R. Dingwall and P. Lewis (London: St. Martin's, 1983); Freidson, *Professional Powers* (Chicago: University of Chicago Press, 1986).

Of particular importance to this study, because of the metaphorical language of the psychologists, are the histories of engineering and medicine. On engineering, most useful have been Edwin T. Layton, Jr., *The Revolt of the Engineers* (Cleveland: The Press of Case Western Reserve University, 1971); Monte A. Calvert, *The Mechanical Engineer in America, 1830–1910* (Baltimore: Johns Hopkins University Press, 1967); Noble, *America by Design*.

The history of the social sciences has also flourished in recent years. The individual historical studies of particular disciplines are too numerous to discuss in detail here, but several synthetic works are worth noting. An excellent introduction is Dorothy Ross, "The Development of the Social Sciences," in *The Organization of Knowledge in Modern America, 1860–1920*, ed. Alexandra Oleson and John Voss (Baltimore: Johns Hopkins University Press, 1979). Mary O. Furner, *Advocacy and Objectivity: A Crisis in the Professionalization of American Social Science, 1865–1905* (Lexington: University of Kentucky Press, 1975), and Thomas L. Haskell, *The Emergence of Professional Social Science: The American Social Science Association and the Nineteenth Century Crisis of Authority* (Urbana: University of Illinois Press, 1977), have been augmented by Dorothy Ross's powerful synthesis, *The Origins of American Social Science*, in which she examines a profoundly ahistorical American social-scientific tradition as against the historically grounded social discourse of European disciplines. In Brown and van Keuren's edited volume *The Estate of Social Knowledge*, practitioners of the several social-scientific disciplines examine the histories and historiography of the human sciences from the interlocking perspectives of those disciplines. (This last collection grew out of the 1986 Summer Institute on the History of Social Scientific Inquiry at the Center for

Advanced Study in the Behavioral Sciences at Stanford, California, sponsored by the Mellon Foundation. See also George W. Stocking, Jr., and David E. Leary, "Summer Institute on the History of Social Scientific Inquiry," *ISIS* 78 [1987]: 76–79; Hamilton Cravens, "History of the Social Sciences," in *Historical Writing on American Social Science*, ed. Sally Gregory Kohlstedt and Margaret W. Rossiter, *Osiris* 8 [1985]: 183–207.)

The journal and case-study literature on the disciplinary histories of the social sciences is vast, and scattered among specialized disciplinary journals, although the synthetic volumes cited above attempt in different ways a more comprehensive approach. *Social Science History* and the *Journal of the History of the Behavioral Sciences* are useful, the former focusing largely on methods, the latter on history. Insightful essays on political science include: James Farr, "The History of Political Science," *American Journal of Political Science* 32 (1988): 1175–95; Stefan Collini, Donald Winch, and John Burrow, *That Noble Science of Politics: A Study in Nineteenth-Century Intellectual History* (Cambridge: Cambridge University Press, 1983); Quentin Skinner, *The Foundations of Modern Political Thought*, 2 vols. (Cambridge: Cambridge University Press, 1983). On sociology, see Robert S. Lynd, *Knowledge for What? The Place of Social Science in American Culture* (1939; Princeton: Princeton University Press, 1970); C. Wright Mills, *The Sociological Imagination* (London: Oxford University Press, 1959); Alvin Gouldner, *The Coming Crisis of Western Sociology* (London: Heineman, 1971); Jan Goldstein, "Foucault Among the Sociologists," *History and Theory* 23 (1984): 170–92; Henrika Kuklick, "Sociology's Past and Future: Prescriptive Implications of Historical Self-Consciousness in the School of Social Sciences," *Research in Sociology of Knowledge, Sciences and Art* 2 (1979): 73–85; Kuklick, "Restructuring the Past: Toward an Appreciation of the Social Context of Social Science," *Sociological Quarterly* 21 (1980): 5–21; Kuklick, "'Scientific Revolution': Sociological Theory in the United States, 1930–1945," *Sociological Inquiry* 43 (1971): 3–22; Kuklick, "Boundary Maintenance in American Sociology: Limitations to Academic 'Professionalization,'" *Journal of the History of the Behavioral Sciences* 16 (1980): 201–19. On geography, see W. G. Roy, "Time, Place, and People in History and Sociology: Boundary Definitions and the Logic of Inquiry," *Social Science History* 11 (1987): 53–62; A.R.H. Baker and D. Gregory, eds., *Explorations in Historical Geography: Interpretive Essays* (Cambridge: Cambridge University Press, 1984); D. Lowenthal and M. Bowden, eds., *Geography of the Mind* (New York: Oxford University Press, 1976); Neil Smith and Anne Godlewska, *Geography and Empire* (Oxford: Basil Blackwell, 1991). William Cronon's *Changes in the Land* (New York: Hill and Wang, 1983) brilliantly incorporates geography both as historical subject and as historiographic method. See also Dorothy Ross, "Historical Consciousness in Nineteenth Century America," *American Historical Review* 89 (1984), and her *Origins of American Social Science* on history and geography. Also useful is Stephen Kern, *The Culture of Time and Space, 1880–1918* (Cambridge, Mass.: Harvard University Press, 1983).

Important synthetic efforts in the history of anthropology include George S. Stocking, Jr., *Race, Culture and Evolution: Essays in the History of Anthropology* (Chicago: University of Chicago Press, 1968, 1982); Marvin Harris, *The Rise of Anthropological Theory* (1969), and *Cultural Materialism: The Struggle for a Science of Culture* (New York, 1980); James Clifford, *The Predicament of Culture: Twentieth-Century Ethnography, Literature, Art* (1988); Clifford Geertz, *Local Knowledge: Further Essays in Interpretive Anthropology* (New York, 1983); Geertz, *Interpretation of Cultures*. See also John S. Gilkeson, Jr., "The Domestication of 'Culture' in Interwar America," and David van Keuren, "From Natural History to Social Science," in *The Estate of Social Knowledge*, ed. Brown and van Keuren. Peter Novick's discussion of Geertz's influence is especially interesting, in *That Noble Dream*, pp. 551–55.

On the discipline of history, Novick's *That Noble Dream* analyzes the political and philosophical controversies engaging American historians since 1884, and the development of social structures of profession. John Higham's *History: Professional Scholarship in America* (Baltimore: Johns Hopkins University Press, 1983) helped frame many of Novick's questions. These two works, and Ross's *Origins of American Social Science*, are the most interesting and broadly inclusive of the histories of history in the United States; there seem to be, ironically, rather fewer thoughtful histories of this discipline than of others. See also Richard Hofstadter, *The Progressive Historians: Turner, Beard, Parrington* (New York, 1968); Berkhofer, *A Behavioral Approach to Historical Analysis*; Hayden White, "The Burden of History," *History and Theory* 5 (1966).

On the history of psychology, an unusually large literature exists; see especially David Hothersall, *History of Psychology* (Philadelphia: Temple University Press, 1984); Donald S. Napoli, *Architects of Adjustment* (1980); Hamilton Cravens, *The Triumph of Evolution: American Scientists and the Heredity-Environment Controversy 1900–1941* (Philadelphia: University of Pennsylvania Press, 1978); William R. Woodward and Mitchell G. Ash, eds., *The Problematic Science: Psychology in Nineteenth-Century Thought* (New York: Praeger, 1982); Thomas Pogue Weinland, "The History of the I.Q. in America, 1890–1941" (Ph.D. diss., Columbia University, 1970); Frank Addams Albrecht, Jr., "The New Psychology in America, 1880–1895" (Ph.D. diss., Johns Hopkins

University, 1960); Thomas M. Camfield, "Psychologists at War: The History of American Psychology and the First World War" (Ph.D. diss., University of Texas at Austin, 1969). Much of the history of psychology is biographical, reflecting the way in which each discipline's history is subject to its own disciplinary assumptions; these monographs are cited above where pertinent.

The history of mental testing also comprises a large literature; the bibliographies in Weinland's doctoral dissertation and in Paul Davis Chapman's *Schools as Sorters: Lewis M. Terman, Applied Psychology, and the Intelligence Testing Movement, 1890–1930* (New York: New York University Press, 1988) and *A Guide to Manuscript Collections in the History of Psychology and Related Areas*, ed. Michael Sokal and Patricia A. Rafail (New York: Kraus International, 1982) are useful starting points, along with the *Journal of the History of the Behavioral Sciences*. Historical accounts of mental testing are very uneven, often expressly written for polemical purposes as professional socialization for educational psychologists, or as policy criticism. With the exception of the work of Franz Samelson, Thomas Camfield, John Burnham, and Leila Zenderland, and a few others, the literature tends either to focus on developments within the intellectual traditions claimed by the psychological profession as its official history or to attack the testing enterprise as the ugliest face of capitalist schooling. For exemplary historical accounts connecting mental testing to broader historical contexts see John C. Burnham, "Psychology, Psychiatry, and the Progressive Movement," *American Quarterly* 12 (1960): 457–65; Thomas M. Camfield, "The Professionalization of American Psychology, 1870–1917," *Journal of the History of the Behavioral Sciences* 9 (1973): 66–75; Robert L. Church, "Educational Psychology and Social Reform in the Progressive Era," *History of Education Quarterly* 11 (1971): 390–405; Paula S. Fass, "The IQ: A Cultural and Historical Framework," *American Journal of Education* 88 (1980): 431–58; Daniel Kevles, "Testing the Army's Intelligence: Psychologists and the Military in World War I," *Journal of American History* 55 (1968): 565–81; Nicholas Pastore, "The Army Intelligence Tests and Walter Lippmann," *Journal of the History of the Behavioral Sciences* 14 (1978): 316–27; Franz Samelson, "Putting Psychology on the Map: Ideology and Intelligence Testing," in *Psychology in Social Context*, ed. Allan Buss (New York: Irvington Press, 1979); Leila Zenderland, "The Debate over Diagnosis: Henry Herbert Goddard and the Medical Acceptance of Intelligence Testing," in *Psychological Testing and American Society*, ed. Michael Sokal (New Brunswick, N.J.: Rutgers University Press, 1987), pp. 46–74. Many of the works are expressly driven by late-twentieth-century policy debates over the value of testing. Both the professional and antiprofessional perspectives are valuable—I am beholden to these scholars in many ways—but they address different, more specific historical issues from the ones that primarily concern me here. In the celebratory professional tradition, see Edwin G. Boring, *A History of Experimental Psychology* (New York: Appleton-Century-Crofts, 1950). In the antiprofessional tradition see Clarence Karier, "Testing for Order and Control in the Liberal State," in *The I.Q. Controversy*, ed. N. J. Block and Gerald Dworkin (New York: Random House, 1976) and entire volume; Stephen Jay Gould, *The Mismeasure of Man* (New York: Norton, 1981); Joel H. Spring, *Education and the Rise of the Corporate Order* (Boston: Beacon Press, 1972); Samuel Bowles and Herbert Gintis, *Schooling in Capitalist America* (New York: Basic Books, 1976); Leon J. Kamin, *The Science and Politics of I.Q.* (Potomac, Md.: Lawrence Erlbaum Associates, 1974).

Several scholarly works on the history of ideas surrounding mental testing are especially useful: Cravens, *The Triumph of Evolution*; Donald K. Pickens, *Eugenics and the Progressives* (Nashville: Vanderbilt University Press, 1968); Daniel J. Kevles, *In the Name of Eugenics: Genetics and the Uses of Human Heredity* (Berkeley: University of California Press, 1985), which has a good bibliography; Mark H. Haller, *Eugenics: Hereditarian Attitudes in Social Thought* (New Brunswick, N.J.: Rutgers University Press, 1963); John Higham, *Strangers in the Land: Patterns of American Nativism, 1860–1925* (1963; New York: Atheneum, 1970). All explore the construction of hereditarian notions of racial identity and their entailment in the social structures of the period. Other important institutional histories include Lawrence R. Veysey, *The Emergence of the American University* (Chicago: University of Chicago Press, 1965); David Rothman, *The Discovery of the Asylum: Social Order and Disorder in the New Republic* (Boston: Little, Brown, 1971).

The Definition of a Profession draws on each of these fields to understand how a very small group of young psychologists around the turn of the century were able to create and market a system for measuring human talent that has permeated American institutions of learning, and influenced such fundamental social concepts as democracy, sanity, justice, welfare, reproductive rights, and economic progress. In creating, owning, and advertising this social technology, the testers created themselves as professionals. The best single collection of early-twentieth-century textbooks, school surveys, master's theses, and doctoral dissertations pertaining to mental testing and school reorganization is found in the Cutter Stacks of the University of Wisconsin Memorial Library in Madison.

The archival materials are scattered, and I have relied on Sokal and Rafail's excellent guide to manuscript collections in the history of psychology, *A Guide to Manuscript Collections*. The American Psychological Association Archive is located in the Library of Congress, as are the papers of Edward Lee Thorndike and James McKeen Cattell. Hugo Münsterberg's papers are at the Boston Public Library. William James's papers are in the Houghton Library at Harvard University. Sir Francis Galton's papers are at the D.M.S. Watson Library at the University College, London. Robert Yerkes's papers are at the Sterling Memorial Library at Yale University, and include his wartime diaries as well as correspondence. Lewis M. Terman's papers are at Stanford University, but are not very useful on his early work; the bulk of material pertains to his later work on the "gifted" study, and he kept no diary. Henry Herbert Goddard's, Edgar Arnold Doll's, Leta Stetter Hollingworth's, and Elsie Oschrin Bregman's papers, and the surviving papers of the Vineland Research Laboratory, are in the Archives of the History of American Psychology at the University of Akron, Ohio. Goddard's papers include a transcription of an interview with his longtime assistant. This institution also houses a collection of "brass instruments" from the early psychological laboratories. Truman Lee Kelley's papers are in the Harvard University Archive. Professor Robert Wozniak of Bryn Mawr College kindly allowed me access to his extensive private library of psychology texts, treatises, and original test forms.

Scholarly and popular scientific journals of the period provided a sense of the relationships between professional psychology's activities and the popular experience of the "IQ." Especially useful were the *Atlantic Monthly, Science, Popular Science Monthly, School and Society, Scientific Monthly*, the *Annals of the American Academy of Political and Social Science, Educational Review, Survey, New Republic, Independent, World's Work, Harper's, The Pedagogical Seminary, The Psychological Clinic, Proceedings of the National Conference of Charities and Corrections*, the *Yearbooks of the National Society for the Study of Education*, and *Proceedings of the National Education Association*. A comprehensive bibliography of primary sources is found in JoAnne Brown, *The Semantics of Profession* (Ann Arbor, Mich.: University Microfilms, 1986).

❖ Index ❖